MAPLE LEAF MOMENTS

MAPLE LEAF MOMENTS

BOB DUFF

BIBLIOASIS
WINDSOR, ONTARIO

FIRST EDITION

Library and Archives Canada Cataloguing in Publication

Duff, Bob, author
Maple Leaf moments / Bob Duff.

Issued in print and electronic formats.
ISBN 978-1-77196-115-8 (paperback).--ISBN 978-1-77196-114-1 (ebook)

1. Toronto Maple Leafs (Hockey team)--History. 2. Toronto Maple Leafs (Hockey team)--Anecdotes. I. Title.

GV848.T6D82 2016 796.962'6409713541 C2016-901866-0
C2016-901867-9

Readied for the press by Daniel Wells
Copy-edited by Natalie Hamilton
Typeset and designed by Chris Andrechek

Canada Council for the Arts Conseil des Arts du Canada
ONTARIO ARTS COUNCIL CONSEIL DES ARTS DE L'ONTARIO
50 YEARS OF ONTARIO GOVERNMENT SUPPORT OF THE ARTS
50 ANS DE SOUTIEN DU GOUVERNEMENT DE L'ONTARIO AUX ARTS

Canadian Heritage Patrimoine canadien

Published with the generous assistance of the Canada Council for the Arts and the Ontario Arts Council. Biblioasis also acknowledges the support of the Government of Canada through the Canada Book Fund and the Government of Ontario through the Ontario Book Publishing Tax Credit.

PRINTED AND BOUND IN CANADA

FSC www.fsc.org
MIX
Paper from responsible sources
FSC® C004071

CONTENTS

INTRODUCTION
THE LEAF PHENOMENON

Jim McKenny witnessed both sides of what he calls "The Toronto Maple Leafs phenomenon."

McKenny was a defenceman with the team from 1966–78, and then for many more years covered the team as a sportscaster for CITY-TV, and like many ex-Leafs and Leaf-fans alike, he can see no end to the Leafs' phenomenon, no matter how many more years the Leafs extend their Stanley Cup drought, currently a 48-year skid.

"They talk about another (NHL) team coming into Toronto, and that wouldn't hurt the Leafs at all," McKenny said.

"Most of the hockey fans in Toronto are Leafs fans. They have real good American League hockey there, and they don't draw flies.

"They have really good junior hockey with the (Mississauga St. Michael's) Majors and they don't draw.

"...People are crazy about the Leafs."

Dave Hutchison, a Leafs defenceman from 1978–80 and again in 1983–84, compared the inflexible devotion of Leafs' fans to those who support another famous lovable loser.

"Have you ever heard of the Chicago Cubs?" Hutchison asked rhetorically.

"Same thing. They're real, true fans, and one day, we're going to turn it around.

"I hope."

Most former Leafs believe that fans start following the team almost from the womb.

"Growing up and watching the games, that was who we watched, the Leafs," said Pat Ribble, who skated on the Leafs' defence for 13 games during the 1979–80 season.

"When I got traded there, it was such a big thrill for me. I was only there for 31 days, but it was a big part of my career, and I really enjoyed it."

Hutchison remembers when the Leafs were dominant.

"When we were kids back in the 1960s, the Leafs won the Cup four times," Hutchison said.

"People from around that era, who would be their 50s now, were watching the Leafs then, and have an influence on their children.

"True Leafs' fans are not jumping around and cheering for other teams when the Leafs aren't doing well. And someday, we're going to reap the benefits of this. And I hope, not too long from now."

Since his playing days ended, former Leafs' defenceman Mike Pelyk has realized how special it was to don the blue and white Leafs sweater and play hockey in Toronto.

"I played there against Gordie Howe and Bobby Hull and I played with and against Pierre Pilote," Pelyk recalled. "Those kinds of things, you take them for granted when you're there. As you get older and reflect, you realize it was something really unique that happened in your lifetime, something you'll treasure for a long time."

Even though he grew up in Leamington, Ontario, a stone's throw from the U.S. border and the Detroit Red Wings, as a youngster Ribble never wavered in his love for the Leafs.

"We've got Detroit that's so close, and there's still a lot of Leafs' fans in the area," Ribble said. "If you're a fan, it's tough to get off that bandwagon. I'm still a fan."

The overdose of Leafs coverage inflicted upon almost every Canadian youngster through *Hockey Night In Canada*, among other places, may also be a double-edged sword and play a role in Toronto's troubles.

"When I was with other teams—Los Angeles, Chicago—coming into Toronto, I always played my best game, because I knew that it was televised coast-to-coast, our family and friends were either in Toronto, or certainly watching it on TV," Hutchison said.

"People get up when they come into the rink. Toronto's a tough place to win, because most of the other players' emotions are running sky high when they come to Toronto to play."

Steve Yzerman experienced this phenomenon as a player with the Detroit Red Wings and has seen it continue during his days as general manager of the Tampa Bay Lightning.

"To be in that city for a hockey game, particularly on Saturday night, there's a lot of atmosphere," Yzerman said.

Johnny Bower's first game as a Leaf was at Maple Leaf Gardens for an opener in 1958. He remembers the nerves he felt as he donned the Toronto sweater for the first time.

"I was just standing there in front of my net, staring at that big picture of Queen Elizabeth," the Hall-of-Fame netminder remembered. "I was so nervous, my legs were shaking."

The atmosphere of game night in Toronto is what former NHL defenceman Dave Lewis recalls most fondly.

"Going through the scalpers outside selling tickets and the buzz around the building," Lewis said. "Then you got inside and saw the pictures.

"That's the stuff I remember."

For nearly a century, Toronto has been the centre of the hockey universe, and that isn't about to change.

FOR BEGINNERS

Toronto's NHL team was nearly a decade old before it became known as the Maple Leafs.

THEY GOT BETTER

The NHL's inaugural season launched on two fronts the night of December 19, 1917. While the Montreal Canadiens were handling the hometown Ottawa Senators 7–4, at Montreal's Westmount Arena, the city's other NHL franchise, the Montreal Wanderers, were playing host to the Toronto Arenas.

Only 700 fans turned out for the contest, a disappointing number considering that all military personnel were admitted free of charge. The few who did show up would be entertained by a non-stop goal fest.

Montreal grabbed an early 2–0 lead and never trailed. The honour of Toronto's first NHL goal went to Reg Noble.

It was 5–3 Wanderers after one frame when Toronto manager Charlie Querrie, who'd curiously dressed two netminders for the game, something that wouldn't become mandatory in the NHL until 1965, opted to hook his starter Sammy Hebert and go with Arthur Brooks. Hebert offered another odd display, taking to the net to start the game wearing No. 9 on the back of his sweater. He's the only regular goalie in NHL history to wear that digit. But that was about the only impression either puckstopper made of lasting importance.

"Neither Hebert, who was the Toronto goalkeeper in the earlier part of the game, nor Brooks, in the second session, stopped the Wanderers' shots as they might have done," noted the *Toronto World* in its report of the game.

At the other end, Bert Lindsay, the father of a player who'd be a long-time Leafs nemesis, Detroit Red Wings forward Ted Lindsay, posted the win. Meanwhile the player-manager for the Wanderers was another who'd develop into a thorn in the Leafs' side for decades, none other than Art Ross, the man who would oversee the fortunes of the Boston Bruins for over three decades.

Ross scored one goal as the Wanderers claimed a 10–9 victory, but the night would hardly be a harbinger of things to come for either squad.

Fire destroyed the Westmount Arena on January 2, 1918, and two days later the Wanderers resigned from the NHL, their opening-night triumph being the only victory in franchise history.

Emboldened by the addition of two future Hall-of-Famers in goalie Harry (Hap) Holmes and forward Jack Adams, the Arenas would rise up and claim the NHL title and then defeat the Vancouver Millionaires in a five-game series to win the Stanley Cup, making them the first NHL champion in league history.

The 10 goals against in a season opener remains the record for the goals allowed by an eventual Stanley Cup championship squad.

BIG MUM WAS TORONTO'S FIRST BIG MAN

They called Toronto Arenas defenceman Harry Mummery the mastodon of the NHL. He was that big.

An original with the Toronto Arenas when the NHL was formed in 1917, Mummery was larger than life.

It was said if Mummery tumbled to the ice, the arena windows rattled. Should Mummery fall on the puck, the vulcanized rubber would resemble a wafer when he arose.

Jack Adams was a rookie forward with the 1917–18 Toronto Arenas when he quickly learned the quirky habits of his Toronto teammate.

Not more than 30 minutes before the puck was to drop for an NHL regular season game, Adams found Mummery in the rink's boiler room, cooking a steak he was holding on the business end of a shovel over the open flame in the furnace.

"Got a little hungry," Mummery told Adams.

Known to down a steak and an entire apple pie with a pint of cream as his pre-game meal, Mummery's weight hovered anywhere between 220–275 pounds during his playing days, depending on the time of the season and what he'd had for dinner.

Yet the man they called Big Mum was surprisingly fast on his skates for someone of his girth.

"He was so big he was frightening at times," Ottawa Senators star Cy Denneny recalled to the *Ottawa Journal*. "There were times when he'd start down the ice and start swaying on one foot or the other, and one of a wingman's worries was that he'd lose his balance and topple on you. You had to watch yourself in between the boards and Mummery."

He wasn't known as a dirty player, though there was one night following a Toronto-Quebec game when Mummery took exception to the work of referee Lou Marsh and sought him out post-game. "It was quite the fight," Mummery told the *Winnipeg Tribune*.

Marsh took the upper hand early in the bout, and knocked Mummery off his feet at least eight times. But Big Mum wouldn't stay down. They kept pounding away at each other until both men were bloodied and on their knees and Marsh finally acknowledged he'd had enough.

"If I'd known Lou was Canada's amateur heavyweight boxing champion at the time, I'd never have faced him," Mummery said. "But as it was I knew I could lick him."

Then Mummery smiled at his memory of Marsh.

"He was a grand fellow," Mummery said.

To help protect his girth, Mummery utilized a rubber band that was 12 feet long and 18 inches wide. Prior to suiting up in his gear, Mummery would hold one end of the rubber band while the trainer held the other and he'd spin like a whirling dervish until his mid-section was encased in his makeshift rubber girdle.

Mummery was not without talent. Though utilized more in a defensive role with Toronto, he collected six assists in five games as Toronto won the Stanley Cup in 1917–18 and scored 15 goals for the Montreal Canadiens in 1920–21, a hefty total for a defenceman. Mummery was also talented enough to play three NHL games in goal, a record for a position player, and he even posted a win as a netminder. Born in Chicago but raised in Brandon, Manitoba, Mummery, who worked the off-season as a CPR locomotive engineer, was the first American-born player to skate for Toronto in the NHL.

His weight was ultimately his undoing. Mummery played for four teams in six NHL seasons, but eventually ate his way out of the league and was shipped to Saskatoon of the Western Canada Hockey League.

Unable to find hockey pants that would fit Mummery, Saskatoon officials commissioned a tent company to fashion a pair out of canvas. The night before his debut, playful teammates snuck into the dressing room and painted a smiley face on the seat of Mummery's pants. When he saw the artwork, Big Mum just smiled, donned his happy pants and was an instant hit with the local fans.

He lasted only four games in Saskatoon and Mummery's playing days were done. "The old man is through," Mummery told the *Ottawa Journal*. "Don't offer me any sympathy. It was all right while it lasted and it's all right with me if I'm through."

Mummery tried his hand at refereeing and one night, when a player accosted him to criticize his work post-game, Mummery boxed his ears. But while he was scrapping with one player, another walloped Mummery across the head with his stick, opening a three-inch gash.

Mummery turned and set off in pursuit of his attacker. The frightened assailant raced out the door of the arena, skates and all, running for his life with Big Mum in hot pursuit. Mummery soon caught the fellow and put a beating on him.

PENNY FOR YOUR THOUGHTS

Forward Ken Randall, an original NHLer with the Toronto Arenas in 1917–18 and a two-time Stanley Cup winner, was also a bit of a stormy petrel.

During that inaugural NHL campaign, Randall accumulated $35 in fines for a variety of miscreant deeds, but steadfastly refused to pay his financial penalty to the league. On February 22, 1918, NHL president Frank Calder decreed that Randall was suspended indefinitely until he paid his fines in full.

Toronto's next scheduled game was the following night, February 23 at Mutual Street Arena, playing host to the Ottawa Senators. When Randall suited up, Ottawa vowed to protest the contest, but Toronto manager Charlie Querrie claimed he'd been granted permission by the league to play his defenceman.

Just before the game was to get underway, Randall skated up to referee Lou Marsh and handed him $35—$32 in bills and a paper bag filled with what Randall told Marsh was three dollars in pennies.

Marsh refused to accept the coinage, so a defiant Randall simply placed the bag of pennies at the referee's feet and skated away. Anxious for the puck to be dropped, Ottawa forward Harry Hyland skated past and swatted the bag with the blade of his stick, sending coppers spilling all over the ice surface.

"A number of small boys were on the ice in an instant, and there was a scramble for the coins, as exciting as a game in itself," noted the *Montreal Gazette*'s report of the contest.

A sheepish Randall left the ice and returned from the Toronto dressing room with $3 in bills and was permitted to play, but didn't figure in the scoring as the Arenas dumped the Senators 9–3.

WHEN TORONTO NEARLY LOST ITS TEAM

Without a title since 1967, long-suffering Toronto fans hoping for a Stanley Cup victory are convinced that winning will herald in a new era of glory days for the team.

The early history of the franchise might undermine this faith. The first Stanley Cup champions in NHL history were the Toronto Arenas, the forerunners to the Maple Leafs, and not only didn't they get a chance to defend their title the next year, they couldn't even finish out the regular season.

Things went south quickly for the Toronto Arenas during the 1918–19 season, despite being the reigning champions of the the newly formed NHL, born in 1917 to replace the National Hockey Association, which had folded up operations.

Hap Holmes, who'd stabilized Toronto's netminding the previous season after being acquired on loan from Seattle of the Pacific Coast

Hockey Association, returned to Seattle for the 1918–19 season, leaving the Arenas—also known at the time as the Blue Shirts—to turn to veteran Bert Lindsay, the father of future NHLer and Leaf tormentor Ted Lindsay. But the elder Lindsay, who'd played pro since 1908 and was a teammate of such early hockey legends as Cyclone Taylor, Lester Patrick and Tommy Phillips, was 38 and past his prime, going 5–11 and posting a 4.99 goals-against average.

The Arenas started the 1918–19 season 1–6 and never were able to get back into the race, winning back-to-back games just twice all season. By February, spectators at Mutual Street Arena were as few and far between as Toronto victories. On February 18, 1919, prior to Toronto's 4–3 overtime loss to the Ottawa Senators, the team announced that wingers Ken Randall and Harry Meeking had been let out of their contracts to sign with Glace Bay of the Maritime Senior League for the rest of the season, though both promised to return for the 1919–20 season. "Randall will leave a big hole in the local team," reported the *Toronto World*.

A 9–2 loss February 20 at Ottawa officially eliminated the Arenas from the playoff picture. The next day, the Arenas opted to throw in the towel. *The Ottawa Journal* reported that the Arenas disbanded immediately after the loss, and that Arenas ownership informed NHL president Frank Calder they intended to forfeit their remaining games.

"I have been notified by telephone by manager (Charlie) Querrie that the Arena club was through, and that their remaining two games away and at home would be defaulted," Calder announced. "I immediately got in touch with the Ottawa and Canadien clubs and suggested that the playoff series should begin at once."

Montreal and Ottawa clashed in a best-of-seven final to determine the NHL champion, the Canadiens winning in five games to advance to the Stanley Cup final.

On November 26, 1919, Fred Hambly, chairman of the Toronto board of education, purchased the Arena Hockey Club for $5,000. Many of the same hockey people, including Querrie, were involved with the new owner. After making an unsuccessful proposal to veteran defenceman Art Duncan of the Vancouver Millionaires to sign on as player-manager, team brass brought on Harvey Sproule as the manager of the team.

On the day they took ownership of the Toronto club, Hambly also applied to the NHL to rename the team the Tecumsehs. But on December 8 he changed his mind and announced that the team would be called the St. Patricks. Frank Heffernan was signed from the amateur ranks as player-coach and given stock in the team as well.

As the St. Patricks, things began to turn around for Toronto. They were a .500 team in 1919–20, going 12–12, and made the playoffs in 1920–21. Finally, in 1921–22 they went all the way, winning the Stanley Cup.

ROLL THEM BONES

Today, any association of gambling with major league sports is frowned on by the powers that be, but when the power went out at the Ottawa Auditorium in the midst of a February 2, 1921 game between the hometown Senators and the visiting Toronto St. Patricks, gambling was utilized to entertain the waiting crowd, which included the Duke and Duchess of Devonshire, the former was the Governor-General of Canada at the time.

The lights first failed during the intermission between the second and third periods, with Ottawa maintaining a 4–3 lead. While workers hastily sought to repair a blown main transformer on Laurier Avenue outside the rink, the band of the Governor-General's footguards entertained the crowd inside, who sang along to the music.

After a ten-minute delay, the third period was barely underway. As Ottawa centre Frank Nighbor broke toward the Toronto net with the puck, the lights failed again, resulting in another delay.

Candles were placed along the boards to light the rink and Toronto goalie Jake Forbes got some laughs as he stickhandled the puck around the rink in his cumbersome goalie gear. Soon afterward, Nighbor and Toronto players Harry Cameron and Reg Noble emerged from the dressing rooms and arranged some of the candles in a semicircle on the ice by the boards in the neutral zone, about to engage in a much different game than hockey.

"Nighbor, Cameron and Noble squatted in the offside area and threw craps," reported the *Ottawa Journal*, "to the delight of the crowd."

Soon after, the lights came on, the game resumed and Toronto crapped out in its bid for a tying goal, falling by a 4–3 tally.

DID SPRAGUE THROW A PLAYOFF GAME?

When the struggling Quebec Athletics transferred to Hamilton for the 1920–21 season and became the Tigers, NHL president Frank Calder was determined to make them a more competitive club. He ordered each of the other three NHL clubs to loan Hamilton players to bolster the club's weak roster.

The Toronto St. Patricks provided goalie Howard Lockhart and forward Joe Matte, while the Montreal Canadiens contributed defenceman Goldie Prodgers.

The defending Stanley Cup champion Ottawa Senators offered nothing.

An NHL governors' meeting was held December 30, 1920 in Montreal and the governors voted that the Senators must immediately send defenceman Sprague Cleghorn on loan to Toronto and forward Punch Broadbent on loan to Hamilton.

Both players refused to report. While Broadbent held steadfast, after about a month, Cleghorn eventually relented and joined the St. Patricks.

Considered the toughest player in the early years of the NHL, Cleghorn was known off the ice as someone of suspect character.

During the 1920–21 season, Cleghorn's wife Evelyn, whom he met in New York and who remained in that city during hockey season, made a surprise visit to her husband only to discover he was living with another woman, Vivian Dalber, who he introduced around town as Mrs. Cleghorn. The couple divorced in July of 1921.

The relationship between the St. Patricks and Cleghorn would also end in controversy and a messy divorce.

Ottawa met Toronto in the NHL final. In those days, NHL playoff series were two-game, total goals affairs—one game in each city, with the team that scored the most goals over the two games advancing to the next round. In the opener of the series in Toronto, Cleghorn appeared disinterested as the Senators romped to a 5–0 victory.

"Sprague Cleghorn did not seem to like going against his former teammates and was, perhaps, the most ineffective man on the ice," reported the *Toronto World.*

The next day, the Toronto club released Cleghorn.

"The release of Cleghorn was the sensation of the hockey world over the weekend," the *Ottawa Journal* noted. "Cleghorn himself states that he told St. Pats he did not want to play against his old team in the playoff, but they insisted on his doing so.

"It was quite evident that Cleghorn was not trying very hard in the last game, and (Toronto coach Frank) Carroll showed poor judgment in keeping him on the ice.

"The committee room juggling that forced Cleghorn to St. Pats proved a boomerang for them."

With Red Stuart occupying Cleghorn's spot on the defence for Game 2 of the series, the St. Patricks gave a much better account of themselves, but still lost the game 2–0 and the set 7–0.

Imagine how delighted the Toronto players must have been to see Cleghorn celebrating with his old Ottawa teammates, his gear back in its stall in the Senators dressing room.

"This is the only club that ever treated me right and I'm never going to play hockey except for Ottawa," Cleghorn told the *Ottawa Citizen*. "It wasn't human to compel me to play against them."

The Senators announced they'd added Cleghorn to their roster for the upcoming Stanley Cup final in Vancouver.

"Sprague Cleghorn returned with the Ottawa party and has been signed on for the trip to the Pacific Coast in defence of the Stanley Cup," the *Toronto World* reported.

The cause of his split with the St. Pats was a monetary issue, according to Cleghorn.

"Cleghorn said that the Toronto club officials had refused to pay him his salary and that he had left the collection of it in the hands of (NHL) president Frank Calder," the *Ottawa Journal* reported.

"The Pacific Coast Hockey Association has consented to the addition of Cleghorn to the Ottawa squad."

There may have been merit to Cleghorn's argument. Toronto players held up the start of Game 2 of the playoff set against Ottawa until ownership of the St. Pats agreed to pay each player one half-week's salary as a playoff bonus.

Still, there can be no question that Cleghorn made little effort in Game 1, offering no support to his teammates and in essence, helping the Senators to an easy victory.

HOCKEY'S FIRST HOLDOUT

With the St. Pats struggling through the 1919–20 NHL season, the team management grew less and less satisfied with the work of either of their netminders, Mike Mitchell or Howard Lockhart.

On February 28, 1920, the St. Patricks signed top amateur puckstopper Vernor (Jake) Forbes, and in his NHL debut he lost a 1–0 decision to the Ottawa Senators, but quickly won over the fans.

"That kiddo is a wonder boy," wrote the *Toronto World*. "Not very big? No. But 100 per cent efficiency and pep. It is very evident from Saturday's game that Vernor keeps his nerve in a garage, also that he will not for a long time have any need for the services of an occultist. He could tell every time just exactly where that wicked little puck was going to hit."

Forbes won the job for the 1920–21 season and backstopped the St. Pats into the playoffs, an accomplishment he felt worthy of financial reward. He sought a one-year contract from the St. Pats for $2,500, but the team scoffed at this, suspending Forbes and signing John Ross Roach, considered the best goalie playing outside of the pro ranks, to a $2,000 pact.

While Roach carried Toronto to the Stanley Cup, Forbes sat and stewed, becoming the first player in NHL history to wait out an entire season in a contract dispute. Traded to the Hamilton Tigers in the spring of 1922 for $2,000, Forbes signed with the Tigers.

He played the next three seasons for Hamilton and in 1924–25, Forbes backstopped the Tigers to a first-place finish, leading the

NHL with 19 wins. But when the players did not receive playoff bonuses from owner Percy Thompson that they insisted they were contractually entitled to, Forbes and captain Shorty Green took the team out on strike prior to the NHL final against the Montreal Canadiens.

NHL president Frank Calder suspended the Hamilton team and awarded the title to Montreal. In anger, Thompson sold the club to New York interests, where the Tigers became the New York Americans for the 1925–26 season.

Forbes spent the next two campaigns as No. 1 goalie for the Amerks, and then Jumpin' Jakie bounced up and down between the NHL and minor leagues for the rest of his career before hanging up his pads for good in 1936.

YOU CAN'T KEEP YOUR HAT ON

His birth certificate read William Roxborough Stuart, but everyone knew him simply as Red.

The owners of the Toronto St. Patricks liked what Red brought to the ice. Signed as a free agent in 1919, Stuart, born in Sackville, New Brunswick but raised in Amherst, Nova Scotia, was an unselfish, clever player, a sensational stickhandler and a fast, powerful skater, equally at home on defence or at any of the three forward positions.

Toronto fans quickly took a shine to Stuart and the St. Patricks' brass wanted them to see Red. In fact, they wanted fans to see all of Red.

Performance clauses being written into contracts are commonplace, but the bonus clause the St. Patricks offered Stuart at the start of the 1921–22 season was certainly hair-raising.

Many NHL players of that era wore ball caps while playing and Stuart was no exception. But with his popularity, speed and flame-red mane, the Toronto brass viewed Stuart as their biggest drawing card, and thought that they had come up with a way to get a few more bums through the turnstiles and into the stands.

So they offered Stuart an odd bonus clause—$100 if he'd play without his ball cap for the 1921–22 campaign.

Stuart agreed, and it paid off for both parties. Paired in the top defensive tandem with Harry Cameron, Stuart posted a career-high ten points in 24 games and attendance increased for St. Patricks games at Mutual Street Arena.

Of course, you could argue that the fact the St. Pats won the Stanley Cup in 1921–22 might have played a role in bringing more people to the games.

DOCTORS IN THE HOUSE

The Toronto St. Patricks won their only Stanley Cup in 1921–22 and the injury-riddled team was forced to count on several seldom-used players during their five-game triumph over Vancouver. One of those super subs was left-winger Rod Smylie, a fierce checker who would lead the team with three assists during the playoffs.

"Smylie played most of the last two periods at left wing and gave his check more than he wanted," the *Winnipeg Tribune* reported of his Game 2 performance. "While he was good on the offensive, it was in his defensive play that he stood out.

"He checked back and stepped into the oncoming Millionaires in no uncertain manner and he slowed up their attacks considerably."

You could say that Smylie moonlighted as a hockey player. While he was helping the St. Pats win the Cup, Dr. Smylie, a graduate of the University of Toronto's medical school, was also serving his internship at Toronto's St. Michael's Hospital. Smylie's brother Cliff, also a physician, covered for Rod on the nights that games conflicted with his shifts.

His medical pursuits limited Smylie to two late-season games for the St. Pats in 1922–23. He signed with the Ottawa Senators in 1923–24 and played 14 games for them before being released.

Returning to Toronto, Smylie rejoined the St. Patricks midway through the 1924–25 season and played 11 games, along with one playoff game. He joined them again for five games during the 1925–26 season when Toronto forward Reg Reid was injured.

That was it for Smylie's hockey career. Medicine became his full-time profession. He would serve as a general practitioner at St.

Michael's Hospital for more than half a century, specializing in the treatment of allergies.

Winning ran in the Smylie family. His sons Doug and Rod Jr. played football for the Toronto Argonauts and were part of Grey Cup winners in 1945, '46, '50 and '52.

Bill Carson was the first player to post a 20-goal season in a Toronto Maple Leafs uniform when he potted 20 in 1927–28, the first full NHL season that the club performed as the Maple Leafs, but nets weren't all that Carson filled.

Dr. Carson was a dentist, which may explain why he didn't turn pro until the age of 26, after two years of persistent pursuit by the Toronto St. Patricks, and also why his NHL days were done by the age of 30.

Carson packed a lot of hockey into a short career. He won two Allan Cups with the University of Toronto Varsity Blues while earning his degree in dentistry and played some exhibition games in 1923–24 with the Toronto Granites, Canada's Olympic gold-medal-winning team in 1924, though Carson did not go with the team to the Olympiad in Chamonix, France.

"One of the greatest players in the game," was how U of T coach Frank Carroll described Carson, whose brothers Frank and Gerry also played in the NHL.

An original Leaf, Carson suffered a fractured skull late in he 1927–28 season and while recovering, lost his spot as the team's number one centre to newcomer Andy Blair. He fell into managing director Conn Smythe's doghouse.

"I will not have a player on this club that doesn't battle all the way," Smythe told the *Toronto Telegram*. "Carson was not giving us his best and a change was the only solution."

Carson was traded to the Boston Bruins on January 25, 1929, for a then-record fee of $25,000 and scored the Stanley Cup-winning goal that spring as the Bruins defeated the New York Rangers.

During his playing days, Carson practiced dentistry in the employ of the Ontario Ministry of Health, travelling to Northern Ontario communities that were without a regular dentist. After his playing days he set up practice first in Aurora, Ontario, and later in Parry Sound.

YOU HEARD IT HERE FIRST

As Valentine's Day arrived on the calendar in the midst of the 1922–23 NHL season, it was a big day for the Toronto St. Patricks. The chances of defending their Stanley Cup title were slipping away.

The Ottawa Senators, who came to Toronto that night, were leading the standings with a 10–6–1 mark. The Montreal Canadiens were holding down the second playoff spot one point back of the Senators at 9–6–2. Then came the St. Pats at 8–8–1, and with seven games to go in the schedule, every game against either Ottawa or Montreal was a virtual must-win for Toronto.

"Standing room only signs will be hung out again at Toronto," noted the *Ottawa Citizen*. "Quite a few Ottawa people will take in the important match."

For the first time in NHL history, those unable to get tickets for the contest wouldn't be left in the dark.

The Toronto Star decided to ramp up its coverage of this pivotal game. The paper had just launched its own radio station, CFCA, and assigned reporter Norm Albert to broadcast the third period of the Ottawa-Toronto match across the airwaves.

It was all Toronto from the outset and the St. Patricks were holding a 5–1 lead after two periods when Albert picked up the broadcast of the game. And he was barely on the air a minute when Toronto's Lloyd Andrews swooped behind the Senators net and fed a pass out to Jack Adams, who made no mistake from close range to make it 6–1.

Ottawa staged a furious rally, Frank Nighbor scoring twice and Punch Broadbent once, but the St. Patricks hung on for a 6–4 triumph in the first NHL game ever carried live on radio.

It was a big night in NHL history and an important win for the St. Patricks, but it wouldn't be enough. Toronto was unable to catch either the Habs or Sens and missed the playoffs.

PRETTY LITTLE LEAF

Back in the day, the Montreal Canadiens cornered the market on players of French-Canadian descent, but one of those who got away ended up making his NHL debut with the St. Patricks.

Pierre Bellefeuille left his home in Trois-Rivieres, Quebec, in 1923 to play senior hockey in Ontario with the Iroquois Falls Papermakers, scoring ten goals in eight games and catching the eye of the management of the Toronto St. Patricks.

He turned down what was reported as a handsome offer, and also one from Leo Dandurand of the Canadiens, but accepted an invite to play senior hockey in London, Ontario for London AAA when he was granted a probationary certificate by the Ontario Hockey Association to transfer teams. But after one season there, the OHA wouldn't permit Bellefeuille to play again in London for the 1925–26 season.

The St. Patricks swooped in with another offer, but once more Bellefeuille rejected it, insisting he wanted to retain his amateur status. Finally in early January of 1926, Bellefeuille's appeal was turned down by the OHA and this time, when Bert Corbeau and Eddie Powers of the St. Patricks showed up in London, they got Bellefeuille's name on a contract on January 9, 1925. Or so they thought.

Bellefeuille initially agreed to a three-year deal worth $4,000 per season, plus a $1,000 signing bonus, but then had second thoughts.

The next day he denied signing any contract with the St. Patricks and asked for the weekend to consider their offer. On January 15, the OHA reconsidered their previous position, granting Bellefeuille a card to play for London, and he rejected the St. Pats' offer. Toronto instead signed Mike Neville, Bellefeuille's London teammate.

Bellefeuille would eventually agree to terms with Toronto in the fall of 1925 and rode the bench until star sniper Babe Dye was felled by flu in early January.

Filling in for Dye, Bellefeuille scored the opening goal of a 3–2 win over the Boston Bruins on January 9, 1926.

"Bellefeuille … played superb hockey," reported the *Montreal Gazette*, "scoring the initial tally of the game and breaking up many of the Bruins' threatening attacks by his persistent backchecking."

Two games later, he scored two goals in a 4–3 win over the New York Americans and added another pair in a 6–2 victory over the Habs two games after that. Armed with a powerful shot that was known to take chips out of the wooden boards when he missed the net, Bellefeuille scored nine goals in Toronto's next nine games and the St. Pats were certain they had a budding star on their hands.

Just like that, the well dried up.

Bellefeuille didn't register a point through the first 14 games of the 1926–27 season and Toronto management loaned him to London of the Canadian Pro League. In January of 1927, just over a month before they became the Maple Leafs, the St. Patricks traded Bellefeuille to the Detroit Cougars.

By 1930, he was out of the NHL for good, and it was a crying shame that Bellefeuille couldn't stick it out in Toronto and be part of the transition from the St. Patricks to the Maple Leafs in 1927.

The English translation of Bellefeuille's name?

Pretty little leaf.

TORONTO'S FIRST EUROPEAN

Long before Borje Salming and Inge Hammarstrom arrived from Sweden in 1973, ushering in a new era of NHL hockey, there was Al Pudas.

The Toronto St. Patricks signed Pudas, a two-time Allan Cup winner with Port Arthur, on October 28, 1926. Born in Siikajoki, Finland, Pudas came to Canada with his family when he was just 18 months old; though he therefore grew up as a Canadian, he wasn't naturalized or made a citizen.

The St. Pats assigned Pudas to the Windsor Hornets of the Canadian Pro League to start the 1926–27 season, where he produced ten goals in 18 games, earning himself a call-up to the NHL.

After playing with the Hornets in a December 28, 1926 2–1 win over Niagara Falls, Pudas reported to Toronto the next day, making his debut with the St. Patricks that night, going pointless in a 4–1 win over the Boston Bruins.

There was a lot of interest in Windsor when Pudas returned with the St. Patricks to Border Cities Arena to face the Detroit Cougars on January 4, 1927, as it was the same rink on which he'd played with the Hornets.

"Border fans who wanted to see "Puddy" Pudas in action with the big league didn't get a chance to watch (him) shine," reported the *Border Cities Star*. "The Toronto St. Pats used (him) for only a few minutes."

Pudas saw brief relief duty on right wing for Ace Bailey, skating on a forward line with Hap Day and Bill Carson.

He played three more scoreless games, before he was dealt to the minor-league Hamilton Tigers for forward George Patterson, who would score the first goal for the Toronto Maple Leafs. Pudas never appeared in the NHL again, though he still would have an impact on the future of the Maple Leafs.

In 1936, Pudas was named coach of the Olympic team that would represent Canada at the Winter Games in Garmisch-Partenkirchen, Germany. To this day Pudas remains the only foreign-born coach ever placed in charge of a Canadian national hockey team.

In order to coach the team, Pudas required some fast diplomatic work by the Canadian government. On January 7, 1936, he was presented with his certificate as a naturalized British subject.

Pudas had believed he'd automatically become a British subject when his father was naturalized in 1911, but the law changed in 1915 and Pudas needed to be fast-tracked through the process in order to acquire the necessary Canadian passport to allow him to travel to Germany.

Glory turned to disappointment when Canada was upset for the gold medal by Great Britain, becoming the first Canadian hockey team to ever lose a game at the Olympics.

In 1941, when Pudas was working as an amateur referee, Jock Stirling, his young officiating partner for a game in Winnipeg, introduced Pudas to a newspaperman.

"Albert coached Canada's last Olympic team," Stirling boasted with pride.

Pudas shuddered.

"For Pete's sake," he begged, "please don't bring that up again."

THE CAPTAIN WORE GOALIE PADS

John Ross Roach's NHL career started under unusual circumstances. The Toronto St. Patricks signed him to tend their goal in the fall of 1921 when veteran Jake Forbes refused to budge in a contract dispute with the team.

Quickly, the St. Pats discovered that had a gem between the pipes.

"One game revealed to the Toronto fans that in the 22-year-old youngster they had found a jewel," wrote the *Seattle Daily Times*. "Two games made them forget Forbes, and the season was not many weeks old until it was discovered that Roach was one of the greatest goalies the game has developed, surpassing (Georges) Vezina of Les Canadiens and (Clint) Benedict of Ottawa, two veterans.

"He is as agile as a cat."

Maybe Roach's success had to do with his approach. He chose to focus his attention solely on the puck and ignore whom the puck-carrier was to ensure facing the NHL's best shooters would not rattle him.

"Most times I don't even know who the player is coming in with the puck," Roach explained to writer Harry Grayson. "I can only tell he's an opposing player by the colour of his stockings."

With Roach in goal, Toronto won the Stanley Cup in 1921–22, and he became the first rookie in NHL history to backstop his team to the title.

Another NHL first would come for Roach a few years later.

On November 19, 1924, he was named captain of the St. Pats, the first goalie ever to captain an NHL team.

"This is really a fine tactical move for the Greenshirts," reported the *Ottawa Journal*, and indeed there was some creativity at work in the decision by Toronto coach Eddie Powers.

NHL rules stated a captain must be on the ice to argue a call with an official. Since Roach never left the ice, that wasn't going to be a problem.

Nicknamed "Little Napoleon," the five-foot-six Roach certainly didn't shy away from fierce debate.

Roach held the captaincy for just the one season. On November 11, 1925, the St. Patricks elected Babe Dye captain, and maybe that didn't sit too well with Roach. The team was barely half a minute into its first workout after Dye was named captain when he was cut open for stitches by Roach's stick.

In 1928, Toronto dealt Roach to the New York Rangers for goalie Lorne Chabot. During the 1931–32 season, Roach would lead the NHL with nine shutouts, but Chabot had the last laugh, backstopping the Leafs to a Stanley Cup win that spring over Roach and the Rangers.

WAIT UP

New York Americans defenceman Joe Simpson and Toronto St. Patricks centre Bill Carson got into a jousting match during the game between the two teams on January 8, 1927, and were immediately handed offsetting roughing minors by referee Cooper Smeaton.

In the days before giant scoreboards that tracked game and penalty times, players in the sin bin relied on the timekeeper seated between them to let them know when their sentences were up.

That's exactly what Eddie Upthegrove, the penalty timekeeper at Mutual Street Arena, did but there was just one problem—Carson was busy tying his skate laces and didn't hear Upthegrove's call.

Simpson did and wasn't about to take advantage of the situation. "Hurry up, Bill," Simpson shouted across the penalty box. "I'll wait for you."

Perhaps Simpson should have found a way to keep Carson off the ice even longer. He scored a hat trick as the St. Patricks dropped the Americans 3–1.

HOW THE LEAFS WERE BORN

Thought it might be hard to imagine it now, the Toronto Maple Leafs were almost finished and packed off to another town before they began, and before they were ever known as the Maple Leafs at all. Late in the 1926–27 NHL season, their immediate predecessors, the Toronto St. Patricks, were struggling at the bottom of the standings when some Philadelphia businessmen made some inquiries about purchasing the club and relocating it to the City of Brotherly Love.

Not wanting this to happen, a group of 14 Toronto businessmen stepped up on February 14, 1927 and pre-empted the Philadelphia consortium by buying the St. Patricks for $160,000. The ownership group included J. P. Bickell, president of the McIntyre Porcupine Mines; lawyers Hugh Aird of Aird, McLeod and Company, and Peter G. Campbell of Campbell, Stratton and Company; stockbroker E. W. Bickle of E. W. Bickle and Company; E. H. Blake, barrister; Lt.-Col. W. G. Barker, president of the Lynodoch Tobacco Company; Major R. Cecil Cowan, vice-president of the Ontario Malleable Iron Company; Allan Case, president of the Pease Foundry Company; Fred Crawford, president of the Standard Mining Exchange; J. S. Beatty, barrister; Max S. Haas, general sales manager of the George R. Hees Son & Company; W. A. H. MacBrien, director of the Port Hope Sanitary Manufacturing Company; T. A. McAuley, president of Arnold Bros. Limited, a steel company; and Blake Jackson of the Jackson-Lewis Construction Company. The new ownership was immediately offered $200,000 for the team by the Philadelphia group, an offer that they quickly rejected.

The new ownership immediately installed veteran amateur hockey mogul and former New York Rangers GM Conn Smythe, who'd helped assemble the new ownership group, as managing director, a move that was to take effect at the start of the 1927–28 season. At the time, Smythe was still busy handling the Toronto Varsity Grads, who'd go on to capture the Allan Cup and win the gold medal for Canada at the 1928 Winter Olympic Games in St. Moritz, Switzerland.

Alex Romeril, a well-known figure in local amateur athletics who'd been a prominent senior hockey player and managed football's Toronto Argonauts, was appointed to manage and coach the team for the remainder of the 1926–27 season.

The ownership picked a new name, logo, and colour scheme for the club—something they planned to unveil at the club's next home game, February 17 at Toronto's Mutual Street Arena Gardens, 78 Mutual Street, against the New York Americans. The new ownership group felt it would be appropriate to launch their lives as the Maple Leafs on home ice.

First, though, there was the matter of a road game set for February 15, against the Detroit Cougars, a first-year NHL franchise that would eventually become the Red Wings.

Since there was as-of-yet no major-league facility in Detroit, the Cougars played all of their home games in 1926–27 at Windsor's Border Cities Arena. Toronto would play this game wearing their green-and-white sweaters with the Shamrock logo for the final time. Secrets about their new uniforms were leaked on the way to Windsor, and the Toronto players checked out their new green sweaters with a maple leaf logo sewn over the Shamrock logo during the train ride to the game.

A crowd of less than 1,000 watched the St. Patricks go out with a whimper, as they took it on the chin in a 5–1 defeat to the Cougars. The honour of scoring the final goal for the St. Pats went to Corbett Denneny.

Two nights later, the Maple Leafs made their debut in Toronto with a 4–1 victory over the Americans. Billy Burch gave the Americans the lead 4:30 into the first period, but George Patterson tied the score, netting the first goal in Maple Leafs history at 9:40 of the second period, taking a pass from Bill Brydge and whipping a wrist shot past Amerks goalie Jake Forbes.

It also happened to be Patterson's first goal as an NHLer. Toronto had acquired his rights from Hamilton of the Canadian Pro League only 16 days earlier.

Ace Bailey tallied a pair of goals, including the game winner with five seconds left in the second period and an insurance goal at 15:50 of the third frame. Bert Corbeau closed out the scoring 15 seconds after Bailey's second goal.

Curiously, the man who scored the farewell goal for the St. Patricks would never play for the Maple Leafs. The Western Hockey League, a major league competitor to the NHL, had folded following the 1925–26 season and the contracts of all of its players were sold to the NHL clubs by Frank and Lester Patrick, who operated the WHL.

The owners of the Saskatoon Sheiks, a former WHL franchise, claimed that they, and not the WHL, held the contracts of their players and therefore the Patricks had no right to sell them to NHL clubs. Saskatoon had joined the Prairie Hockey League, a minor loop, after the collapse of the WHL, and wanted their players back, so they took the NHL to court.

On February 17, 1927,—the day the Leafs debuted—a Toronto court ruled that Denneny was the property of the Saskatoon club and was ordered to return to the team immediately.

Had Denneny played just one game for the Leafs he would have been the only man to suit up under all of Toronto's NHL nicknames—Arenas, St. Patricks, and Maple Leafs.

THE FIRST LEAF

Carl Voss was the first winner of the Calder Trophy as the NHL's rookie of the year with the Detroit Red Wings in 1932–33. But six years prior to that, Voss was the first player signed by the Leafs.

February 17, 1927 was the night Toronto's NHL club were set to abandon their previous St. Pats identity, and to be reborn as the Toronto Maple Leafs. Earlier in the day, the Leafs announced the signing of Voss, a versatile defenceman-forward who was toiling with the Toronto Marlboros, playing for the team in both the junior and senior divisions of the Ontario Hockey Association during the 1926–27 campaign, to a $1,200 contract for the remainder of the season.

Voss was born in Chelsea, Massachusetts but moved to Canada as a teenager. His NHL debut coincided with the Maple Leafs' debut against the New York Americans, a 4–1 Toronto win at Mutual Street Arena. "Carl Voss, former Kingston junior and latterly with the Marlboros of Toronto, signed by the Maple Leafs today, came on for defence relief and made a good impression," noted a report of the game in the *Montreal Gazette*.

It would be the lone occasion he was called out for any positive comment as a Leaf. He'd play 12 more games in 1926–27 and then two more in 1928–29 without collecting a point, before being banished to Buffalo of the International League, where he went on to win the scoring title with 41 points in 46 games in 1931–32.

That caught the eye of the New York Rangers, who traded for Voss, but after just 10 games they dealt him to Detroit, where he'd finish with 23 points and earn the NHL's first rookie award.

Moss never grew under Voss' feet. Over the next five seasons he would serve tours of duty with the Ottawa Senators, St. Louis Eagles, New York Americans, Montreal Maroons, and Chicago Blackhawks.

Chicago proved to be Voss's final NHL stop, and it was there that he came back to haunt the Leafs. His farewell goal that spring proved to be the Stanley Cup winner as the underdog Blackhawks stunned the heavily-favoured Leafs in the 1937–38 final series.

This also allowed Voss to claim a rarity. Since he'd won the Grey Cup with the Queen's Golden Gaels in 1924, he joined Lionel Conacher—brother of Leafs great Charlie Conacher and father of Brian Conacher, a forward with the Leafs' 1966–67 Stanley Cup winner—as the only men to have their names engraved on both the Grey Cup and the Stanley Cup.

Voss was done as a player, but was hardly done with the NHL. From 1950–65 he served as the NHL's referee-in-chief and is credited with dramatically improving the calibre of officiating within the league, by increasing the scouting of amateur officials and the training implemented with professional arbiters.

Voss was inducted into the Hockey Hall of Fame in 1974.

HE DIED WITH HIS BOOTS ON

When they traded to acquire his rights from the Montreal Maroons on October 1, 1928, the Leafs had high hopes for the potential of forward George (Shorty) Horne.

Horne—who stood five-six, hence his nickname—had scored 32 times for Stratford the previous season to lead the Canadian Professional League in goals.

In his first season with the Leafs, Horne finished fourth on the team with nine goals and tied for sixth with 12 points.

"I would say he was one of the most promising players we had," Leafs defenceman Hap Day told the *Ottawa Journal*.

Sadly, that promise would be snuffed out after just one season with the team.

In the summer of 1929, Horne landed a job as a prospector with a Northern Ontario mining company, assessing claims. On July 31, he set out with friends Jack Jessop and Jack Stafford and fellow prospector Vic Perdue in a canoe on Lake Sagatosky, near Gogoma, Ontario, about 150 kilometres northwest of Sudbury.

A sudden and unexpected storm materialized and the high waves capsized their heavily-loaded canoe. Approximately 100 metres from shore, after clinging to the side of their capsized canoe, the men opted to swim for it, doffing their clothing and boots. Horne, though, was unable to remove his boots. Struggling as he swam due to the cumbersome footwear, he grew weary.

Perdue swam back to Horne to try and help him along, but then decided to head for shore and grab a log for Shorty to hang on to while they brought him ashore.

As he neared Horne with the log stretched out in front of him, Perdue could only watch in horror as Horne disappeared below the water and did not resurface.

The three men searched frantically for their friend to no avail. Eventually, they opted to hike through the woods in search of help.

Friends and family joined local police in a futile search for the NHLer, but had no luck. Four days after the search began, a water plane was sent north by the Ontario government to provide aid and curiously, when it landed on the lake, the wake caused by its large pontoons brought Horne's body to the surface.

Horne's funeral was held in Sudbury, and among those in attendance was Leafs managing director Conn Smythe as well as Leafs players Day, Ace Bailey, Art Smith, and Red Horner.

GETTING THE GEARS

Tim Daly described his job as "the life of Reilly."

When Daly started work as trainer for Toronto's NHL club in 1926, they were still known as the St. Patricks. He stayed on the job until 1960, and summered in baseball, mostly with the Maple Leafs of the AAA International League, but also served as trainer of the New York Giants in the 1912 World Series as well as a season with American League's Detroit Tigers.

But hockey was his passion and the Leafs were his first love.

"Pullman cars, staying in the best hotels?" Daly boasted. "If a fella had a million bucks he couldn't do nothing more than that."

Life was good for Daly, though there was a night when it all went wrong.

The Leafs were at Madison Square Garden on January 10, 1929 to play the New York Americans. Late in the first period, Leafs goalie Lorne Chabot raced from his net to clear a loose puck and was accidentally clipped over the right eye by the stick of Amerks forward Billy Burch.

Bleeding profusely, Chabot skated off the ice and went to the Toronto dressing room for first aid. Meanwhile, sub goalie Benny Grant, a rookie who'd yet to see NHL action, was also instructed to head to the dressing room just in case he needed to don his gear.

"But Daly is out there telling everyone that Chabot isn't hurt, and that he'll be out there in no time," former Leafs defenceman King Clancy recalled to the *Ottawa Journal* in 1946. "He keeps applying the towels to Chabot's face, but the eye keeps swelling up and Lorne can't see. Tim just keeps saying that Lorne will be fine."

Of course, Chabot was not fine, and what wasn't dandy—and the reason behind Daly's assurances that he'd get Chabot healed up—became apparent when Leafs managing director Conn Smythe finally ordered Grant to suit up.

Daly had forgot to bring Grant's goalie equipment on the trip.

Grant was forced to don the equipment of the much larger Chabot to tend goal in his NHL debut. "Poor Benny has to go out there with Chabot's belly pad down to his knees and the pads sticking up to his stomach and Chabot's skates several sizes too big for him.

The Americans beat the Leafs 2–0, and Rabbit McVeigh's game winner and the first goal Grant ever allowed in NHL competition left the rookie feeling a tad embarrassed.

McVeigh shot from mid-ice and when Grant went to catch the puck with Chabot's glove, it bounced off his hand and into the net.

ROLLY'S TALLY

As an NHL goal scorer, Rolly Huard batted 1.000. For many decades, he was the only player who could boast of this unique mark.

When injuries left the Leafs minus forwards Charlie Conacher, Joe Primeau, and Baldy Cotton, coach Art Duncan reached out to

Mickey Roach, manager of the Buffalo International League team, for some assistance.

Roach offered the loan of centre Huard, who just three seasons earlier potted 21 goals for the Windsor Hornets of the same league.

Just past the nine-minute mark of the opening period in their December 14, 1930 contest against the Boston Bruins, Huard, on a spectacular individual effort, beat the Boston defence and slipped the puck past Bruins goalie Tiny Thompson to give the Leafs a 1–0 lead.

It wasn't a sign of things to come for the Leafs, or for Huard. Boston rallied for a 7–3 victory and two nights later; Huard was back on the Buffalo roster, never again to see NHL duty.

He remained the only player in NHL history to play one game and score a goal in that game until 1989, when current NHL referee Dean Morton did likewise for the Detroit Red Wings. Brad Fast of the Carolina Hurricanes added his name to this unique list in 2004.

A TWO-SPORT LEAF

Toronto's Babe was a Leaf on more than one occasion and in more than one sport.

Cecil (Babe) Dye is the only man to play both hockey and baseball for the Toronto Maple Leafs. His ability at the latter sport also explains how he got his nickname, a reference to baseball legend Babe Ruth.

Dye, a hard-shooting right-winger, broke into the NHL with the Toronto St. Patricks in 1919–20, scoring 11 goals in 23 games, but he was slow afoot and there were questions about his intestinal fortitude as well.

The St. Pats loaned Dye to the Hamilton Tigers for the 1920–21 season, but when Dye potted a pair of goals in a season-opening 5–0 win over the Montreal Canadiens, St. Pats manager Charlie Querrie reconsidered and recalled him. It proved to be a wise move, because Dye went on to pot back-to-back 30-goal campaigns and, in the spring of 1922, scored nine goals in Toronto's five-game Stanley Cup final series win over the Vancouver Millionaires, equaling the total of the entire Vancouver team, a record that still stands today.

"Dye could shoot a puck as hard as anyone who ever lived," former teammate Jack Adams said.

In game two of that series Dye made another piece of Stanley Cup history. In the second period, with Toronto trailing 1–0 thanks to a first-period goal by Vancouver's Jack Adams, Dye broke into the clear, but was hauled down from behind by Vancouver defenceman Art Duncan. Referee Cooper Smeaton immediately pointed to centre ice, awarding a penalty shot. Though not yet an NHL rule, it was part of the Pacific Coast League rulebook being used to govern the even-numbered games of the five-game series. It was the first penalty shot ever awarded in a Stanley Cup final series.

Adding to the drama, Dye went to the bench and picked out a new stick for his penalty shot opportunity. But for once, Dye's hard, accurate shot eluded him and he sent his drive on the free shot sailing over the net. After Corb Denneny knotted the score in the third period, the Toronto sniper made up for the miss. Dye scored 4:50 into overtime to give the St. Pats a 2–1 win.

Dye led the NHL in goals (26) and points (37) in 1922–23, and then he shocked the hockey world on Sept. 6, 1923. Believing he was on the brink of making the major leagues after batting .318 with 16 homers for Buffalo of the International League, he announced that he was giving up hockey to focus on his burgeoning baseball career. On New Year's Day 1924, assured that he would be staying with Buffalo's ballclub, Dye reconsidered and signed with the St. Patricks.

"The best goalkeepers in the world admit that Dye is a dangerous man, and it will be bad news to them to learn that he will play again," the *Montreal Gazette* reported.

Dye see-sawed between the ice rink and the ball diamond his entire professional career.

He was actually a triple threat in 1920, the season after he debuted with the St. Patricks. Dye also played halfback for the Toronto Argonauts and broke into pro baseball with the Brantford Red Sox of the Michigan-Ontario League.

A speedy outfielder with a stout bat, Dye first played baseball for the Toronto Maple Leafs of the International League later that year. He then moved on for four seasons with Buffalo—for whom Dye hit over .300 from 1922–24—before rejoining the baseball Leafs in 1926. He struggled after his return, however, batting only .220 before being released in July and joining the Baltimore Orioles. In August, Dye's ninth-inning, two-out single to right field for the O's broke up a no-hit bid by Reading Keystones pitcher Al Maumax.

His primary weakness as a ballplayer was his work in the field, especially when it came to corralling ground balls.

In 1927, after a season playing in Chicago with the Blackhawks, owner William Wrigley invited Dye to try out for his team, the Chicago Cubs, but he ended up playing the season with Mobile of the Southern Association. Six years earlier, Connie Mack offered Dye $25,000 to give up hockey and sign with the Philadelphia Athletics.

Dye broke his leg in a training-camp collision with Blackhawks teammate Art Townsend in 1927 and was never the same player. Traded to the New York Americans he scored just one goal in 40 games for the Americans, in 1927–28 and was relegated to minor-league New Haven the following season. Meanwhile, a back injury curtailed his swing and scuttled his baseball career.

As the 1930–31 NHL season was about to begin, Leafs managing director Conn Smythe offered that he'd developed a new approach to running a bench during a game.

"I'm tired of carrying players I don't use, don't want to use, and don't have to use," Smythe told Dick Gibson of the *Border Cities Star*, explaining that he would go with just three subs. Besides, Art Duncan, now the Leafs coach, could also suit up in a pinch.

Dissatisfied with the work of forward Shrimp McPherson and Howie Grant in training camp, Smythe reached out to Dye and signed the veteran forward on the eve of the regular season. It was hoped that the veteran presence of Dye would help educate Toronto's young forwards and that he might rediscover his goal-scoring touch. It quickly became clear, however, that Dye's body was too broken down and that he could no longer keep up. After six scoreless games, Dye was released.

Though his NHL days were over, that brief return to Toronto allowed Dye, who was elected to the Hockey Hall of Fame in 1970, to become the only two-sport Leaf.

THE OTHER GUY WHO COACHED THE LEAFS AND WINGS

Before Mike Babcock, there was Art Duncan. Before Bobby Orr, there was Art Duncan.

In both instances, they are the only men who can claim to have accomplished their particular feats.

In 1926, Duncan was named player-coach, captain, and general manager of the expansion Detroit Cougars, who would become the Red Wings in 1932, two years after Duncan was named coach of the Leafs.

Prior to Babcock being hired in 2015 to coach the Leafs after a decade behind the Detroit bench, Duncan had been the only man to coach both franchises.

Before arriving in the NHL, Duncan was already a nine-season veteran of major-league hockey, playing in the Pacific Coast Association and Western Canada Leagues, competitors to the NHL for the Stanley Cup. And in 1923–24, skating for the Vancouver Millionaires, Duncan made big-league hockey history, posting 21–10–31 totals in 30 games to lead the PCHA in scoring.

Duncan was the first defenceman to ever win a major-league scoring title. It wouldn't happen again until Orr of the Boston Bruins led the NHL and won the Art Ross Trophy with 120 points in 1969–70.

Duncan and Orr would share another mark. On March 11, 1922, Duncan scored three goals as Vancouver won the WCHL-PCHA Stanley Cup semi-final over the Regina Capitals by a 4–0 count. A defenceman wouldn't record a hat trick again in Stanley Cup play until April 11, 1971, when Orr put three pucks past Ken Dryden as the Bruins downed the Montreal Canadiens 5–2 in Game 4 of their quarter-final series.

Duncan could fly on the ice and in the sky. Commissioned as a lieutenant in the 228th Battalion (Canadian Railway Troops) in the Great War, with his sensational hand-eye coordination Duncan was soon transferred to the Royal Flying Corps and was promoted to captain in the Royal Air Force.

Flying a mission at 6,000 feet at the rear of the German lines, Duncan got separated from his formation while flying through a cloudburst. Alone in the air, with a double-seater German plane set prey upon him, Duncan out-manoeuvred the enemy pilot, got above him and swooped down in attack, riddling the plane with a hail of bullets.

Duncan then trailed the German plane to the back of the British lines, where he forced the disabled craft to land and the ship and crew were taken prisoner.

For his bravery, Duncan was decorated with the Military Cross, and awarded a Bar, both for "conspicuous gallantry and devotion to duty." During the war he was credited with 11 victories in aerial combat.

HOCKEY'S GASHOUSE GANG

The Maple Leafs of the 1930s enjoyed their fun, maybe too much, which might explain why they appeared in seven Stanley Cup finals during the decade, but lifted Lord Stanley's mug just once.

HOW IRVINE DREW AN ACE

Irvine (Ace) Bailey was the Leafs' first shooting ace, leading the NHL scoring race in 1928–29 with 22–10–32 numbers. Some thought that was where his nickname originated, as the ace among goal scorers.

There was another legend that Bailey gained the handle because of his uncanny ability to draw an ace whenever the boys would deal out the cards.

In truth, it was for neither of these reasons.

"I got it from a fellow in Toronto," Bailey explained to writer Jimmy Thompson in 1930. "This chap was always going broke—of course there's nothing unusual about that in these days—and every time he saw me, he'd always touch me for a couple of dollars.

"His friends becoming curious as to where he got this money, asked where he got it, but all they could get out of him was that it came from his "Ace" in the hole.

"Gosh," Irvine Bailey finished, "that reminds me, he owes me 20 bucks right now."

THE KIDS WERE ALRIGHT

The Leafs weren't having much luck making any headway in the NHL standings in the late 1920s. Meanwhile, the Toronto Marlboros were dominating the junior ranks.

Frank Selke Sr., who ran the Marlies and was also Conn Smythe's right-hand man as the Leafs assistant GM, suggested to his boss that he fortify his squad with some of his Memorial Cup champion Marlboros.

Smythe listened, adding defencemen Alex Levinsky and Red Horner and two-thirds of what would become the most dangerous forward line in the NHL with left-winger Harvey (Busher) Jackson, 19, and right-winger Charlie Conacher, 20.

Placed on each side of centre Joe Primeau, at 24 the elder statesmen of the unit, the trio quickly garnered the nickname the Kid Line.

They were big boys. Conacher tipped the scales at 198 pounds, while Jackson weighed in at 196.

Conacher could score by going hard to the net or via what was simply the hardest shot in hockey.

"Conacher could shoot like none of the others," former Leaf Frank Finnigan told the *Ottawa Journal*. "He could vary a shot. He'd play the goalies with a couple of knee-high shots. When he wanted, he'd drill one high. But those low ones would take an ankle off you when he was levelling for a goal."

Jackson's forte was speed. He could leave any defenceman flat-footed.

"I never ran up against a wingman who could come up to you and then leave you like the Busher," Finnigan said.

Former Leafs defenceman King Clancy was still with the Ottawa Senators the first time he encountered the competitiveness of Jackson. "He takes this shot and (Ottawa goalie) Alex Connell makes the stop," Clancy recounted to the *Brandon Sun*. "The puck ended up on top of the net.

"I'm standing there, minding my own business when I see Jackson swoosh in and try and hand mashie that puck into the net the back way. I gave him the old dingaroo with the stick. Broke his thumb.

"'Uh uh' I yelled at him. 'Rookies don't go around trying tricks like that.'"

While Conacher and Jackson were robust, Primeau was cerebral, providing the perfect mix of personalities for the group.

"With their size and speed they needed a centre who could hesitate," Finnigan explained. "Primeau could do that. He could stop and give it to either side.

"The wings didn't need to hesitate. Joe would see to that."

They dominated the 1930s like no other forward line. Between 1930–31 and 1936–37, at least one member of the Kid Line was among the NHL's top 10 scorers. From 1931–32 through 1936–37, there was always a member of the Kid Line on the NHL's First or Second All-Star Teams.

"They were the best players in the league," teammate Red Horner said.

In 1931–32, Jackson and Primeau finished first and second in the scoring race and Conacher's 34 goals were an NHL high. Conacher and Primeau ran first and second in scoring in 1933–34 and Conacher defended his scoring title in 1934–35.

Three times Primeau topped the league in assists. Five times Conacher led the NHL in goals.

"It was a real talent to be a hard-shooting player like Conacher was," Horner said.

The litmus test, the coming out party for the kids came in the 1932 Cup final, when Toronto faced off against the New York Rangers and their sensational unit of Frank Boucher between the Cook brothers Bill and Bun.

It was no contest. Toronto swept the best-of-five series, with the Kid Line dominating. Jackson scored five goals in three games, Conacher added three of his own and the trio finished with 16 points.

"They could really go after goals," said Finnigan, a member of that 1931–32 Leafs team. "You could be three goals up and then they'd suddenly cut loose.

"You never could be sure when they'd bear down. They were the top line in my book."

SUB ZEROES

The Leafs put their stock of whitewash to rapid use to start the 1930–31 season. Toronto posted five straight shutouts to open the season, an NHL record from the beginning of the campaign.

What made it an even more curious achievement was that Toronto did so while alternating goalies, a practice that wouldn't become commonplace in hockey until well into the 1960s.

Lorne Chabot got the nod in goal for the season opener, a scoreless tie with the New York Americans. Then the Leafs turned to Benny Grant and he kicked aside 31 shots for a 4–0 verdict over the Philadelphia Quakers.

Taking their show on the road, Chabot was back between the pipes for a 3–0 verdict at Montreal over the Maroons. Going back to Grant, he turned in a 40-save performance in another scoreless tie against the Americans. Then it was Chabot's turn to shine again as he blanked the Ottawa Senators 2–0.

Surprisingly, the team that would ultimately make a claim for the title of the worst club in NHL history would be the one to halt Toronto's record stretch. Hib Milks scored on Grant 11:42 into the first period as the Philadelphia Quakers, who'd win just four times in 44 games during the season, edged the Leafs 2–1.

Including the two 10-minute overtime periods from the scoreless ties, Toronto's shutout streak lasted 331 minutes and 42 seconds, still the club record.

In the remaining 39 games of the season, the Leafs would post just three more shutouts and the rotating goalie plan would come to an end after Grant coughed up double digits in a 10–1 loss at Detroit on Christmas Day.

BUSHER'S HEROIC BRUSH WITH FIRE

As a member of Toronto's famous Kid Line in the 1930s, Harvey (Busher) Jackson was a hero to many. But on the night of May 24, 1931, Jackson was a life-saving hero to J. A. Fraser and J. B. Saulter of Toronto.

The two men were sleeping in their Wasaga Beach, Ontario, cottage when it was engulfed in flames.

Jackson was one of two men who joined an Ontario Provincial Police constable in a bid to save the trapped men. While one man went to arouse the local fire department, the police officer and Jackson entered the burning building.

Fraser was overcome by smoke, as was the police officer. Jackson carried one man to safety and then re-entered the burning structure to carry the other man out of the inferno. Saulter was able to escape the fire of his own accord.

Aside from his heroics on the ice—in 1931–32, Jackson, then 21, became the NHL's youngest scoring champion—it was one of the rare times when Jackson acted heroically.

He earned his nickname via his youthful petulance. Injured and unable to play, Leafs trainer Tim Daly asked the ailing Jackson to help him carry the sticks from the dressing room to the bench.

"I told him I wasn't a stick boy, I was a hockey player," Jackson remembered to *Canadian Press*. "So he said I was nothing but a fresh busher and the name stuck."

After retirement, a passion for exotic cars, alcohol, and making bad investments deprived Jackson of his hockey income. "I wish I had gotten into a good business when I was going good," Jackson said late in his life. "I haven't got a pretzel."

In 1954, he was arrested for assaulting his wife, Marie. Four years later, he was charged with threatening the wife of his landlord.

It was these sorts of actions that drove Leafs managing director Conn Smythe to launch a campaign to keep the four-time NHL First All-Star selection from gaining enshrinement in the Hockey Hall of Fame.

"I'm a hero-worshipper myself," Smythe said, explaining his rationale to writer Scott Young in 1970. "I have been all my life. And I think that has often been the thing that has kept me from doing things I shouldn't do. So I'm not going to help anybody give kids today a hero that isn't worth their worship."

The Hall of Fame finally enshrined Jackson in 1971, five years after his death. As a result, Smythe immediately tendered his resignation from the Hall's selection committee.

GARDENS OPENING WAS A GALA AFFAIR

Tom Gaston remembered well the night that Maple Leaf Gardens opened on November 12, 1931.

"There were lots of soup and fish," Gaston recalled in a 1998 interview. "That was slang in those days for tuxedos and top hats and tails."

Gaston, who worked for years as an assistant at the Hockey Hall of Fame, attended the first Leafs opener at the corner of Church and Carlton Streets.

He was there in his usual seat in section 94 in the west greys when the Leafs played their farewell opener at the Gardens against the Stanley Cup champion Detroit Red Wings to launch the 1998–99 NHL season, Toronto's final one at the famous hockey shrine.

Born in 1917, Gaston's family had season tickets at Mutual Street Arena, where the Leafs played before moving to the Gardens.

"It was a real event," Gaston said of the Gardens opener. "My dad made sure I had a suit and tie to wear.

"Everything smelled so new and the seats—the reds, the greens and the greys—were all so bright."

Opposing the Chicago Blackhawks, Toronto fell behind on Mush March's goal. "I can still see (Chicago centre) Doc Romnes winning the faceoff in their zone," March recalled in 1999. "(Tommy) Cook flipped the puck over to me. I shot it, I looked, and I was very surprised when it went in."

Charlie Conacher tied the score, and then Vic Ripley netted the winner in a 2–1 Chicago decision that sent the 13,233 Leafs fans home unhappy.

Prior to that night, the Blackhawks had never won a game in Toronto, going 0–9–1 at Toronto's previous home, Mutual Street Arena Gardens.

"It was just one of those things," March said of his historic goal. "It was something where you happen to be in the right place at the right time for something special."

A Silton, Saskatchewan native, March seemed to have a knack for coming up with something special.

He scored twice in the final NHL game at Mutual Street Arena Gardens—a 2–2 tie in a Stanley Cup game March 24, 1931 between Chicago and Toronto. But the honour of the final goal in that barn went to Toronto's Andy Blair. And March netted the first goal ever scored at Chicago Stadium, in a 6–5 loss to the Ottawa Senators November 21, 1929.

March—whose nickname was derived from the Dick Tracy character Mush Mouth—also tallied a fairly famous marker against the Detroit Red Wings, beating Wilf Cude at 10:05 of the second overtime period on April 10, 1934 to give the Blackhawks a 1–0 victory in Game 4 of the final series that year, clinching Chicago's first-ever Stanley Cup triumph.

CONVOY FOR CONVEY

Left-winger Eddie Convey was a junior hockey sensation. Playing on the same line for the Toronto Marlboros with future Leafs Charlie Conacher and Busher Jackson, as well as future Leafs Red Horner and Alex Levinsky on defence, Convey led the team with 12 assists as the Marlies won the 1928–29 Memorial Cup.

He never could translate that success into regular duty as an NHLer, and his Leaf buddies wanted to help their old pal make the grade.

When Convey, who had been recalled from the minor-league New Haven Eagles by the New York Americans, arrived to face the Leafs and his old teammates on December 22, 1931, Toronto had its way with the struggling New Yorkers, winning 9–3.

The quartet of ex-Marlies in the Leafs dressing room, led by Conacher, hatched a plan to help out Convey and everyone on the team bought into the scenario.

"If we get a few goals up, let's make it easy for Convey," Conacher said. "Let's help him score a couple."

Toronto raced to a 4–0 lead and the first time Convey got on the ice in the second period, right-winger Conacher abandoned his post, allowing Convey free reign to carry the puck into the Toronto zone. When he got to the defence, King Clancy let him slip past, giving Convey a breakaway. If that wasn't enough help, as Convey closed in on goal, Toronto netminder Lorne Chabot stayed to one side of his goal, leaving Convey the other half of the net wide open.

He fired wide.

The next time Convey got the puck, Conacher missed him with a bodycheck, Clancy stumbled and Chabot hugged his post tightly, leaving three-quarters of his net available.

Once more, Convey missed the target.

A third opportunity presented itself. Conacher missed his check, and Clancy did likewise. Chabot opted to go for a skate, leaving his cage unattended.

Convey bore down on the vacated net and fired a shot right over top of it.

Former Ottawa Rough Riders star Frank Dunlap heard Clancy regale a banquet audience with this tale one night and was certain it was fiction. By chance, he happened to run into Convey on a trip to Toronto and queried him on the subject.

"That's really true," Convey sheepishly admitted. "But I don't tell it nearly as well as Clancy does."

SNEAKY DICK

In his spare time, Leafs coach Dick Irvin's favourite pastime was working with his pigeons. He maintained a poultry farm back home in Regina and raised racing pigeons and champion poultry, often entering his prized birds in Toronto's famous Royal Winter Fair.

The night of February 18, 1932, Irvin sought to play the NHL for pigeons. Ever the crafty strategist, Irvin knew that the NHL rules of the day stated any player who jumped over the boards to create a too many men on the ice scenario would be assessed a major penalty.

Irvin also knew that two of his star players—right-winger Charlie Conacher and defenceman Red Horner—sat with two major penalties on the ledger for the season; Three majors called for an automatic one-game NHL suspension.

With the playoffs closing in, Irvin didn't want either player assessed a third major late in the season, as it might result in losing them for a key game. And it just so happened at the moment that both Conacher (broken hand) and Horner (fracture clavicle) were injured and on the shelf.

Irvin struck upon a brilliant idea. He suited up his two injured stars for a game against the New York Rangers. Neither player left the Toronto bench during the pre-game warm-up or the game, and then late in the contest, just before the time on the game clock expired, Irvin sent both Horner and Conacher over the boards and into the fray without taking any players off the ice. Prior to the game, Irvin informed game officials Eusebe Daignault and Odie Cleghorn of his plan, and both players were immediately assessed major penalties.

Hailed as a crafty genius in the media, Irvin was sure that he'd performed an end run on the rulebook, outsmarting those who ran the league, but NHL president Frank Calder didn't see it that way.

The day after Irvin's ploy, Calder advised Irvin that he didn't know the rules as well as he thought he did and issued the following statement:

"Because players Horner and Conacher, presumably both physically unfit to play, were sent on the ice in order to incur their third major penalty at Toronto last night, it does not follow that the inevitable suspension will apply to the "next" game in which they are presumably also able to play.

"While it has been customary to suspend a player incurring his third major penalty for one game, and that (being) the "next" one, the rule does not specifically provide that the suspension shall be for the "next" game—or for only one game. That point seems to have been overlooked.

"Both players are now undoubtedly under automatic suspension—but the duration of the suspension is for the time being, made indefinite pending further investigation."

His message sent, Calder did not make the punished players sit for long. Horner was reinstated February 23 and Conacher on February 25.

NOW IN GOAL ...

The Three Musketeers they weren't. More like the Three Stooges.

The Leafs were in Boston for a late-season game against the Bruins on March 15, 1932. The contest was barely underway when Boston centre Cooney Weiland lagged leisurely in the Toronto zone and Leafs goalie Lorne Chabot playfully tripped the Bruin. Referee Bill Stewart failed to see the humour in the act and called a minor penalty on Chabot.

In those days, the goaltender served his own penalty, so while Chabot cooled his heels in the sin bin, three Leafs defencemen set out to prove why they didn't pursue puckstopping as a profession.

First up was rugged Red Horner, who'd protected the net flawlessly once previously in a two-minute stint on January 29, 1928 at

Ottawa after Chabot took umbrage with the work of referee Billy Bell and fired the puck at the official.

Things started out just fine when Horner made a save on a Weiland shot. But just seconds later, Eddie Shore slipped the puck to Marty Barry, who scored easily to make it 1–0.

That was enough for Horner, who handed off Chabot's oversized cudgel to teammate Alex Levinsky.

He'd barely taken up the position when Weiland fed Barry and he whistled a long shot past Levinsky. He then turned over the goaltender chores to King Clancy.

Clancy was a veteran of the pipes. Famously in the 1923 Stanley Cup final for the Ottawa Senators he'd kept a clean sheet for two minutes while goalie Clint Benedict served a penalty, essential work since the final margin of victory over the Edmonton Eskimos in the Cup clincher was 1–0.

Maybe it was simply a matter of first time lucky for Clancy, because the Bruins also made short work of him. Shore carried the puck down the boards and fed a wide-open George Owen on Clancy's doorstep and he made no mistake.

With Chabot off the ice, Leafs' managing director Conn Smythe decided he couldn't bear to watch and retreated to the Boston Garden concourse, but every so often curiosity got the better of him and he'd come back for a peek, each time with disastrous results.

"Connie Smythe started through one runway just in time to see a puck zing past Red Horner," Clancy recalled to the *Ottawa Journal*. "He blinked as if he couldn't believe it and tried another runway in time to see another goal whiz past Alex Levinsky.

"Connie came out a third runway just as another goal went by me. They were blasting from six to 10 feet out at point blank range."

The Bruins scored three power-play goals in 1:31 on three different goalies, though applying the term goaltender to describe this trio is generous use of the word.

Later in the game, Chabot risked another penalty when he punched Owen in the nose, but it went undetected by the officials in the midst of a goal-mouth scramble.

The Boston fans took notice and rode Chabot hard the rest of the game. He revelled in their distaste and at the end of the game, a 6–2 Boston win, Chabot skated to centre and took a bow before heading to the dressing room.

JOE'S BROTHER THE FATHER

When Joe Primeau was awarded the Lady Byng Trophy for sportsmanship in 1931–32, the Leafs centre broke a four-year stranglehold on the award by New York Rangers centre Frank Boucher. In fact, it would be the only time in an eight-season span that Boucher didn't win the Lady Byng.

They called him Gentleman Joe, but Primeau's brother answered to an even higher calling. Cecil Primeau gave up his hockey career in 1926 and left his Toronto home to enter the Jesuit novitiate in Guelph, Ontario.

In 1932, Cecil Primeau, in his last year of training for the priesthood and studying philosophy in Toronto, was granted special permission to attend a December 29 game at Maple Leaf Gardens between the Leafs and Montreal Maroons.

It was the first time he'd ever seen his brother play an NHL game, a 1–0 win on a King Clancy goal and a 20-save shutout by Lorne Chabot.

By the early 1940s, Rev. Cecil Primeau was serving as a missionary among the Ojibway Indians in northern Ontario.

CHABOT'S BUSIEST NIGHT

Lorne Chabot was the goalie when the Maple Leafs won their first Stanley Cup in 1931–32 and the netminder who posted a 93-save shutout in the longest game in franchise history, a 1–0 Stanley Cup six-overtime victory over the Boston Bruins on April 3, 1933. But neither of those rated as Chabot's most impressive work as Toronto's puckstopper.

The Leafs travelled to Ottawa to face the Senators on November 20, 1928, but early in the game, several Leafs ran afoul of the rules in short order and were sent to the visitor's penalty box by referee Jean Dussault, who was making his NHL debut as an arbiter.

It started when Ottawa forward Bill Touhey got behind the Leafs' defence and Toronto captain Hap Day spilled Touhey, drawing a tripping major. Art Duncan soon followed Day, called for tripping Hec Kilrea.

With the Leafs two men down, Frank Finnigan finished a three-way passing play for an apparent Ottawa goal, but it was waved off because official Billy Bell had whistled the play dead before the puck entered the net for a tripping penalty on Toronto's Art Smith, who had upended Senators' defenceman King Clancy. Ottawa defenceman George Boucher also thought he had scored seconds later, but the play was ruled offside. Then Jack Arbour tripped Ottawa's Clancy and now a fourth Leaf was in the bin.

There was no limit to how many men short a team could be in those days, so the Leafs found themselves four men down, Chabot and rookie forward Andy Blair, playing in just his third NHL game, left to fight off five Ottawa attackers. It was about to get very busy around the Toronto net.

"Toronto had four men in the box and the rink was in an uproar," reported the *Ottawa Journal*. "Finnigan went in on a pass, and Chabot saved. Chabot saved three times off Finnigan and Clancy in sensational style. Ottawa showed too much anxiety in going in close to shoot and rattled a lot of shots of Chabot's pads."

The *Ottawa Citizen* noted that the Senators "buzzed around Chabot like a hive of bees. Lorne Chabot's great stand against five Ottawa gunmen in the first period was simply sensational. The Port Arthur boy was bouncing all around in his net, knocking out drives pelted here and there."

Finally, Frank Nighbor fed Clancy for the lone Ottawa power-play goal during this five-on-one situation, the only advantage of that size to ever occur in NHL history.

"The (Ottawa) crowd gave Chabot a great ovation for his glorious feat," noted the *Citizen*.

During the game, a 4–1 Ottawa victory, Chabot faced 54 shots.

"I'll never forget that as long as I live," Chabot said afterward. "That was my hottest five minutes of hockey."

ONE KIDNEY, SEVEN SCORING TITLES

Were he playing in today's NHL, Charlie Conacher would be the owner of five Rocket Richard Trophies and a pair of Art Ross Trophies. But in his era there were no awards for the NHL's top goal scorer or scoring leader.

Leafs' right-winger Conacher led the NHL in goals five times in six seasons from 1930–31 through 1935–36, putting up some impressive totals in that span. Four times he topped 30 goals, netting 31 goals in 37 games in 1930–31, 34 in 44 games in 1931–32 and 36 goals in 1934–35. He scored six times in seven games as the Leafs won the Stanley Cup in the spring of 1932. Conacher also finished as the NHL leader in points in 1933–34 with 52 and 1934–35 with 57.

"He had everything," Hall-of-Fame goaltender Alex Connell told the *Ottawa Journal*. "He had the class that goes to make a great hockey player. He was strong and he was big. He wasn't rough but when anything started on the ice he was right in the middle of it. Believe me, the other players respected him."

The Big Bomber, as Conacher was known, was considered the owner of the hardest shot in hockey during the 1930s and he utilized it to pile up those impressive scoring totals.

"He was the best right wing I ever saw," Connell said. "He was as fast on his skates as a 150 pounder and there was never anyone with a more wicked shot. He drove them at you like a bullet. On top of his size and his strength and his speed, he was brainy.

"You never knew how he was coming in on you with the puck. One time he'd play you one way. The next time he'd come down on you in an entirely different way. He was a fellow that it was almost impossible to get set for, and then he had that blazing shot."

Perhaps most amazingly of all, Conacher accomplished all of these feats despite undergoing surgery for the removal of his left kidney on April 29, 1930.

"The loss of one kidney will not affect his future," vowed Charlie's brother, Montreal Maroons defenceman Lionel Conacher. "He'll play hockey again."

A power forward long before the term ever came into vogue, the 6'1", 195-pound Conacher played the game with a fearless courage, driving the net and accepting the punishment required to do so without giving it a thought. But he paid a price for his no-holds-barred style of play. As a junior with the Toronto Marlboros, he crashed hard into a goalpost and it was the injuries suffered from that collision that saw Conacher fall seriously ill not long after the conclusion of the 1929–30 season, and eventually costing him a kidney in life-saving surgery. Over the years he also suffered a broken hand, fractured wrist, separated shoulder, broken collarbone and a bout of blood poisoning from an infection that developed in a cut across his hand.

Eventually the years of injury and illness took a toll on Conacher. He scored just three times in 15 games in 1936–37 and had seven goals through 19 games in 1937–38, when he stunned the hockey world by calling it quits.

"We are resigned to that Charlie won't play next season or the season after that," Leafs managing director Conn Smythe told the *Winnipeg Tribune*. "We don't expect a miracle."

It was another collision with a goalpost during the 1937–38 campaign that brought about the demise of Conacher's days as a Leaf.

When Conacher returned to action, the familiar drive was gone from his rushes. It was evident that there was something seriously wrong.

"He is in no condition to play hockey ever again," pronounced team physician Dr. J. W. Rush. "The strain on that one kidney over a period of strenuous years has been too much. The kidney stopped functioning properly.

"Charlie needs a long rest in a warm climate. I told him he must give up violent exercise of all kinds."

After taking the rest of the season off, Conacher did return to the NHL, playing one season with Detroit Red Wings and two with the New York Americans, mostly as a defenceman, but he was never the same player who had dominated the league as a Leaf. He retired from the NHL in 1941 at the still young age of 30.

Conacher enjoyed a lengthy coaching career, leading the Oshawa Generals to the 1944 Memorial Cup and later taking the helm of the NHL's Chicago Blackhawks from 1947–50. He was inducted into the Hockey Hall of Fame in 1961 and the Canada Sports Hall of Fame in 1975.

THE MIGHTY MOLECULE

There was nothing big about Ken Doraty. He wasn't a big-time star, spending much of his time toiling on the bench, and he certainly wasn't big in stature, standing 5'7" and tipping the scales at a meagre 133 pounds. But when it came time to come up big, Doraty frequently loomed large.

During 103 regular-season NHL games, Doraty scored just 15 times, an average of one goal every 6.8 games played. But in 15 playoff games as a Leaf from 1932–35, Doraty scored seven times, an average of just under one every two games, impressive considering that the amount of ice time he usually saw was extremely limited.

Among those seven tallies was one of the most famous in both Leafs and NHL history.

The Leafs faced the Boston Bruins in Game 5 of their Stanley Cup semi-final series at Maple Leaf Gardens on April 3, 1933. A Toronto win would clinch the series and send the defending Cup champion Leafs on to face the New York Rangers in a rematch of the 1932 final.

A throng of 14,500 gathered, the largest at that time to ever witness a hockey game in Canada, and they'd wait well into the evening—in fact into the wee hours of the early morning—before they'd see a goal. And it would be the only one they'd see, at least the only one that would count.

After 104 minutes and 46 seconds of overtime, at 1:50 a.m., Toronto forward Andy Blair intercepted a pass from Boston defenceman Eddie Shore in the neutral zone and headed toward the Bruins end. As Blair entered the Boston zone, the diminutive Doraty, known as the Mighty Molecule, darted toward the Boston net. He took Blair's pass in stride and drove a low shot into the corner of the net past Boston goalie Tiny Thompson, ending what at the time was the longest game in NHL history.

Seldom-used during regulation time, Doraty seemed to have fresher legs than anyone else on the ice and four times during the overtime session prior to his goal got in alone, only to be foiled by Thompson.

Each team scored once prior to Doraty's tally. Alex Smith tallied for Boston in the third period but referee Odie Cleghorn ruled that Smith had been offside. In the fourth overtime session Toronto defenceman King Clancy put the puck in the Bruins net after the whistle had already been blown.

After the fifth overtime, there was a long delay as debate was waged about whether to continue. As the delay lingered, fans started clapping in unison, seeking a return to the ice of the two teams.

In the dressing rooms, talk of a coin flip was put forth.

"The Boston club made this suggestion," NHL president Frank Calder explained. "Toronto was willing but I pointed out to them the rules say each game must be played to a finish so they went on playing."

Two years later, facing elimination against the Detroit Red Wings, Doraty scored twice as the Leafs downed the Wings 3–1. "Boy I'm telling you Doraty is the best pinch-hitter in hockey," Detroit coach Jack Adams said. "In a playoff series of this kind, Doraty is the ideal player.

"Doraty was the deciding factor. He has been before in an important series and he will be again. We never fool ourselves that the little fellow isn't in there. We know he is."

Doraty was occasionally deadly in regular-season action as well. Earlier in the 1933–34 season, on January 16, he scored a hat trick against the Ottawa Senators. What made this three-goal performance even more memorable was that Doraty scored all his goals in the ten-minute overtime period after Toronto and Ottawa were deadlocked 4–4 in regulation.

Doraty is the only player in NHL history to record a hat trick during an overtime period.

THE LEAF WHO ALMOST DIED

Frank Selke Sr. was in Toronto when he took a cryptic phone call from his boss, Leafs managing director Conn Smythe.

"Look Frank," Smythe said from Boston. "I want you to make arrangements to get (Ace) Bailey's body back to Canada."

"Is he dead?" Selke asked.

"Not quite," Smythe replied. "But it's only a matter of time."

There was always bad blood when the Leafs faced the Boston Bruins. Blood was often spilled when the two teams clashed. But no game ever played between the two was more horrific than on the night of December 12, 1933.

Boston defenceman Eddie Shore was taken out of the play with solid bodycheck from Leafs rugged Red Horner. Getting to his feet in a sour mood and looking to exact revenge, the first Leaf Shore spotted was Bailey.

He stepped into Bailey from behind with his right shoulder and the Toronto forward flipped, his head crashing into the ice with a dull thud that echoed throughout the rink. Bailey lay on the ice, his body writhing in convulsions.

Spotting the smug look on Shore's face, Horner rushed toward him, decking Shore with one punch. His head also cracked on the ice and blood began pooling under him.

A brawl seemed certain, but Boston's Vic Ripley, realizing that Bailey was in serious jeopardy, acted the role of peacemaker.

"Both Shore and Bailey were unconscious," recounted Selke in his biography *Beyond The Cheering*. "But the Toronto player was more badly hurt."

Sixteen stitches were required to patch up Shore's head, but it was quickly evident serious medical attention would be required to save Bailey's life. Moved to a dressing room for treatment, his facial colour paled and one side of his body was slowly turning a bluish hue.

"If this boy is a Roman Catholic, we should call a priest," suggested Boston Garden house physician C. Lynde Gately.

Bailey briefly regained consciousness, and was visited by Shore, who expressed his regret for what he'd done. "I'm awfully sorry," Shore said. "I didn't mean it."

"It's all right Eddie," Bailey told him. "It's all in the game."

When Bailey relapsed into unconsciousness, he was rushed by ambulance to hospital.

He was diagnosed with a fractured skull and a cerebral haemorrhage. There was a five-inch crack in Bailey's right frontal and parietal bones that started in the forehead over the right eye and extended beyond the right ear. There were signs of internal bleeding and pressure on the brain was three times its normal rate. Fluid was drawn off by puncturing the skull at the base of the spine to relieve pressure on the brain. There were no signs of paralysis.

"They would have charged Shore with manslaughter if Bailey had died," Horner said. Indeed, Boston police did investigate.

"I see nothing criminal in this case," Boston Police inspector John J. McCarthy said. "There was no criminal intent on Shore's part to injure Bailey."

Two delicate brain operations were performed in order to save Bailey's life.

"I think he'll pull through," Smythe predicted of Bailey. "He certainly is a remarkable fellow."

It was touch and go for about a week, but Bailey did survive. "As far his condition is concerned, as soon as he gets over his convalescence he will have made a complete recovery," neurosurgeon Dr. Donald Munro, who performed both surgeries on the Leaf player, told *United Press*.

Shore sat out a 16-game NHL suspension for his hit on Bailey, but Bailey wasn't in the market for retribution.

"I didn't see Eddie and he didn't see me and we crashed, and that's all," Bailey said. "I don't remember anything leading up to the play or anything about the game, except from what (Boston manager Art) Ross told me.

"There never was any hard feeling between Shore and myself."

Smythe, who faced assault and battery charges for punching fan Leonard Kenworthy as he tried to fight through the crowd to get to the injured Bailey, charges that were later dropped, was less forgiving.

"This judgement is a joke," Smythe said of Shore's suspension. "There isn't any mention of compensation for the Maple Leaf hockey club or for Ace Bailey.

"The Toronto Maple Leafs have been penalized enough already with incurring a further loss of what I figure will amount to $8,000.

Who is going to pay the hospital bill and all the expenses resulting from Bailey's injury? We will have to pay the salary of a hockey player who won't be on the ice for a single minute during the rest of the season. Bruins will have Shore back January 28 and besides that, we lost Horner for six games (his suspension for striking Shore). Is there any justice in that?"

The Bruins helped relieve the financial burden, turning over the gate receipts of $6,741 from their December 19 game with the Montreal Maroons to Bailey to help defray his medical costs.

By mid-January, Bailey was up and about and holding press conferences. "Tell the Toronto fans I'll never forget their kindness," Bailey said on January 12 , 1934. "I'm getting better.

"I feel so good now I expect to be back on the ice before the season is over."

Bailey's injuries would prevent him from ever playing hockey again.

Years later, Bailey wondered whether protective headgear might have made the whole matter moot.

"Had I been wearing a helmet, it is likely that my injuries would have been slight," Bailey told *CP* in 1968. "My feet were swept from under me and I struck my head on the ice. A helmet would have cushioned this.

"I didn't lose a drop of blood. I had tried a helmet earlier in my career, but didn't wear one for very long."

FIT FOR A KING

Suggesting that St. Patrick's Day was King Clancy's favourite night of the year wouldn't be a stretch, but on March 17, 1934, it truly was King Clancy Night at Maple Leaf Gardens.

The Leafs honoured their veteran defenceman prior to their game against the New York Rangers. With his father Tom, the original King Clancy watching, Clancy was presented an array of gifts including a tea service from the Knights of Columbus, a chest of silver from the Maple Leafs directors, a grandfather clock from his teammates and a radio to be installed in his automobile from a local car dealer.

A pre-game parade to the ice featured colourful floats such as a giant Irish potato, a harp, and an old boot. Finally, the Leafs' defenceman arrived in a sleigh, Clancy riding in behind the man at the reins, crown on his head, sceptre in his hand. He began the game garbed in a deep green Leafs sweater, with a white shamrock on the back, but the Rangers complained that they found the jersey distracting and after one period Clancy switched to his regular Leafs sweater.

The Leafs won the game 3–2 on a third-period goal by Ken Doraty.

Afterward, 13-season veteran Clancy predicted the end was near for him. "I love the game, but I've been in it a long time and I figure two more years is as much as I can stand," he said.

True to his word, Clancy retired in 1936.

CONACHER A LIFE SAVER

Though his brother Lionel was the one known as the Big Train, on April 20, 1934, it was Charlie Conacher who came up big on the train.

The Leafs and Detroit Red Wings were travelling westward for a post-season exhibition series in British Columbia when Conacher noticed a man atop the speeding train preparing to leap from the observation platform. Acting quickly, Conacher raced to the top of the train and lunged for the man, grabbing him just as he was about to fall to his death.

It was later revealed that the man was being transferred to the Essondale, British Columbia, psychiatric hospital.

GOODFELLOW CONVINCED KING TO ABDICATE

Edward VIII of England wasn't the only King to abdicate his throne in 1936. Maple Leafs legend Francis (King) Clancy also chose that year to hang up his skates.

It was a shot by his old Ottawa buddy Ebbie Goodfellow of the Detroit Red Wings that convinced the Leafs defenceman to call it quits as an NHL player on November 24, 1936.

Two nights earlier, from a faceoff in the Toronto end, Goodfellow beat Clancy to a loose puck and rifled a shot into the Leafs' net.

"I am in good condition," Clancy explained to *Canadian Press*. "I feel fine and I think I could play the rest of the season, but that incident convinced me that I was not as fast as I used to be.

"It started me thinking and today I made up my mind to retire while I was still on top and my health was good. So I told (Leafs managing director Conn) Smythe that I had decided to hang up my skates and make room for a younger fellow.

"No one influenced me in my decision. I realized I had just about reached the end of the rope and could do more for the club by pulling out and making room for a better man."

Clancy did admit that he felt badly about leaving the team at a time when the Leafs sat at the bottom of the NHL's International Division with just three points, but felt it was best for the team.

"I think when the team hits its real stride and gets back to the top, everyone will be grateful for the move I have made," Clancy said.

Smythe indicated that Clancy would continue to travel with the Leafs and would be in charge of team morale and also serve as a goodwill ambassador.

"I hate to see him not back of the blue line for us, but there was nothing I could do," Smythe said. "He told me of his decision and I said it was entirely up to him."

It was Smythe who purchased Clancy from the Ottawa Senators for a record price of $35,000 in 1930. In the process of building a championship team, Clancy was the straw who stirred the drink for the young Leafs, a veteran presence with two Stanley Cup wins to his credit.

Solidifying the team and bringing character to the room, Clancy helped the Leafs to the 1931–32 Stanley Cup and was a four-time NHL All-Star selection.

"Clancy has given us six years of great hockey and I cannot complain of any action he takes," Smythe said. "Major league hockey loses one of its greatest players and one of its finest sportsmen and like everyone else I am sorry to see him go."

A 15-year NHL veteran, at 34, Clancy was the oldest active player at the time of his retirement.

"He was the most colourful, most loyal and most courageous player ever to perform," NHL president Frank Calder said.

Leafs' centre Joe Primeau saw Clancy as the man who turned Toronto's young core into champions. "The first year he was with us, we reached the playoffs," Primeau told the *Ottawa Journal*. "The next year we won it, and we were in the finals for four out of five years.

"His dynamic personality and drive inspired us."

After a stint as coach of the Montreal Maroons and as an NHL referee, Clancy returned to the Leafs organization in the 1950s and worked with the franchise in a variety of capacities, including as coach, assistant coach, assistant general manager and vice-president until his death in 1986.

SHORE TAKES LEAVE OF HIS SENSES

Leafs coach Dick Irvin called it "the greatest feat any team ever pulled anywhere."

Boston Bruins' defenceman Babe Siebert took a completely opposite view. "It was highway robbery," Siebert griped to writer Elmer Dulmage. "We were robbed, there's no doubt of that.

"Nothing like it has ever happened before."

The Bruins rolled to a solid 3–0 victory over the Leafs in the opening game of the two-game total goals Stanley Cup quarter-final series between the two arch-rivals on March 24, 1936.

When Bill Cowley scored the only goal of the first period of Game 2 two days later at Maple Leaf Gardens to extend Boston's lead in the series to 4–0, things looked grim for the blue and white.

Finally, the Leafs caught a break in the second period. All-Star Boston defenceman Eddie Shore was banished to the penalty box by referee Odie Cleghorn, and while he was off, both King Clancy and Charlie Conacher connected on the power play.

Shore returned to action, but the Leafs tallied again, Red Horner banging home the rebound of an Art Jackson shot. Shore protested vehemently, insisting that Horner was in Tiny Thompson's goal crease when Jackson shot and therefore the goal shouldn't count.

Cleghorn, however, would hear none of it. Sensing that the infamous Shore temper was reaching a boiling point, Clancy deployed a little bit of the Irish blarney.

Sidling up next to Shore, Clancy agreed that Horner's goal should never have counted and insisted to Shore that Cleghorn was giving the Bruins the shaft.

"That was a cheesy penalty," Clancy opined regarding the minor that Shore was serving when the Leafs scored twice. As he talked and fuelled Shore's anger, Clancy calmly placed the puck at Shore's feet.

"Don't let the bum get away with the thing like that."

Seething and seeing red, a frustrated Shore cradled the puck with his blade and fired a shot toward the referee, connecting squarely with Cleghorn's backside.

Instantly, Shore was assessed a ten-minute misconduct. With their backbone in the bin, the Bruins faltered and the Leafs poured in three quick goals to take control of the game and the series.

Toronto went on to win the game 8–3 and take the round 8–6.

"I've been around a lot and I've never seen anything like it," Clancy said.

Shore was still fuming after the game's conclusion.

"I got the misconduct for telling Cleghorn that Horner was in the crease on his goal," Shore complained. "Sure, I told him off.

"He never could referee and never will be able to."

Leafs' managing director Conn Smythe couldn't resist getting in a dig at his old foe Boston manager Art Ross as the two shook hands in the Leafs' dressing room.

"Well I guess a couple of home referees did us more good than they did you," Smythe said with a grin. "You got the breaks in Boston and we got them here."

THE BENTLEY WHO GOT AWAY

In 1947, the Leafs traded for Chicago Blackhawks star and 1945–46 Hart Trophy winner Max Bentley, a two-time NHL scoring champion, and he helped the Leafs win three Stanley Cups. But long before they acquired Max, the Leafs let his older brother Doug slip through their fingers.

Doug, the leading scorer in the Saskatchewan Senior League in 1936–37 with the Moose Jaw Millers, headed to camp with the Maple Leafs full of optimism and hope.

He was engaged in conversation in the dressing room with Toronto forward Art Jackson on the first day of training when players began to arrive.

"A great big good-looking guy came through the door, glowered around the room until he came to me and then went over to the trainer (Tim Daly)," Bentley recalled to the *Winnipeg Tribune* in 1943. "'Daly,' he said, 'get out my equipment. I feel like playing rough today.'"

Shaken, Bentley turned to Jackson. "Who's that?" he asked. "That's my brother (Busher)," Jackson answered.

Bentley continued his tale of woe.

"Just then, an even bigger guy came through the door. He had a great big, black, tough cigar in his mouth and he looked at me and shouted to the trainer, 'Daly, get my equipment. Somebody's going to get hurt today.'

"I looked at Jackson and said, 'Who's that?' 'That's Charlie Conacher,' he said.

"The third guy who came in was just as big as Conacher, and he stood in the doorway and flexed his muscles and looked at me. 'Daly,' he said. 'Get out my heavy pads. I'm going to do some bodychecking.'

"Jackson didn't wait for me to ask. 'That's Red Horner,' he said.

During the workout, the frightened Bentley stayed out of the corners and shied away from the puck. That evening, he caught the first train home to Delisle, Saskatchewan.

Signed by Chicago in 1939, Bentley would win the NHL scoring title in 1942–43 and was a three-time NHL First All-Star Team selection. He was inducted into the Hockey Hall of Fame in 1964.

ALL ABOUT ALFIE

As the Chicago Blackhawks began preparations for Game 1 of the 1938 Stanley Cup final on April 5 against the Leafs at Maple Leaf Gardens, they realized that there was a problem.

Goaltender Mike Karakas, who'd broken the big toe of his right foot two days earlier in Chicago's semi-final triumph over the New York Americans, couldn't get his skate on over the swollen digit. Since Chicago was travelling without a back-up goalie, coach Bill Stewart and GM Bill Tobin discussed contingency plans with Leafs GM Conn Smythe earlier in the day, and insisted that they'd been granted permission to use Dave Kerr of the New York Rangers as an emergency replacement.

Kerr joined the Blackhawks in their dressing room and began to don his gear, but outside the door, trouble was brewing.

The Leafs claimed no knowledge of such an agreement and refused to allow Chicago to use Kerr.

Unbeknownst to the Chicago brass, the Leafs had secreted away journeyman minor-league goalie Alfie Moore in a separate dressing room and had him all suited up and ready to go.

Leafs' assistant GM Frank Selke Sr. had phoned Moore, who was back home in Toronto after his Pittsburgh Hornets were eliminated from the International League playoffs, in the afternoon to see if he was available to play.

Moore claimed Selke had told him that Kerr was ruled to be ineligible, and Moore would have to guard the Chicago net.

"Finally I entered Chicago's dressing room and they didn't even know I was to play," Moore explained to *Canadian Press*. "Kerr was getting dressed.

"Right then I knew I had been made the sucker."

The Blackhawks were furious over what they felt was an attempt by the Leafs to sabotage their earlier agreement.

"Nobody told us Kerr was ineligible to play," Chicago vice-president Bill Tobin said. "Instead (Toronto managing director Conn) Smythe orders Moore here while we are away at our hotel, banking on having Kerr in the nets. We get to the Gardens and Kerr starts to get ready. Then Moore walks in to tell us he has been ordered here to play."

Selke flatly denied Moore's claims that he was the one who'd informed the goalie he'd be in the net for Chicago.

"I didn't tell Moore he had to play," Selke insisted. "I told him he might have to play if Kerr was ruled ineligible."

Tobin, Chicago manager Bill Stewart, Moore, and Smythe ended up in a shouting match inside the Blackhawks' dressing room.

It seemed as though things had settled down, but when Stewart and Smythe crossed paths in the corridor some minutes later a second argument ensued. When Selke got involved, the tension ramped up.

"You're a liar," Stewart hollered at Selke.

"You can't call my pal Selke a liar and get away with it, Smythe shouted and Stewart and Smythe came to blows.

The Chicago coach came out of the fray with a black eye, a cut cheek, and a bruised forehead.

Meanwhile NHL president Frank Calder finally settled the matter, ruling that Kerr would not be permitted to fill in for Karakas.

Eventually, the game began with Moore, a 12-season minor-league veteran with just 18 games of NHL experience, between the pipes. And Chicago's worst fears appeared realized when Toronto's Gordie Drillon whacked the rebound of a Bob Davidson shot past Moore just two minutes into the contest.

But that was it. Moore settled in and kept a clean sheet the rest of the way. Johnny Gottselig scored twice and Paul Thompson netted the game winner in a 3–1 Chicago victory.

Stewart wasn't done scrapping. In the first intermission, he bellowed loudly in the hallway outside the dressing rooms about, "the Toronto racketeers who were Smythe's bodyguards," counting former Leaf forward Baldy Cotton among that group.

Cotton overheard the accusation and charged at Stewart, landing a solid right hand that bloodied Stewart's nose, resulting in yet another fight.

When the game was done, Moore fired a few verbal jabs in the Leafs' direction.

"It isn't fair to the Hawks," Moore told the *Chicago Tribune*. "They wanted Kerr and I was picked because I'm a bum."

This self-proclaimed bum was ruled ineligible for Game 2. Farmhand Paul Goodman got the start and was lit up in a 5–1 Leafs victory.

It was all Chicago from that point onward. Karakas returned and the Blackhawks took the next two games to capture the best-of-five series and skate off with the Stanley Cup.

FUN WAS ALWAYS NO. 1

As great as they were on the ice, the Leafs of the 1930s were far more dangerous away from the rink.

"There was no need to expand the stories because a team with guys like Charlie Conacher, Busher Jackson, King Clancy and Baldy Cotton was certain to have a great deal of fun," centre Joe Primeau once told writer Frank Orr.

Pranks were always the order the day. Leafs' defenceman Clancy won a chicken at a church social. He tucked the prize bird into trainer Tim Daly's underwear while the latter was asleep.

"You couldn't repeat what Tim said," Clancy recalled to the *Ottawa Journal* in 1947. Daly vowed he'd get even.

"I was afraid to get on a rubbing table for the rest of the winter," Clancy said.

Checking forward Cotton was often the brunt of his teammates' practical jokes. During a road trip to New York, Clancy and Conacher hung Cotton's trousers out a high window. They knew Cotton was afraid of heights. He pleaded with his teammates to pull his pants back to safety, since his money was in the pockets.

On another road trip, Cotton, who fancied himself a stylish dresser, purchased a sharp new hat. Before the train ride home, Conacher slipped out to a haberdashery and bought a cheaper hat that bore a striking resemblance to Cotton's new fedora and they pulled the old switcheroo when he wasn't looking.

Then the Leafs players proceeded to play soccer on the train with the hat, kicking it to and fro while Cotton begged them to stop.

"You fellows get all the money on the club and I play for peanuts," Cotton complained. Just as the train was pulling into Toronto, someone reached up into an overhead compartment and pulled Cotton's new bonnet out from its hiding place.

Leafs' defenceman Red Horner felt that their obsession with having a good time was the main reason the Leafs didn't spend more time with Lord Stanley's mug in the 1930s.

"We had a very fine offensive team," Horner said. "We led the league in points for about six or seven years. But we seemed to not be able to swear off the fun and get down to business once we got into the finals.

"We knew we were going to get our goals but we probably should have defended better than we did. It was always disturbing to me that we didn't win the Cup more than once."

CLANCY NEVER WON A FIGHT, BUT AT LEAST HE CAME IN SECOND

Often described as 150 pounds of muscle and conversation, Leafs' defenceman King Clancy never backed away from a fight. Yet despite all of his scrapping, no one could ever confirm a fistic victory for the King.

Many a steak was utilized over a blackened eye on Clancy's person following a punch-up.

"At my weight, I never won one of them," Clancy admitted of his fistic encounters. "I made a career of starting but never finishing fights."

Even when his teammates came to his aid, Clancy couldn't help but lose. The Leafs were facing the Montreal Maroons, perhaps the NHL's roughest and dirtiest team in the 1930s. During a line brawl, Clancy ended up paired off with Maroons defenceman Allan Shields and as was almost always the case, on the bottom of the wrestling match.

Seeing their friend in need, Leafs forwards Charlie Conacher and Busher Jackson left the bench to come to Clancy's aid. They pulled Shields from atop of Clancy and while one pinned Shields to the ice, the other lifted Clancy up and placed him atop Shields.

Before the officials took notice, Jackson and Conacher beat a hasty retreat to the Toronto bench to avoid penalties of their own, but just as they were stepping off the ice, Jackson tapped Conacher on the shoulder and pointed back toward the fray.

"Don't look now," Jackson said. "But guess who's on the bottom again?"

Not every one of his opponents bought into this "woe is Clancy" routine.

"For a guy who couldn't fight, King could sure look after himself," former Montreal forward Toe Blake said. "And I know guys who have the scars to prove it."

THE RED MENACE

The tough guy never considered himself to be all that.

From 1932–33 through 1939–40, Leafs defenceman Red Horner led the NHL in penalty minutes each campaign—eight seasons in succession.

Only Wayne Gretzky, who led the NHL in assists for 13 consecutive seasons, can lay claim to a longer run atop any of the league's statistical categories.

Yet when you tried to convince Horner, who died in 2005 at the age of 95, of his legendary toughness, you had a tough time of it.

"I don't know about that," Horner claimed in a 2002 interview. "There were many players in the league who were tough.

"I wasn't any tougher than anyone else."

History would beg to differ.

As a 14 year old, Horner delivered groceries by bike to several Toronto homes, including that of Frank Selke Sr., the assistant GM of the Leafs and the GM of the junior Toronto Marlboros.

Horner would consistently corner Selke whenever he saw him to talk hockey and badger the man to give him a tryout with the Marlies. Eventually, Horner wore Selke down and the youngster earned a spot with the club in 1926 at the age of 17.

With Dinty Moore and Whitey Field anchored along the defence, Horner saw little ice time, until Field suffered a broken collarbone in December.

Facing North Bay in the Sportsmen's Patriotic Association Cup final, Horner would fill in for Field. Joe Verdun was considered the toughest player on the North Bay roster—some claimed he was the toughest player ever to come out of Northern Ontario—and on the first rush of the game, he drove a high stick into Horner's neck. Horner dropped his gloves and the two tangled. In fact, they'd fight so many times—there was no three-fight limit in hockey in those days—that Horner opted to take to the ice for the third period barehanded, eliminating the need to drop his gloves.

The Marlboros won 10–3, but the North Bay fans were certain that Horner wouldn't have the courage to make the trip to their town for the second leg of the final, let alone dare try anything with Verdun on his home rink.

The Marlies arrived and Horner took up his spot on the blue line. Verdun grabbed the puck from the opening faceoff and headed down Horner's side of the rink for the Toronto goal. Horner met him with a bodycheck so devastating that it rendered Verdun unconscious, and that was that.

By 1928, Horner, 19, was captain of the Memorial Cup champion Marlboros and also skating in the Toronto Brokers League, as well as earning $25 a week at the Toronto Stock Exchange as a clerk for Solway Mills, a local brokerage firm.

He was playing in a Brokers League game one Saturday afternoon a couple of weeks before Christmas when Conn Smythe, managing director of the Leafs, came to watch. Afterward, Smythe, whose team was in need of defensive help, approached Horner.

"He said, 'We'll pay you $2,800 for the rest of the season,'" Horner recalled. "That sounded pretty good to me and we shook hands on that."

The Leafs were playing the Pittsburgh Pirates that night and Smythe wanted Horner to start work immediately. There was just one problem.

"I didn't have a car," Horner explained.

Smythe solved that problem quickly. "He said, 'I'll pick you up at your house,'" remembered Horner, likely the only player to get a ride to his NHL debut from one of the owners of the team.

"They started me off on defence with Art Duncan," and Horner started off intimidating the opposition immediately.

Standing six feet tall and weighing in at 176 pounds—massive for that era—Horner had picked up a little trick during his junior days. "When I bodychecked someone, I'd stand over them and stare down at them, daring them to get up and do something," Horner recalled. "Not one of the Pittsburgh players did a thing about it."

Horner's second NHL game would be against the rugged Montreal Maroons, and they'd quickly show him how the cockiness of youth could be corrected.

"I started out doing the same thing whenever I hit someone," Horner explained. "I was coming up the ice with the puck in the second period when I was chopped across the hands. I felt a sharp pain and fell to the ice.

"(Maroons centre) Nels Stewart (the 1926–27 NHL penalty

minute leader) had got me. Slashed me and broke my hand. Then he stood, towering over me.

"That'll be enough of that, you son of a bitch," Stewart advised the rookie Toronto defender.

Realizing he had lightning in a bottle, a rugged enforcer willing to stand up and protect his highly skilled team, Smythe sought to beef up Horner. Horner landed a summer job at Camp Wanapitei, about 20 miles north of Sudbury.

Five days a week, Horner would paddle an 18-foot prospector canoe 100 miles. He would cover two-mile portage routes carrying the canoe by himself.

When he returned to the Leafs, Horner had bulked up to 190 pounds and set out to paddle the rest of the NHL.

He paired on defence with King Clancy on Toronto's first Stanley Cup winner in 1931–32, and Horner captained the Leafs for two seasons prior to retiring in 1940. While Horner may have downplayed his legendary toughness, those he protected remained forever indebted to him.

"No one, not even the toughest guys in the NHL, took liberties with the Leafs," Clancy once told the *Toronto Star*. "Do one of us dirt and you had to deal with Red.

"That was absolutely no fun at all. He was as tough as any man who ever played the game, an excellent bodychecker who fought only when necessary."

COMING THROUGH IN THE CLUTCH

Coach Dick Irvin figured three of the finest clutch scorers in hockey history suited up for the Leafs during the 1930s.

"I had three great ones when I was coaching the Toronto Maple Leafs," Irvin told writer Dink Carroll. "They were Charlie Conacher, Syl Apps, and King Clancy. Any one of them could produce when the going got tough."

When Irvin coached the Leafs to the 1932 Stanley Cup title, in Game 2, the New York Rangers were leading 2–0 in the second period when the Leafs rattled in six straight goals for the win. A Conacher goal tied the score and Clancy netted the game winner.

During the 1942 Cup final, Apps, who'd joined the Leafs in 1936, helped key the Leafs' rally from a 3–0 series deficit for a 4–3 decision over Detroit in the Stanley Cup final.

In Game 4, Apps netted the tying goal and figured in the winner by Nick Metz as Toronto won 4–3. He picked up two goals and three assists in a 9–3 Game 5 verdict.

In the deciding game of the 1948 final, also against the Red Wings, in what would prove to be the final game of his NHL career, just two minutes after Leo Reise scored to narrow Toronto's advantage to 3–1, Apps beat Harry Lumley to end any thought of a Detroit rally.

"You can have those guys who get the fifth, sixth and seventh goals when you win a hockey game by a 7–2 score," Irvin said. "I'll take the guy who scores the winning or tying goal. That's when it counts."

THE FIRST SLAPSHOT?

Debate over the origin of the slapshot is almost as fervent as the one over the site of hockey's birthplace. But Leafs' defenceman King Clancy insisted he was in on both the birth and the brief demise of the power shot while a Leaf during the 1930s.

"It happened at a team practice," Clancy claimed in a tale he spun for the *Brandon Sun*. "I had gone in with big Charlie Conacher.

"I accidentally lost the puck off my stick, and kept going in on the defence. Charlie, steaming up, slapped at the puck and whistled it in behind (goalie) Lorne Chabot."

Figuring they'd hatch a plan of brilliance, the duo couldn't wait to try out their new play in a game.

Lining up against the Boston Bruins, the strategy was for Clancy to crash the Boston defence, dropping a pass back to Conacher for a one timer just as he caused the chaos up ahead.

Clancy charged forward with the puck, slipped a quick pass back to Conacher a split second prior to impact, and Charlie promptly drove a powerful shot into the seat of Clancy's pants.

They gave up on their idea after that one game.

BE-LEAF IT OR NOT

Truth is often stranger than fiction, but the fact of the matter is these things really happened.

HELPING HAND

Several Leafs enlisted and joined the Canadian war effort during World War II, but even those who stayed home during the conflict chipped in and did their part.

A group of a dozen British children, all around the age of ten, uprooted by the war and sent to Canada to study and board at Upper Canada College, were invited to skate with the Leafs at Maple Leaf Gardens on November 17, 1940.

Outfitted with skates, the kids, most of whom had never been on the ice before, joined Leafs' coach Hap Day and players Bingo Kampman, Gord Drillon, and Nick Metz for a skate.

With all 12 kids on the ice at the time opposing the three Leafs, it turned into more of a combination of roller derby and rugby, and the puck was somewhat neglected during the entire process.

IF THE SHOE FITS

When the Leafs were afforded a two-man advantage against the Montreal Canadiens late in the second period of the March 6, 1941 game between the two teams at the Montreal Forum, angry Habs' fans showered the ice with programs and the protective winter rubbers from their shoes.

The game was halted while arena workers came out to clean up the mess, but Toronto right-winger Gordie Drillon, known as an opportunistic goal scorer, saw a chance and took it.

Drillon cruised around the ice surface sizing up rubbers, holding them up to the bottom of his skates to measure them for size.

When he found a pair that fit, Drillon skated to the bench and handed them off to a teammate for safekeeping.

GUS WORKS FAST

Others may have gotten off to better starts in their NHL careers but none got off to a quicker start than Gus Bodnar.

Just 15 seconds into his NHL career on October 30, 1943, Leaf rookie forward Bodnar whipped a shot past New York Rangers netminder Ken McAuley for the fastest goal ever scored by a player in his NHL debut.

Bodnar would finish the 1943–44 season with 20 goals and 62 points, the latter an NHL rookie mark that would stand until 1968–69, and would remain the Leaf standard for first-year players until bettered by Peter Ihnacak in 1982–83.

Bodnar won the Calder Trophy ahead of future Hall-of-Famers Bill Durnan and teammate Teeder Kennedy.

"I thought I was pretty big stuff," Bodnar told Frank Orr of the *Toronto Star*. "I had my hair long and all slickered down with goo.

"I figured I was about the hottest rookie ever to hit the pros, even though I weighed only 145 pounds."

Fast became Bodnar's trademark. On January 12, 1946, against Detroit, he scored 3:17 into the contest to launch what would be the fastest six goals in Leaf history. The outburst came in a span of 7:16, with Billy Taylor (twice), Gaye Stewart, Syl Apps, and Jack Hamilton also scoring.

"He was a great player with good hockey sense and very skilled—a high-class player," Kennedy told the *Globe & Mail*. "And he was the same off the ice—a class gentleman."

Traded to Chicago in 1947, Bodnar would be involved in another outburst of goal-scoring quickness, setting up all three of Bill Mosienko's 21-second hat trick goals against the New York Rangers on March 23, 1952.

"I just won the faceoff, handed the puck to Mosienko, who skated in and scored, and then waited for him to come back," Bodnar said.

He still holds the NHL record for the fastest three assists.

HELPING HAND FROM HABS

Imagine the Hatfields lending their lawn mower to the McCoys. Or Itchy inviting Scratchy over for lunch.

It could happen. Hey, in 1943 the Leafs were in desperate need of a goaltender and who stepped up to help them out?

Why the Montreal Canadiens, of course.

When Canadiens netminder Paul Bibeault was discharged from the Canadian Army in the fall of 1943, the Habs no longer had a spot for him, what with rookie Bill Durnan playing at a level that would earn him a Vezina Trophy and NHL First All-Star Team selection at season's end.

Benny Grant, who first played goal for the Leafs in 1928, was trying to fill the void left when Turk Broda enlisted in the military, but at 35 his best days were behind him, as were far too many pucks.

So on December 22, 1943, the Canadiens loaned Bibeault to the Leafs for the remainder of the season.

In his second game as a Leaf, Bibeault blanked the New York Rangers 4–0, just the second shutout of the NHL season. But it was probably his second shutout for Toronto, a 5–0 win over the Canadiens, that left the Montreal brass wondering whether they'd made a mistake.

The fear turned to panic when the first-place Canadiens opened the Stanley Cup semi-finals at home against the Leafs and Bibeault's 41-save performance gave Toronto a 3–1 victory and Montreal's first loss at the Forum all season.

"If he's hot we'll win," Toronto coach Hap Day predicted of his netminder, but it would turn out that Montreal had little to fear.

In Game 2, Habs superstar Rocket Richard put five past his good friend Bibeault and Montreal posted a 5–1 victory.

The Canadiens won the two games at Maple Leaf Gardens and in Game 5, which would prove to be Bibeault's farewell as a Leaf netminder, they slammed double digits behind him in an 11–0 victory.

At the end of the season, Bibeault was named to the NHL's Second All-Star Team. The Leafs offered the Canadiens $15,000 for Bibeault, but the Habs turned it down.

Bibeault didn't leave Toronto empty-handed. He met his future wife while a Leaf—a Maple Leaf Gardens switchboard operator by the name of Evelyn Selke who just happened to also be the daughter of Leafs' assistant GM Frank Selke Sr.

I KNOW THAT ONE

Leafs' captain Bob Davidson was the guest of honour at a father-son service club banquet that featured a hockey quiz with the following question:

"Who scored five playoff goals in one game?"

"Maurice Richard," Davidson blurted out quickly. "I know, because I was supposed to check him."

Richard scored all five goals as the Montreal Canadiens downed the Leafs 5–1 in Game 2 of their Stanley Cup semi-final series on March 23, 1944.

ALL BETS ARE OFF

For years, law enforcement looked the other way as illegal gambling waged unfettered in the so-called "bull ring" at Maple Leaf Gardens.

So bold were these gamblers that bookies freely bellowed out odds and money openly exchanged hands.

Finally, in the mid-1940s, police began to take exception to this law-breaking, spurred into action after Toronto defenceman Babe Pratt was suspended by the NHL for wagering on games. John Chisholm, Toronto police commissioner, requested a hearing into these illegal activities that were openly taking place in a smoking and refreshment area at the east side of Maple Leaf Gardens while NHL games were waging on the nearby ice surface.

A February 1, 1946 Toronto Police Commission hearing into the bull ring revealed that the gambling ring was frequented by "some of the most prominent men in Toronto," a group the often included Leafs' managing director Conn Smythe, a well-known gambler.

"For some time this betting was carried on in a very open manner and to such an extent that they were calling out the odds on the game and waving money in the air," reported Toronto police inspector John Vernon. "A large number of businessmen of all callings were involved.

"During the past two or three years, because of the efforts of the police, this practice has been considerably curtailed but the betting has continued in a more underhanded manner."

On January 30, 1946, Pratt, who'd won the Hart Trophy in 1943–44, setting an NHL record for points by a defenceman with 57, was expelled from the NHL by president Red Dutton for conduct prejudicial to the welfare of hockey.

"I feel that I am innocent of any charge of having conducted myself prejudicially to the game of hockey," Pratt said in a statement.

No argument was put forth that Pratt hadn't gambled on games. In fact, Leafs players recalled a game during the 1943–44 season when the team learned close to game time that minor leaguer Maurice Courteau would tend goal for Boston against them and Pratt was miffed that there wasn't time to get a couple of hundred dollars down on the Leafs.

"I never made a bet against the Leafs in my life," insisted Pratt, who appealed his suspension. "I also assured Dutton I would never make a wager on hockey again and that I would not ever be seen in the company of known gamblers."

Pratt felt that he was the fall guy when others were also guilty of the same offence. "It looks to me as if I'm the guy they want to get rid of. I'm not saying what other players have done or who made bets or anything like that. I'm not talking about anybody else but myself. What else can I say but that it looks like I'm being made the goat?

"What can I, a lone player, do against the millions that are represented against me in this affair?"

Dutton was unmoved by Pratt's words. "The good name of professional hockey can't be jeopardized to protect one player," Dutton told *Canadian Press*. "(Pratt had) ignored warnings against wagering.

"I was faced with reports that Pratt was gambling. I appointed an investigator, who brought me the evidence. Pratt admitted he had been gambling."

Pratt did admit he'd been approached with a bribe to throw a game, but insisted he'd never bet against the Leafs. Dutton acknowledged that was also what his investigation had revealed.

"There was no evidence he was betting against his own team," Dutton said.

Just 16 days later, his appeal was heard and the NHL's board of governors reinstated Pratt, 30.

ME AND MY SHADOW

Harry Watson didn't need help from Sherlock Holmes to recognize that something wasn't right.

He kept hearing about how he supposedly lived in the Detroit suburbs, and how people would run into him at restaurants and golf courses in the Motor City.

There was a time when it was true. In 1942–43 and 1945–46, around his stint in the military during World War II, Watson spent two seasons with the Detroit Red Wings. But after being traded to the Leafs in the fall of 1946, Toronto became his home, right up until his death in 2002.

So what was up with the Detroit stuff?

Turns out Watson had a double—an impersonator who for decades went around telling people he was the Hockey Hall-of-Famer and five-time Stanley Cup champion.

Don Wadsden was golfing one day near his home in Royal Oak, Michigan when someone approached him and asked whether he was the NHLer Harry Watson. Wadsden answered in the affirmative. Soon, people were buying him drinks and picking up tabs.

Wadsden, who bore a striking resemblance to Watson, admitted he'd allowed his ruse to get out of hand when he was outed in 1994 by Saskatoon *Star-Phoenix* reporter Doug McConachie.

"It wound up snowballing," Wadsden said. "I got in too deep."

Wadsden gave media interviews as Watson. He studied Saskatchewan, where Watson was originally from, concocting an entire back story to cover his lie. He told people his real name was Wadsden and it had been changed when he made the NHL to make it easier for reporters to spell. When questioned about the fact that Watson lived in Toronto, he claimed to have homes in Toronto and Detroit.

"It was all made up," Wadsden told McConachie, "and I want to apologize to him and everybody in Canada."

Lucky for Wadsden, Watson, who finished second in Lady Byng Trophy voting in 1948–49, wasn't a fellow to carry a grudge.

"I don't hold any animosity toward the guy," Watson said. "I guess it's been some time in the spotlight for him. Why not, eh? No harm done.

"I'm going to just let him be."

DID HOWIE MEEKER REALLY SCORE FIVE?

Up until Darryl Sittler's record six-goal night in 1976, it stood as the mark for the most goals scored by a player in a Maple Leafs uniform.

During a 10–4 rout of the Chicago Blackhawks on January 8, 1947, Leafs rookie forward Howie Meeker put five goals past Chicago netminder Paul Bibeault.

Or did he?

No way, former Leaf Wally Stanowski insisted right up until his dying day in 2015 at the age of 96.

"I scored two of them," Stanowski told the *National Post* in 2015.

Indeed, there is evidence in the *Canadian Press* game report from that night to support Stanowski's thesis.

"Howie Meeker, twice wounded war veteran, sparked the Toronto attack with five goals from his right wing post," *CP* reported. "His first two goals were originally credited to Wally Stanowski but after a conference between players and officials at the close of the second period, it was ruled that both of Stanowski's shots were deflected into the Chicago net by Meeker."

Stanowski explained why he was so vehement that he was robbed of a pair of tallies.

"The first goal, pretty much, was standard," Stanowski said. "The puck went in and I came back to the bench and Hap Day, our coach, tapped me on the shoulder and said, 'We are going to give that goal over to Meeker.'"

On the second goal, Stanowski explained that the puck two-hopped its way into the net, but never touched anyone from the time it left his stick to when it dented the twine.

Once again, Stanowski allowed, when he got back to the bench he was told by Day they were going to lobby the officials to change the goal to Meeker and Stanowski was sure he knew why.

"They were lying," Stanowski said. "They were building Meeker up for the rookie award. Eventually he won it, with the five goals there he made it."

Meeker was voted the Calder Trophy in 1946–47, beating out a group of rookies that included a pair of future Hockey Hall-of-Famers—Gordie Howe and Bill Gadsby.

For his part, Meeker insists both shots in question hit him en route to the net.

"Those were two horseshit goals," said Meeker. "One deflected off my stick and the other hit me in the ass.

"The only reason I was standing in front of the net was because Wally's shot couldn't break a pane of glass. If he had any spit on his shot, he would have scored a million goals."

HE WASN'T HORSING AROUND

The Leafs and centre Max Bentley were facing the Detroit Red Wings, the same team they'd defeated in the 1947–48 Stanley Cup final, in a February 12, 1949 game at Maple Leaf Gardens when he was presented with a unique offer.

Charlie Hemstead, a Toronto racehorse breeder, was seated next to the Leafs bench and while Bentley idled beside him awaiting his upcoming shift Hemstead leaned over and suggested, "Max if you score a goal right now I'll give you a yearling."

Always known as someone with a knack for potting timely goals, a few seconds after taking the ice, Bentley fired a shot past Detroit goalie Harry Lumley for what proved to be the game winner in Toronto's 3–1 victory.

The 14,191 in attendance likely wondered why Bentley was pounding his chest with such excitement after the tally. Bentley quickly skated to the bench and shook hands with Hempstead, one of the top thoroughbred breeders in the city. The story soon made the rounds.

"I've got about 12 good yearlings and Max will get a good one," Hemstead said.

Bentley was so pumped up by his acquisition that he added the insurance goal for the Leafs in the third period.

Three days later, Bentley travelled to Hemstead's breeding farm in Thornhill, Ontario, and picked out his yearling, naming the thoroughbred Four-Bo.

In nine previous games that season against Detroit, Bentley had only scored one goal, but that one, a game winner in a 2–1 decision over the Wings on December 25, also earned him a racehorse as a Christmas present.

Bentley named that runner Lucky Teeder after Leafs captain Teeder Kennedy. The horse was was gifted to him by Toronto-based publisher George McCullagh.

"If it hadn't been for Teeder Kennedy I might not have been getting it," Bentley explained to *Canadian Press* as to his rationale for the horse's name. "He happened to mention to Mr. McCullagh that I was interested in buying a horse the night I scored the winning goal against Detroit a couple of weeks ago.

"Mr. McCullagh came over to me in the dressing room and told me not to bother buying one, he was going to give it to me."

Bentley raced both horses at tracks in Calgary and Winnipeg, eventually losing both of them in claiming races.

"I made some money with them," Bentley said. "I did all right."

THE LEAFS' FIRST TV GOAL

Taking a line made famous by Maxwell Smart, another television character, Bob Hassard missed it by that much.

Hockey Night In Canada took to the TV airwaves in Toronto for the first time the night of November 1, 1952, as the Leafs edged the Boston Bruins 3–2.

The game was joined in progress just in time to see a gaggle of Leafs joyously celebrating Hassard's goal at 6:22 of the second period to open the scoring.

"The puck has just gone in the net, now the broadcast starts," Hassard explained to writer Stu McMurray in 2001. "The goal has just gone in about two or three seconds before the thing came on and we were patting each other on the back."

About eight minutes later, Max Bentley put a shot past Bruins goalie (Sugar) Jim Henry to make it 2–0 and earn the right to be the first Leaf to dent twine in front of a national television audience.

Hockey Night In Canada did not commence broadcasting entire games until 1968.

THE ONTARIO MAPLE LEAFS?

The Leafs held training camp for the 1956–57 NHL season in Sudbury, Ontario, which didn't seem to sit well with the people who ran the local paper.

In an editorial, the *Sudbury Star* insisted that Toronto was no good and called upon the Maple Leafs to change the team's name to the Ontario Maple Leafs.

"The name leaves a bad taste in Northern Ontario," the paper wrote, insisting it was why most people in the area held rooting interests with the Montreal Canadiens or Detroit Red Wings.

"Looking for the reason, it would be found that the name Toronto, associated with Hogtown, is the main beef against friendship with the once-famed Queen City."

The paper claimed that people who came from the surrounding parts of the country became usurped as Torontonians once they tasted some success in the big city and their hometowns were discredited because of this factor.

"Girls from Vancouver and North Bay become the Miss Torontos, athletes who make the headlines of fame become Toronto boys and girls if they happen to be living in the suburban areas or are temporarily residing within the city."

While understanding the difficulties that such a name change would entail, the paper nonetheless called upon Leafs' management to begin the arduous task immediately if the team wanted to grow more popular within the province.

"We are fully aware of certain legal difficulties to be overcome in changing the name of such an established institution as the Toronto Maple Leafs. Still, the dividends in increased fan support throughout the province would be a rich reward of the Ontario Maple Leafs."

It is not an idea without precedent. In Phoenix, for example, the NFL's Phoenix Cardinals became the Arizona Cardinals and more recently, the NHL's Phoenix Coyotes were renamed the Arizona Coyotes.

On the other hand, considering how popular the Leafs have grown to be nation-wide—NHL teams in Western Canada often complain that they feel like the visiting club in their own building whenever the Leafs come to down—it would appear that in their logic, the *Sudbury Star* was actually barking up the wrong tree.

ROUTING THE RANGERS

It didn't start out as a record-setting night. The Leafs went to the dressing room after one period of their March 16, 1957 game at Maple Leaf Gardens with a 2–0 lead over the New York Rangers.

That's when the fireworks ignited.

The Leafs, who came into the night as the lowest-scoring NHL team with 150 goals in 63 games, scored six times in the second period and rifled another half-dozen goals past Rangers netminder Gump Worsley in the final frame to skate away with a 14–1 victory, the largest offensive output in franchise history.

Toronto's 37 scoring points tied an NHL record set by the Detroit Red Wings in a 15–0 shutout of the Rangers on January 23, 1944. The 14 goals were a franchise mark and the combined 15 goals were the most in an NHL game since Detroit beat Chicago 10–6 on March 16, 1947.

Every Leaf with the exception of goalie Ed Chadwick and defenceman Jim Thomson collected a point. Brian Cullen and Sid Smith each registered hat tricks. Ron Stewart and Tod Sloan scored two apiece and single tallies came from George Armstrong, Rudy Migay, Dick Duff, and Al MacNeil.

THEY NEARLY GOT BURNED

The Chicago Blackhawks knew the Leafs were hot when they raced out to a 2–0 first-period en route to a 3–1 win October 11, 1959, at Chicago Stadium, but they probably didn't know how hot the Leafs nearly got en route to the contest.

The Pullman railway car carrying the Leafs from Toronto for the game burst into flames early the morning of the game as the train was passing through Valparaiso, Indiana. The fire broke out in the linen closet of the Canadian National Railways car and gutted the car before it was extinguished by volunteer firefighters from nearby Griffith, who fought the blaze for nearly three hours.

Damage was estimated at $20,000 and though all the players escaped without injury, most lost their personal belongings in the fire.

Another car was sent for the Leafs and they continued on to Chicago, where Bob Pulford opened the scoring with a short-handed tally and Ted Hampson made it 2–0 before the end of the opening frame. Bert Olmstead also scored and Johnny Bower got the win in a 3–1 victory.

The Leafs truly were off to a hot start. Coupled with their 6–3 win over the Blackhawks on home ice opening night, Toronto's 2–0 record left the team atop the NHL standings.

KID DYNAMITE

Few athletes accomplished the variety of achievements that Gerry James was able to assemble.

He won four Grey Cups with the Winnipeg Blue Bombers. He won a Memorial Cup. And he played in the Stanley Cup final.

At 17, the youngest player in CFL history, in 1954 James was named the league's outstanding Canadian. The following spring, he won the Memorial Cup with the Toronto Marlboros.

At the conclusion of the 1955 football season, James signed a contract with the Leafs. "He's my kind of hockey player," Leafs coach King Clancy told the *Lethbridge Herald*. "I'm tickled pink that he saw fit to turn pro with us. He's a rugged, hard-hitting right winger."

James admitted that he didn't expect to be as big a star on the ice as he was on the gridiron. "I know they have fellows who can play better than I," said James, who in 1957 would turn down an offer from the NFL's New York Giants. "If I'm good enough to make it, I figure I should last 10 years in the NHL."

James had already played one game with the Leafs while still a junior and would spend the 1955–56 and 1956–57 seasons with Toronto.

He split time between the Leafs and AHL Rochester Americans in 1957–58 and missed the entire 1958–59 hockey season after suffering a leg injury playing football. But in 1959–60 James would enjoy a magical campaign. He won his second Grey Cup in the fall of 1959 as the Blue Bombers beat the Hamilton Tiger-Cats 21–7, James converting two touchdowns and booting a field goal.

That Grey Cup game was played in Toronto and in the spring, James would help the Leafs return to the Stanley Cup final to face the defending champion Montreal Canadiens. James played in all four games as the Habs swept the Leafs. He remains the only man to play in the Grey Cup and Stanley Cup in the same season.

"Just playing in that 1960 final against such a great Montreal Canadiens team was a highlight," James told the *Toronto Sun*.

He played one more year of pro hockey with the WHL's Winnipeg Warriors and played in the CFL until 1964. Known as Kid Dynamite because he was the son of Canadian football legend Eddie (Dynamite) James, in 1981 he would join his father in the Canadian Football Hall of Fame.

THE BIG M—AS IN $1 MILLION

It sounded like a scene straight out of an Austin Powers movie.

There was Chicago Blackhawks owner Jim Norris, telling a Toronto official that if they would give him all-star left-winger Frank Mahovlich, he'd supply the Maple Leafs with the unheard-of sum of one million dollars.

It all unfolded during an after party in the hospitality suite of the Royal York Hotel following the October 5, 1962 NHL All-Star Game dinner in Toronto. According to those at the party,

Norris offered someone from the Leafs organization $1 million for Mahovlich, holder of the club single-season record for goals, scoring 48 during the 1960–61 season, backing up his bravado by peeling off ten crisp $100 bills and placing them in the fellow's hand.

"I have offered the Leafs one million dollars for Mahovlich," Norris confirmed to reporters.

Toronto president Stafford Smythe was unreceptive to the idea when he was approached about the offer by the media. "I will not consider such a deal at a party," Smythe said.

The next day, Chicago GM Tommy Ivan stopped by Maple Leaf Gardens with a certified cheque for $1 million made out to the Toronto Maple Leaf hockey club. Smythe indicated he'd have to run such an offer past the MLG board, but seemed sceptical, insisting Chicago's offer was nothing more than a publicity stunt.

"We'll get the World Series off the sports pages," Smythe proclaimed.

Others in hockey felt the shenanigans were giving the game a black eye.

"It's bad for the sport," insisted Detroit Red Wings GM Jack Adams.

Norris insisted his offer was the real thing. "I made a deal, gave my word and I'll stick to it," Norris told the *Boston Record American*.

At the time, Mahovlich was among many Leafs players who were contract holdouts. He was seeking a deal similar to the $30,000 pact signed by New York Rangers defenceman Doug Harvey, and seemed unconcerned about the seven-figure war being waged over him.

"I'm not getting any of the money," Mahovlich said, adding that he'd be happy to become a Blackhawk if the deal were indeed done. "What's wrong with Chicago? I don't care where I'm playing as long as I'm getting my bucks."

Smythe indicated that he never approached the team's board of directors with the offer. Instead the Leafs turned down the $1 million package and signed Mahovlich to a four-year pact worth $110,000.

Chicago's million-dollar offer to the Leafs didn't sit well with Blackhawks superstar Bobby Hull. "Can you imagine the Hawks quibbling over $200 when they were signing me to a contract this year?" Hull complained.

Others in the game scoffed at the notion that any player was worth that kind of dough.

Boston Bruins' GM Lynn Patrick thought long and hard about whether any hockey player should be valued at a $1 million price tag.

"Eddie Shore," Patrick finally answered, referencing the Bruins' defenceman who won four Hart Trophies in the 1930s.

Someone quickly begged to differ. "Thanks for the compliment," Shore said. "But I don't think any hockey player's worth one million dollars, or even half that."

Phil Watson, coach of the last-place Bruins, jokingly suggested he knew where to find a bunch of $1 million babies.

"I've got 19 of them on my team," Watson said with a smile.

THE LEAFS OF GOVERNMENT

A Maple Leaf was the initiator of the drive to put the maple leaf on the Canadian flag. Leafs centre Red Kelly was elected to Canada's House of Commons on June 18, 1962, as the Liberal member for York West, unseating two-term Tory John B. Hamilton.

Kelly's maiden speech as a Member of Parliament called upon Canada to develop its own national flag. Amazingly, he served as an elected official while still playing for the Leafs, commuting back and forth on a regular basis between Toronto and Ottawa.

Even though Kelly was a Liberal, Conservative leader John Diefenbaker was in Kelly's corner at the 1964 Stanley Cup final series against Detroit. "Off the parliamentary ice, we're all for Kelly," explained former Prime Minister Diefenbaker.

Kelly served in Parliament until 1965. "I felt like a canoe in a sea trying to make waves," Kelly said. "But I really couldn't. There were open doors but too many other problems.

"It needed more time."

Before Kelly, Leafs' forward Howie Meeker was elected as Conservative member for Waterloo South in November 1951, serving one term through 1953. At 28, he was the youngest Member of

Parliament and took some good-natured ribbing while on the ice, such as the night Meeker was called for a faceoff violation. "Would you kindly keep out of the circle until I drop the puck, your honour," chastised referee Red Storey.

The first Leaf to be elected to the Canadian government was Wilfred (Bucko) McDonald, a Toronto defenceman from 1938–44, who was elected as the Liberal Member of Parliament for Parry Sound, Ontario in 1945 and re-elected twice, serving until 1957.

McDonald, who played senior hockey in nearby Hull, Quebec while serving in Ottawa, was known as a bruising defender. "I was the kind of guy who'd sooner throw a bodycheck than score a goal," McDonald told the *Montreal Gazette*. "I scored two against George Hainsworth when Detroit was playing Toronto in a Stanley Cup final (in 1936).

"Poor George was thinking of retiring and that probably helped him make up his mind."

COAST-TO-COAST LEAFS

The Leafs were always on the cutting edge of the broadcast media. They were the first team to carry radio play-by-play of one of their games, and the first to broadcast Saturday night games to the masses via Foster Hewitt and *Hockey Night In Canada* in the 1930s.

As Toronto marched toward its third consecutive Stanley Cup in the spring of 1964, the owners of the team sought to ramp up coverage of their team for a ravenous nation that couldn't seem to get enough of the Leafs.

Leafs' president Stafford Smythe announced plans to provide radio coverage of each of the team's 35 regular-season road games during the 1964–65 NHL season. CFRB in Toronto would be the flagship station with Hewitt handling the play-by-play duties, but the adventurous plan called for selling the broadcast rights to the games to 50 stations stretching from Newfoundland to British Columbia.

"I can promise you we will have a new sound and a new approach," said David Poyntz, vice-president of Walsh Advertising, which was spearheading the venture for Maple Leaf Gardens.

Smythe indicated the plan was spawned because of the tremendous number of requests from Leafs' fans across the country that desired to hear their favourite team over the airwaves on a regular basis.

THE SWEDISH EXPERIMENT

A decade before Borje Salming and Inge Hammarstrom arrived on the scene, the Leafs were already seeking some Swedish delight.

In the fall of 1963, the defending Stanley Cup champions invited Swedish left-winger Carl Oeberg and goalie Kjell Svensson, both long-time members of the Swedish national team, to training camp and they were given long looks during the exhibition campaign.

Apparently, they turned some heads.

"A pair of Swedes have astounded the experts by their play in exhibition contests," wrote *Windsor Star* sports columnist Jack Dulmage. "Left-winger Carl Oeberg and goalie Kjell Svensson have been tendered pro contracts with their destination likely Rochester Americans, Toronto farm club in the American League."

The Swedes admitted that North American hockey was more demanding than what they played back home. "You have to put a little more effort into here," Oeberg told *Canadian Press.* "In Sweden you practise only two or three times a week. Toronto practised twice a day."

As events unfolded, both Swedes decided North American hockey wasn't for them and opted to return home. By maintaining their amateur standing, both Oeberg and Svensson played for Sweden at the 1964 Winter Olympic Games in Innsbruck, Austria, earning silver medals.

That same year, Swedish forward Ulf Sterner became the first European-trained NHLer, playing four games for the New York Rangers.

FOES AND FRIENDS

When rugged Montreal Canadiens' forward John Ferguson tried to run roughshod over the Leafs, the guy who most frequently stood up to the NHL's toughest customer was Eddie Shack.

Their regular clashes produced a feud as famous as the Hatfields and the McCoys, but when the skates came off, the antagonism ended.

Ferguson even suggested that he admired Shack.

"In fact, I think he is a fine hockey player," Ferguson said while playing the Leafs in the 1966 Stanley Cup playoffs. "I attend many banquets over the season and the player I am most asked about is Eddie Shack. I always answer that Eddie is a fine player. But he has become a productive player and he must be stopped."

Hearing of Ferguson's praise, Shack was somewhat taken aback.

"Aw, is that right?" Shack asked. "Did he really say that?"

Then Shack headed to the trainer's room to get treatment on an ankle injured earlier in the season.

The player who delivered the slash that led to Shack's ankle ailment? That would have been Ferguson.

UP A CREEK WITHOUT ORR

Growing up in nearby Parry Sound, Ontario, Bobby Orr was an instant hockey hit.

"I put on my first skates when I was four and began playing hockey the following year," Orr told the *Boston Herald*. "All I've ever wanted is to be a hockey player."

According to his family, Orr would have loved nothing more than to wear the blue maple leaf on the front of his hockey sweater.

"Bobby's father and grandfather were diehard Leafs fans," explained former Leafs' GM Gord Stellick. "It would have been their dream to see him play for Toronto."

The Leafs received an unsolicited letter in 1960, advising them about the budding 12-year-old defenceman playing in nearby Parry Sound. The Leafs responded with a form letter, indicating they might check out the lad when he was a few years older.

"They didn't even go take a look at him," Stellick said.

In 1962, the Boston Bruins signed the youngster and instead of being his dream come true, the Leafs became Orr's nightmare.

It was during Orr's rookie season in the NHL, on December 4, 1966, in a game against the Leafs, that he'd suffer the first of the numerous knee injuries that would ultimately curtail his career at the age of 30 when he was bodychecked hard into the boards by Toronto defenceman Marcel Pronovost.

"He kept coming down and going to my side," Pronovost explained in his book "*A Life In Hockey*." My partner on the right was (Larry) Hillman, so I told him to drop off and open up the middle for (Orr).

"I could skate with Orr but I was tired of chasing him. So what I did was I went up a little higher and picked him up a little earlier. What he didn't realize was that I could skate as fast backwards as he could forward.

"He got right in front of the Boston bench, just by the blue line and turned outside and that's when I knew I had him."

Pronovost nailed Orr with a hip check and pinned him into the boards.

"I hit him squarely," Pronovost said. "I caught him with my hip and just about threw him into their bench."

Orr suffered sprained internal ligaments to his left knee, was left on crutches and out for three weeks.

"I still remember it," Orr said. "I was just trying to slip past him. My leg dragged behind me and he pinned it to the boards. That was it."

The Leafs would go on to win the Stanley Cup that spring while the Bruins would finish in last place, but two seasons later, the skates were on the opposite feet.

The second-place Bruins played host to the fourth-place Leafs in Game 1 of their Stanley Cup quarter-final series on April 2, 1969, at Boston Garden.

Late in the second period, with Boston leading 6–0, Bruins superstar Orr came down ice with the puck, his head down. Burly rookie Toronto defenceman Pat Quinn assumed he was fair game, focused his bombsights on the target and delivered his payload, leaving a wounded Orr puddled in the fetal position.

Next thing you know, they're re-enacting the Boston Massacre.

"Everybody wanted a piece of me," recalled Quinn, who insists to this day the hit was clean, figuring referee John Ashley assessed him an elbowing major in order to save both of their lives.

"The fans were screaming for my head. The ones behind the penalty box were pounding on the glass and it came loose and fell in on me. I'm trying to hold the fans back and I look to the cop in the penalty box, but he's yelling at me for hitting Orr, too."

Orr suffered a concussion and spent the night under observation at Massachusetts General Hospital.

Quinn had caught Orr with a similar check in a March 15 game that season in Toronto and the two ended up dropping the gloves and scrapping, but it was Orr who would enjoy the last laugh.

The night Quinn laid out Orr in that playoff game, the Leafs lost 10–0. The Bruins went on to sweep the series.

HOME AWAY FROM HOME

Maple Leaf Gardens served as home base for the Leafs from 1931 to 1999. It's where the Leafs won eight of their Stanley-Cup-clinching games. The Gardens also played host to seven NHL All-Star Games, numerous Memorial and Allan Cup finals, a Canada Cup, and 1972 and 1974 Summit Series contests. And surprisingly, it also served as a home to two other NHL teams.

In the spring of 1950, the upstart New York Rangers stunned the Montreal Canadiens in the Stanley Cup semi-finals to earn a surprise trip to face the Detroit Red Wings in the final series.

There was just one problem—the circus was coming to Madison Square Garden and the Rangers had nowhere to play.

Aware that Detroit had fallen to Toronto in both the 1948 and 1949 Stanley Cup finals and had just edged Toronto in a hate-filled seven games series to garner the other 1950 final berth, the Rangers chose Maple Leaf Gardens, figuring the Toronto crowd would be anti-Detroit and therefore pro-New York by default.

Even though the Rangers won just once all season in Toronto, they still felt it was a good move. "It doesn't mean a darn thing in the playoffs," Rangers GM Frank Boucher said. "Anyway, we're not playing the Leafs."

Detroit GM Jack Adams was not at all pleased when he heard his Wings would be required to play Games 2 and 3 of the final set in the home of their arch-rivals, but the Rangers weren't worried about keeping Adams happy.

"They're our games and we'll play them wherever the hell we like," Rangers coach Lynn Patrick said.

The strategy seemed to pay off when Edgar Laprade scored twice and New York took a 3–1 verdict in Game 2, but Detroit was all over the Rangers in Game 3 for a 4–0 shutout victory.

Detroit ended up winning the set in seven games, with the other five contests all played at Olympia Stadium.

The Philadelphia Flyers were new to the NHL in 1967–68 and so was their stadium, the $12 million Spectrum. But when high winds ripped holes in the roof of the rink, the Flyers needed to find a temporary home.

The Flyers moved the majority of their games to the rink of their Quebec AHL farm club, one to Madison Square Garden and a March 7, 1968 game against the Boston Bruins to Maple Leaf Gardens.

While the Bruins posted a 2–1 victory, no one remembered the final score. Everyone was talking about the horrific first period stick-swinging duel between Flyers' defenceman Larry Zeidel and former Leafs' forward Eddie Shack of Boston that left both players bloodied.

Each was ejected from the game and then the physical battle became a verbal one between both sides.

"How many swipes was Shack supposed to take from the guy before he retaliated?" Boston coach Harry Sinden asked.

Zeidel, the only Jewish player in the NHL at the time, insisted the Bruins had taunted him with anti-Semitic slurs.

"It was inevitable that something was going to happen, the Bruins have been jibbing me," Zeidel told the *Boston Record American.*

The feud between Shack and Zeidel stretched back a decade to an October 2, 1958 pre-season game in Niagara Falls, Ontario, between Shack's New York Rangers and Zeidel's AHL Hershey Bears that also resulted in both men swinging their sticks at each other's heads.

Their latest bout led to a four-game suspension for Zeidel and a three-game sitdown for Shack, who was absolved of all racism charges by Zeidel.

"Eddie wasn't involved in anything like that verbally," Zeidel said. "He was just the one who did the dirty work."

Two Toronto fans seated at rinkside, Mary Patterson and Mike Meade, sent written statements to NHL president Clarence Campbell confirming that they heard Bruins players direct racial slurs at Zeidel.

But after an investigation, Campbell ruled that there was no evidence to support Zeidel's claims.

PELYK'S FREEBIE

Of all his Maple Leaf Gardens memories, Mike Pelyk's favourite was his first National Hockey League goal—but not for the obvious reason.

Pelyk's first NHL tally came well into his second NHL campaign, on December 18, 1968, in a 5–2 victory over the Oakland Seals.

"Gary Smith was their goalie and he and (Leaf defenceman) Jim McKenny were pretty good friends," Pelyk recalled. "I'm sure Jimmy said to Gary, 'If the game's out of reach and Mike gets a shot, let it go in and break the bubble.'

"With about three minutes to go in the game, I got a shot from the point. It was wide open. I got pretty good wood on it, but it was right along the ice. Gary kicked his foot out to stop it, but it went right underneath and into the net.

"Of course, I go to retrieve the puck and I could hear him laughing behind his mask.

"Howie (McKenny) and I used to sit next to each other in the dressing room and I said, 'Jeez, Howie, Smitty shouldn't have missed that one, right?' and Howie just looked at me and smiled."

TIPTOE TO THE LEAFS

He was tipping more than tiptoeing on October 7, 1969, when singer Tiny Tim—famed for his hit song "Tip Toe Through The Tulips"—donned skates and took to the ice with the Leafs following their annual Blue-White game.

Unable to balance on his blades, the unstable Tiny Tim was supported around the rink by Leaf defenceman Jim McKenny and centre Mike Walton.

Tiny Tim's passion for the Leafs developed as a youngster growing up in New York City. He listened to Foster Hewitt's radio call of Leafs broadcasts, annually acquired a Leafs calendar via mail order and even took out a subscription to *The Hockey News* to follow his heroes.

"It was love at first sight," Tiny Tim explained in 1968 to *Weekend Magazine*. "I picked the Toronto Maple Leafs because the name was so close to nature.

"As long as the Leafs are in there, I'm pulling for them. Hockey means so much to me. When I'm on stage I have this wonderful feeling that I'm in the hockey nets. My ukulele is my hockey stick.

"I have such a passion for hockey. When I'm on stage, I'm Mr. (Punch) Imlach. I'm thinking about how to get the best out of my material.

"If I had one final dream, it would be to put on the goalie pads some day and have someone shoot at me. Someone like Mr. (Jean) Beliveau or Mr. Bobby Hull. It would be such a thrill. Or Mr. (Tim) Horton. Those shots go a hundred miles an hour.

"Everybody would say: He was stoned on the ice as well as off. What a dream that would be."

SPINNER'S DAD SPINS OUT OF CONTROL

What should have been the most rewarding weekend of Brian Spencer's NHL career turned into the most tragic time of his life.

Spencer, 21, a rookie left-winger with the Leafs and playing his third NHL game, was interviewed during the first intermission of *Hockey Night In Canada*'s broadcast against the Chicago Blackhawks on December 12, 1970.

Back home in Prince George, B.C., Spencer's family didn't get to see their son on television because the local CBC station, CKPG-EV, was carrying the game between the expansion Vancouver Canucks and the California Golden Seals.

Roy Spencer wanted to see his son play, and was willing to do anything to do so. Wielding a .45-calibre pistol, Spencer drove the 100 km from his home in Fort St. James, British Columbia, to the television station and forced his way into the building.

"I don't like the CBC's hockey games," Spencer told newsman Tom Haertel. "Why don't you broadcast more Toronto games?"

Spencer then walked into the newsroom and demanded of news director Stud Fawcell that they take the Canucks' game off air and replace it with the Leafs' game. "I am very disturbed with the CBC coverage," Spencer, 59, told Fawcell. "There is going to be a revolution unless it's changed."

While this was going on, program director Don Prentice dialled the police.

Backing out of the studio, Spencer warned, "I don't want to kill anyone. I've killed many times before in the commandos."

As police arrived at the building, Spencer fired his gun, wounding RCMP constable Dave Pidruchny in the leg. Police returned fire and Spencer was struck twice in the chest.

He was pronounced dead on arrival at Prince George Regional Hospital.

The next night, Spencer collected two assists as Toronto blanked the Buffalo Sabres 4–0.

HOLIDAY TREATS

The NHL stopped playing games on Christmas Day in 1971, but the Leafs certainly enjoyed their final holiday treat.

A 5–3 victory at Maple Leaf Gardens over the Detroit Red Wings on December 25, 1971, featured the first NHL hat trick ever recorded by Toronto forward Billy MacMillan.

One year earlier on Christmas Day, Leafs' centre Norm Ullman beat Gump Worsley to become the seventh player in NHL history to ascend to the 400-goal plateau, but it was in vain as the Leafs fell 6–3 to the Minnesota North Stars.

WHEN 13 WAS THE LEAFS' LUCKY NUMBER

It looked like the Leafs were headed for a solid victory, leading 6–0 over the Detroit Red Wings after two periods of their January 2, 1971 game at Maple Leaf Gardens.

A torrid third period would turn it into a record-setting performance.

The Leafs scored seven goals in the final frame to post a 13–0 triumph, the largest shutout win in franchise history and the worst setback in Wings history.

Balance was the key to Toronto's scoring exploits. Norm Ullman, Paul Henderson, Darryl Sittler, and Billy MacMillan each scored twice. Ullman added two assists and Jim Harrison collected a goal and three assists. Harrison's goal was the 13th and added insult to Detroit's injury when Wings' forward Nick Libett bounced the puck into their own net off the skate of teammate Garry Unger, Harrison getting credit for the tally as the last Leaf to touch the puck.

MacMillan (2–1–3), Henderson (2–1–3), Sittler (2–1–3), Dave Keon (1–2–3), and Brian Spencer (1–2–3) who scored his first NHL goal, all collected three points.

Jim Rutherford got the hook from the Detroit net after allowing three first-period goals and Don McLeod was left in to take the brunt of the Leaf assault.

Amazingly, at the other end, Toronto also used two goalies. Bruce Gamble came in for the third period to replace Jacques Plante, who'd struck his head on the ice in a goalmouth scramble, so it went in the books as a shared shutout.

THE BAY STREET BALLERINAS?

Angered by the inability of the Leafs to put up much of a fight in the quarter-finals of the 1975 Stanley Cup playoffs against the Broad Street Bullies, a.k.a. the defending Stanley Cup champion Philadelphia Flyers, one frustrated Leafs' fan took coach Red Kelly and his team to task via the written word.

Addressed to "Mrs. Red Kelly and the Toronto Maple Leafs," a three-inch, one-column ad that ran in the *Toronto Sun* expressed one fan's disgust with the team.

"Have you lost your pride and respect? What happened to all the press reports that if Philadelphia was to use force we would stand up to the task? If that is force, I suggest the entire Leaf team do a ballerina dance up Yonge Street at 12 o'clock noon on any Saturday afternoon and they would supply the same entertainment."

The Leafs responded to being called out in print by getting shut out 2–0 in the next game of the series and ultimately were swept aside in the minimum four games of the best-of-seven set.

PYRAMID POWER

The Leafs were swept from the 1975 Stanley Cup playoffs by the eventual champion Philadelphia Flyers at the quarter-final stage, so when the same two teams met again in the 1976 quarter-finals, no one was surprised to see the Flyers race to a quick 2–0 series lead.

Little did the fellows from the City of Brotherly Love know that Toronto coach Red Kelly had a sneaky trick up his sleeve. Or was it a pyramid scheme?

Upon returning to Toronto for Game 3, Kelly made a move that was part voodoo, part good-luck charm and mostly a psychological ploy.

"It was a plastic model of a pyramid," recalled Darryl Sittler, Leafs' captain at the time. "Red brought it into our dressing room and hung it up."

The idea was that if you stood under the pyramid it would serve as a source of energy and strength. Kelly had pyramids placed under the Toronto bench and when the Leafs won the next two games to even the series, the Toronto players began buying into what their coach was selling.

A 7–1 loss in Game 5 at Philadelphia's Spectrum brought the Leafs to the brink of elimination, so Sittler decided it was time to ramp up the mumbo jumbo.

He dug out the tie he'd worn earlier in the season when he'd produced an NHL-record ten points in a game at Maple Leaf Gardens against the Boston Bruins and raced to the dry cleaners to pick up the suit he'd worn with it en route to his record night.

Upon arrival at the rink, Sittler elected to test the power of the pyramid.

"I took the six sticks I was going to use in the game and put them under the pyramid," he explained. "Then I stood under the pyramid. You were supposed to stand under the pyramid for four minutes—not any more, not any less—to get its vibrations.

"A lot of guys on our team saw what I was doing and soon each guy was standing under the pyramid."

Sittler took to the ice and scored five goals and six points to gain a share of a pair of Stanley Cup records as the Leafs whipped Philly 8–5.

His six points tied the playoff mark set by Dickie Moore of the Montreal Canadiens on March 25, 1954, and Phil Esposito of the Boston Bruins on April 2, 1969.

Sittler also tallied three goals in the second period, equalling the Stanley Cup mark for goals in a period, originally established by Toronto's Harvey (Busher) Jackson on April 5, 1952, and tied by five other players prior to Sittler.

"I can still feel the vibrations from this stick," Sittler claimed after the game, but the good vibrations would soon come to an end for the Leafs.

Pyramid power was not the shape of things to come. Back on home ice, the Flyers hammered the Leafs 7–3 in Game 7 to wrap up the series.

SOLVING THE SPECTRUM JINX

The Leafs were the picture of perfection when they travelled to Philadelphia to face the Flyers on December 19, 1971.

Guy Trottier scored twice, Norm Ullman and Dave Keon notched singles, and Jacques Plante turned aside all 25 shots he faced for a 4–0 Toronto victory.

It would be a long time before they'd know the feeling again. No rink would haunt the Leafs more during the 1970s than Philadelphia's Spectrum.

The skid began February 21, 1972, when Bobby Clarke netted a couple of goals as the Flyers dropped the Leafs 3–1.

The Flyers handed the Leafs a pair of 5–2 setbacks during the 1972–73 season and then a 10–0 drubbing on March 4, 1973, the second-worst shutout defeat in Toronto franchise history.

Philly inflicted a 2–0 loss on Toronto's first visit to the Spectrum in the 1973–74 campaign. A brief respite from defeat was earned March 17, 1974, when Borje Salming's power-play goal earned the Leafs a 2–2 tie at the Spectrum.

Two more losses, by 5–1 and 3–1 counts, were suffered there in 1974–75, as well as 6–3 and 3–0 defeats in the Stanley Cup quarter-finals that spring.

The next season would prove no friendlier. The regular season saw 6–2 and 4–2 losses at Philadelphia, and although the Leafs extended the defending Cup champion Flyers to seven games in the quarter-final playoff series, Toronto lost all four games played at the Spectrum.

There was a 7–4 setback the first time the Leafs ventured to Philadelphia for the 1976–77 season, so when Toronto arrived in town for a March 7, 1977 game, the Leafs were a dismal 0–16–1 in their last 17 games at the Spectrum.

Deadlocked 2–2, Jim McKenny's second goal of the game late in the second period put the Leafs in front. Mike Palmateer held the Flyers off the scoresheet the rest of the way and when Ian Turnbull stuck one into the empty Philadelphia net for a 4–2 triumph, the city of Brotherly Love had finally shown the Leafs some.

"We knew how long it had been since we'd won here," Toronto defenceman Brian Glennie told *AP*. "I was just hoping we wouldn't do what we usually do here—play two good periods and then fold."

The two teams met in the Stanley Cup quarter-finals again that spring and when Toronto grabbed a 2–0 series lead by taking 3–1 and 4–2 decisions at the Spectrum, there was a notion that the Leafs had finally found Philadelphia freedom.

But it turned out that this time, they played two good games and then folded. The Flyers roared back to win the series in six games.

WELL, THAT WAS A LONG TIME COMING

When Rick Vaive whipped a shot past St. Louis Blues goalie Mike Liut on March 24, 1982, it was an historic moment in Leafs' history, as he became the club's first 50-goal scorer.

It was a goal that ended a lengthy drought.

The Leafs were the last of the so-called Original Six NHL teams to have a player produce a 50-goal season, and Vaive's magical moment came 48 years and six days after Maurice (Rocket) Richard of the Montreal Canadiens became the NHL's first 50-goal shooter in 1944–45.

Bobby Hull gave the Chicago Blackhawks a 50-goal scorer in 1961–62 and Phil Esposito added the Boston Bruins to the list in 1971–72. Vic Hadfield recorded the first 50-goal season for the

New York Rangers in 1971–72 and Mickey Redmond posted back-to-back 50-goal campaigns for the Detroit Red Wings in 1972–73 and 1973–74.

In fact, by the time Vaive put the Leafs in the 50-goal club, 12 expansion teams—the Philadelphia Flyers, Buffalo Sabres, Pittsburgh Penguins, Los Angeles Kings, New York Islanders, Atlanta Flames, Hartford Whalers, Edmonton Oilers, St. Louis Blues, Quebec Nordiques, Washington Capitals, and Minnesota North Stars—had already beaten the Leafs to the milestone.

MAPLE LEAF MCCARTHYISM?

Tom McCarthy was the man in demand when the Toronto media arrived at Leafs' practice on November 1, 1982, which is unusual for a fellow who worked as one of the team's equipment managers.

Toronto radio station CFRB broke the news earlier that morning that the Leafs had acquired Minnesota North Stars forward Tom McCarthy, a 23-goal scorer during the 1980–81 season as the North Stars reached the Stanley Cup final.

There was just one problem—no trade had been made.

The Maple Leaf Gardens switchboard lit up, curious and puzzled Leaf fans demanding to know whether it was true that the struggling Leafs had acquired McCarthy from a Norris Division rival, since only CFRB was reporting the deal.

It turned out that the fuss was all about the wrong Tom McCarthy. The Leafs hadn't acquired centre Tom McCarthy, 22, from the North Stars, but they did employ Tom McCarthy, 25, on their training staff.

The Leafs figured that the rumour stemmed from their passenger list for an upcoming Air Canada flight to Los Angeles to begin a three-game road trip.

"We've got an assistant trainer named Tom McCarthy who's listed in the party that will be travelling to Los Angeles," Leafs executive assistant Gord Stellick explained to *Canadian Press*. "That passenger list went to Air Canada."

McCarthy was a last-minute addition to the manifest and that's likely where the confusion happened. The Leafs were certain that an Air Canada employee had leaked the misinformation to someone at CFRB, but couldn't prove it.

"It looks to me as if somebody has got that passenger list, saw a Tom McCarthy was travelling with the team, put two and two together and phoned CFRB," Stellick said. "That's the only explanation I can see."

On this occasion, two and two didn't turn out to be four.

McCarthy the player remained with the North Stars and scored a career-high 39 goals for them during the 1983–84 season.

THEY SHOOT, THEY SCORE, AT RECORD PACE

Goals were plentiful during the NHL of the 1980s, but nowhere did they come as fast and as furious as during the October 15, 1983 game at Maple Leaf Gardens between the Leafs and Chicago Blackhawks.

It was 6–3 Leafs late in the second period when Gaston Gingras netted his first of the season for Toronto at 16:49. Denis Savard replied for Chicago just 23 seconds later and 15 seconds after that goal, Steve Larmer tallied for the Blackhawks. Another 15 seconds elapsed and Savard scored again.

Finally, Toronto's John Anderson quelled the Chicago resurgence when he scored at 18:13 of the frame.

The end result was five goals in a span of one minute, 24 seconds, an NHL record that remains on the books today.

The Leafs carried on to record a 10–8 triumph and just about everyone figured in the scoring. Twenty-six of the 36 skaters dressed garnered a point and Toronto's Greg Terrion scored on a penalty shot. Both goalies—Chicago's Tony Esposito and Mike Palmateer of the Leafs—also collected assists.

THE CONN GAME

He made his share of enemies, but Conn Smythe also made the Leafs into the scourge of the NHL.

SMYTHE VS. ROSS

Perhaps hockey's most famous feud, and perhaps it's longest-running battle was the tilt that pitted Leafs' managing director Conn Smythe against Boston Bruins' general manager Art Ross.

So how did it all begin?

For years, Smythe was in charge of the Toronto Varsity Grads, the 1928 Allan Cup winners and also the Olympic gold medallists that year representing Canada in St. Moritz, Switzerland. While in Boston to play against the local university side, Smythe issued a challenge to Ross, coach of the first-year expansion Boston NHL club—he'd put up $1,000 for a winner-takes-all game between the Grads and the Bruins.

Ross declined and years later in a 1949 conversation with George C. Carens of the *Boston Traveler*, Smythe admitted he'd overstepped his boundaries.

"I have to laugh at my brashness," Smythe said. "That was a pretty insulting episode, much like Harvard challenging the Red Sox in baseball."

The two men finally buried the hatchet during World War II, when both Smythe and Ross' offspring enlisted in the Canadian Armed Forces.

"The feud went up in thin smoke when Art's sons flew into combat in the latest World War," Smythe explained.

WHEN SMYTHE LEFT ROSS OWEN

One of the few times that Boston Bruins' GM Art Ross got the better of Leafs' managing director Conn Smythe was when he scooped Harvard star George Owen away from Toronto in 1929.

"Actually it was Conn Smythe of the Toronto Maple Leafs who sold me on playing pro hockey, and I was going with them when they came into Boston the next time," Owen explained to the *Boston Herald*.

"But just by chance, my father ran into Ross on the street and said, 'George is going to sign with Toronto.' Next thing I knew, Ross called me, and said, 'Come over and let's discuss this.'"

Ross dealt the rights to forwards Eric Pettinger and Hugh Plaxton to the Leafs for the rights to Owen and installed him on his defence.

"It would have been fun with the Leafs," Owen said. "Smythe didn't want me as a defenceman. I had played centre, and the next year he was bringing up Busher Jackson and Charlie Conacher and he wanted me to centre for them.

"That would have been something, playing with those two."

Instead, it was Joe Primeau who was installed between Conacher and Jackson on Toronto's fame Kid Line during the 1930s.

SMYTHE'S RARE JEWEL

The Leafs were an up-and-coming team as the 1930–31 season got underway, but they were young and managing director Conn Smythe sought a veteran who would serve as a calming presence and also provide leadership.

He set his sights on Ottawa Senators' defenceman King Clancy, a two-time Stanley Cup champion and the next-best rearguard in the NHL after Boston's Eddie Shore.

Smythe knew that the Senators were a cash-strapped team in a small market and the onset of what would become the Great Depression left the team in even more dire straits. But the asking price for Clancy—$35,000—was unheard of in NHL circles.

Ever the gambler, Smythe had just acquired a thoroughbred racehorse for $250 named Rare Jewel. She hadn't lived up to her name—finishing last in five of her six starts and next-to-last in the other—but Smythe was urged by jockey Dude Foden to enter the filly in the September 20, 1930, Coronation Stakes, a top race for two-year-olds slated for Toronto's Woodbine Racetrack.

A maiden, meaning she'd never won a race in her career, Rare Jewel went off at post-time odds of 106–1. Smythe bet a bundle on her.

Rare Jewel showed little until the horses reached the top of the stretch. She let out a tremendous burst of speed at the three-quarter pole, raced to the front and was never headed again, covering the six furlongs in 1:15.

Rare Jewel returned $214.40 for every $2 bet ticket—at the time the highest winning price ever paid out on a Canadian horse race—$46.75 on place bets and $19.95 on show bets.

Smythe had bet her across the board—$50 to win, $30 to place and $50 to show—and he pocketed a cool $6,240. Coupled with his $3,570 winner's share of the purse, Smythe took home $9,810.

He was able to borrow the rest of the money from the bank and Smythe now had the cash to acquire Clancy.

Clancy would be named to the inaugural NHL First All-Star Team at the conclusion of his season as a Leaf, and would lead them to a Stanley Cup triumph in 1931–32, but things didn't turn out so well for Rare Jewel.

The filly came down with a case of pneumonia and couldn't fend off the illness, succumbing November 14, 1930, at Toronto's Thorncliffe Park racecourse, where Smythe stabled Rare Jewel.

The Coronation Stakes victory would be the only win of her brief career.

A STEW WITH STEWART

The Leafs were in Boston during the 1931–32 season and managing director Conn Smythe didn't take kindly to a penalty call referee Bill Stewart made against the Leafs.

As Stewart was following the play up ice and skated close to the Toronto bench, Smythe reached out and grabbed Stewart by the sweater. Instantly, Stewart ejected Smythe from the game. Smythe refused to depart and when Stewart ordered some of the Boston Garden ushers to forcibly remove Smythe from the premises, the Toronto players swarmed to the scene. Smythe threw a punch and connected with Stewart's face. Baldy Cotton climbed up on the boards, ready to wallop anyone who came his way.

The Boston crowd began to surge toward the ruckus and Bruins president Charles Adams arrived as well, accompanied by some of the local constabulary. Working as a mediator, Adams was able to quell the riotous situation and when all was said and done, Smythe was permitted to remain on the bench.

A $3,500 MALTED MILK

After the Leafs won the Stanley Cup in the spring of 1932, captain Hap Day hatched an investment plan with managing director Conn Smythe.

"I'm a pharmacist by trade," Day, who earned a degree in pharmacy from the University of Toronto, explained to the *Boston Traveler* in 1941. "And Smythe is a student of the Bible. He knew the story of the man with the talents—about how one man invested his talents and profited thereby, and the other buried his without profit.

"So, back in 1932, when I had an idea of breaking into business, Connie put up some of his hard-earned money and we became partners in a drug store."

Smythe's reasoning for bankrolling the operation was at heart a simple one. "I'd always wanted to be able to go into a drug store and order a malted milk without paying for it," Smythe said.

Day laughed. "But every time he came in for a malted milk we made him pay for it."

This was in the midst of the Great Depression, and like many businesses, the Hap Day Pharmacy found it difficult to make ends meet.

"Finally after four years of struggling, our investment showed $7,000 in red ink, and we decided to close the doors," Day said. "On the day we were to put up the shutters, Connie came in and ordered a double malted."

The clerk asked Smythe for 30 cents to cover the cost of his milkshake.

"You can put this one on the cuff," Smythe snorted. "I'll always call it my $3,500 malted milk."

ROSES FOR A THORN IN THEIR SIDE

Before the start of the January 26, 1933 game at Boston Garden between the Leafs and Bruins, Leafs' managing director Conn Smythe sent a bouquet of roses to the Boston bench for Bruins' manager Art Ross, who was convalescing from minor surgery.

Smythe told defenceman King Clancy to deliver the flowers, a curious gesture since on Toronto's previous visit to Boston, a 5–1 loss on December 12, 1932, Clancy and Ross exchanged punches, resulting in a $50 fine for the Bruins' boss.

That incident began when Toronto's Red Horner and Boston's Joe Lamb scuffled with sticks and fists. Heading to the Boston bench to explain the penalties to Ross, referee Cooper Smeaton was followed by Clancy.

"Tell him to keep out of this," Clancy advised Smeaton to pass on to Ross. "Go back to your tree," Ross countered to Clancy, emphasizing his point by firing a right-hand punch over Smeaton's shoulder and smack into Clancy's face. Clancy countered with a right of his own that failed to connect with Ross but landed strongly on Smeaton.

And then it was on. Ross threw a left that hit Clancy and a right that caught Smeaton. Both benches emptied and even Smythe clomped out on the ice to join in the fray. Boston police entered the fracas, one of the local constabulary ending up on the business end of a punch from Leafs forward Baldy Cotton.

Once calm settled over the situation, Smythe doffed his fedora to the Boston fans as he headed back to the comfort of the Leafs' bench.

Two years earlier, Ross and Smythe had come to blows following another Bruins-Leafs game in Boston and the next day, Smythe recalled Leafs' back-up goalie Benny Grant from his loan to Boston's farm club in the Can-Am League.

Now it was time for bygones to be bygones. Or so it appeared from afar.

Up close, the messages delivered were much more personal.

Skating up to the bench, Clancy smiled and said, "With our compliments, Art." Ross declined the roses and delivered an invective of epithets in the direction of the Toronto defenceman. According to those with the Bruins, it was an appropriate response to the salty message Smythe had written on the card accompanying the bouquet.

Clancy eventually handed the flowers over to arena announcer Eddie Cummings, who in turn passed them along to a woman with a rinkside seat—hopefully minus the nasty card.

The fun didn't last for the Leafs, who squandered a 2–1 lead and fell 4–2 to Boston.

IS THAT SMYTHE, OR MR. PEANUT?

When Chicago Blackhawks' owner Major Frederic McLaughlin suggested that what the NHL lacked was dignity, Leafs' managing director Conn Smythe picked up the gauntlet and answered the Major's challenge.

For a January 19, 1937 game at Boston Garden against the Bruins, Smythe moved behind the Leafs' bench garbed in top hat, white tie and tails, swinging a gold-headed cane by his side.

"I'm eager to provide hockey with some much-needed refinement," Smythe explained.

Recalling the incident years later, Smythe was amazed he got out of Beantown alive. "I shudder to think of the consequences if the Boston fans had not possessed a keen sense of humour."

Even Smythe's bitter rival, Bruins' GM Art Ross, chuckled with delight at his adversary's garb.

"If someone had thrown an over-ripe tomato the result would have been disastrous to my own dignity," Smythe said. "Instead my attire tickled the risibilities of the Boston crowd and so upset the Bruins that the Leafs got three goals in the opening period and went on to win the game that night."

Toronto were 6–2 winners in a game that ended with a line brawl sparked when Boston's Hooley Smith tore into Toronto's Red Horner.

So much for dignity.

SMYTHE ON THE ICE

The Leafs lost 2–1 to the New York Rangers on February 6, 1938, but when everyone left Madison Square Garden that night it wasn't the game that was the topic of conversation.

In the first period, shortly after Toronto forward Syl Apps returned to the ice from serving a penalty, Leafs' managing director Conn Smythe was angry that no penalty had been called on what he perceived to be a foul by the Rangers, so Smythe jumped the boards and set off in pursuit of referee Billy Boyd, who just by coincidence was an ex-Ranger.

As Smythe got to Boyd and tried to stop, he lost his footing on the slippery ice and tumbled, grabbing onto Boyd as he fell, taking the official down with him.

"A little bird told me to do it," Smythe claimed afterward, insisting he was, "just trying to straighten Boyd's necktie."

BRUIN TROUBLE

It was no secret that there wasn't any love lost between Leafs' managing director Conn Smythe and Boston Bruins' long time coach-GM Art Ross. They feuded for decades but perhaps the dastardliest trick pulled by one on the other occurred December 19, 1939.

That night the Leafs were slated to play the Bruins at Boston Garden and in that day's *Boston Globe,* Smythe took out the following ad:

"ATTENTION, HOCKEY FANS

If you're tired of seeing the kind of hockey the Boston Bruins are playing, come to the Garden tonight and see a real hockey club, the Toronto Maple Leafs."

Smythe twisted the knife a little deeper during an interview he conducted at the paper while placing the ad.

"Mind you, we'll get no financial return from this ad because the visiting club doesn't get a share at all in the receipts," Smythe said. "But if we've got to carry the whole National League while the other clubs fall asleep and try to scare the customers away, then we're willing to put out the dough.

"I'm referring particularly to that game the Bruins played in Toronto last Thursday night. That, my friends, was a living disgrace. It was a perfect exhibition of how to drive the customers away in droves. Sure, I know the Bruins have lost Eddie Shore and Roy Conacher, but they're still the champions, aren't they? Everybody calls them champions. Why can't they play like champions then, both on the road and at home?"

Smythe even took a shot at Boston's legendary Kraut line of Milt Schmidt, Bobby Bauer, and Woody Dumart.

"We have anywhere from 500 to 1,000 fans from Kitchener every time the Bruins are in town to see the Sauerkraut Line. All they saw last Thursday night (in a 1–1 tie at Maple Leaf Gardens) was the 'Sauer' part. I guess Ross is so busy inventing things that he doesn't find time to make his players play hockey. Well, if that's the way they want to play, we'll carry the load and show the customers hockey as it should be played."

Evidently, the so-called Kraut line got fired up, scoring two goals in Boston's 3–2 overtime win over the Leafs before a season-high crowd of 14,107.

"Connie's piece of managerial master-minding exploded in his face last night, all because the Bruins possess a great hockey team and one of the greatest lines in hockey," noted the *Boston Herald*.

Two days later, Ross went before NHL president Frank Calder, demanding that Smythe be fined $1,000 for his actions, but nothing ever came of it.

LET'S BE FRANK—SMYTHE MISSED SELKE

For two decades, Frank Selke Sr. was Conn Smythe's right-hand man. They first crossed paths in 1914 when Smythe's University of Toronto team beat Selke's Kitchener Union Jacks in the OHA junior playdowns.

The New York Rangers hired Smythe as GM in 1926 and Selke helped him find players. After Smythe was let go in New York, Selke tipped him off that the Toronto St. Patricks were for sale and Smythe assembled a syndicate to purchase the franchise in 1927, renaming them the Maple Leafs.

Smythe convinced Selke to give up his job as an electrician and come to work for the Leafs full-time. He ran Toronto's minor-pro and junior franchises and developed many players who made a significant impact for the Leafs in the 1930s, including the entire Kid

Line of Joe Primeau, Charlie Conacher, and Busher Jackson, and defencemen Red Horner and Alex Levinsky.

Selke served 18 years as Smythe's assistant manager with the Leafs and during that time Toronto appeared in nine Stanley Cup finals, winning three titles.

Selke often called himself the "chore boy" of Maple Leaf Gardens, handling everything from publicity to booking hotel rooms for road trips. "I do the work around there that others won't do," he told the *Ottawa Journal*. "I'm like the lance corporal in the army in that respect."

Smythe left Canada to head to Europe to fight in World War II, leaving Selke in charge of the Leafs. Selke made several moves during that time to assemble another Leaf dynasty that would win four Cups between 1947–51, though he wouldn't be around to enjoy the fruits of his labour.

Returning from combat, Smythe bristled at some of Selke's moves, especially his decision to deal rugged defenceman Frank Eddolls to the Montreal Canadiens. The player Selke got back from the Habs was Teeder Kennedy, who'd captain the Leafs and be the backbone of Toronto's team for over a decade.

It was clear to Selke that he was being frozen out of the Toronto scheme. He showed up at the Gardens one morning to discover his desk had been turned over to another employee.

The Canadiens were in the market for a new boss and Selke jumped at the chance, signing to take over as the man in charge of running the Montreal franchise in the summer of 1946.

It didn't take long for the bad blood between the two men to boil over. Early in the 1946–47 season, Smythe launched into a tirade about the nefarious tactics of the Habs, labelling them the NHL's worst stick men.

"No wonder there is a shortage of pulp and paper in the country," Smythe told *Canadian Press*. "Canadiens have called in all the woodchoppers.

"They use sticks 30 percent stronger than any team in the league."

"I wish we did, because we'd save considerable money," fired back Selke, who insisted the Leafs were kings of holding and that he might resort to signing popular French-Canadian wrestler Yvon Robert to have someone on his roster trained in breaking free from holds.

"If Selke trots out Yvon Robert, we can always get Whipper Watson," Leafs forward Bud Poile joked.

What the Canadiens would wrestle away from the Leafs under Selke's tutelage would be claim to the throne as the NHL's top franchise. With Selke in charge, Montreal played in ten straight Stanley Cup finals from 1951–60, winning six titles, including an unprecedented five in a row from 1956–60.

PUNCH OUT

Leafs' managing director Conn Smythe was livid when a coach from the Quebec Senior League arrived at his training camp in 1948 and sought to lure players away with offers of $3,500 contracts and jobs in the city.

Smythe indicated that Dean McBride and Ray Hannigan were the Leaf prospects approached by the Quebec coach.

"We had a big investment in these players and have jobs ready for them at comparable rates of pay," Smythe said.

Oh, that Quebec coach who angered Smythe so? It was Punch Imlach, the same guy Smythe would lure away from the Boston Bruins' system a decade later to run the Leafs.

SMYTHE IS DYNAMIC

The honour caught Conn Smythe completely by surprise and believe it or not, left the managing director of the Leafs on the verge of speechlessness.

"Words fail me," Smythe told reporters after they voted him Canada's most dominating sports personality of 1949. "And I'm a man of a few million words."

Smythe was given the news of his award just prior to embarking on his annual health-building month of vacation in Florida.

"No wonder everyone was telling me to take a good holiday down south and stay as long as I could," Smith said. "Maybe my dominating personality is wearing on my friends."

DON'T FORGET TO DUCK

When Conn Smythe ran the Maple Leafs, he took guff from no one, including the city of Toronto.

In 1949, when the city increased the tax assessment on Maple Leaf Gardens, Smythe countered by moving the free tickets he provided for Leaf games to city councillors from the prime reds into the second tier blues.

This didn't sit well with councillor Norman Lamport, who returned his tickets to Smythe. Later, Smythe claimed during a heated session at city council, "Lamport telephoned Smythe and in a most aggressive manner he objected to be shifted back to the blues.

"We moved these fellows from the red seats to the blue seats because we had 5,000 seats in the blues and only 600 in the reds."

Lamport countered that claim. "(Smythe) wants to make people believe that it's not a matter of dollars and cents with him. Yet when I sent my tickets back in a letter, he wrote me to point out that the city had increased the assessment on Maple Leaf Gardens."

After Lamport returned his tickets, Smythe removed him from the Gardens' list of complimentary subscribers.

Controller David Balfour attacked Smythe's demand that a thank you letter should be sent his way in future for any free tickets provided. He stated in future he'd only attend games at the Gardens if Smythe writes him a properly worded invitation.

Smythe cackled at such a notion.

"Mr. Balfour is thereby doing a public service by making two more tickets available to the general public."

Balfour also accused Smythe of hypocrisy for being against Sunday sport in Toronto when his team frequently played Sunday games in the United States.

"Now I know why they want Sunday sport," Smythe spouted about the politicians. "So they'll have somewhere else to go for free."

Mayor Hiram McCallum sat back and didn't utter a word during the dispute, other than to advise his councillors to "duck" whenever Smythe had them in his firing line.

OH DANNY BOY

In the days prior to the entry draft, amateur players became tied to NHL teams via what was known as a C form. Players could sign these—with the consent of their parents—at a young age and would be tied to that team, basically becoming indentured servants, forced to play where they were assigned by the pro team for which they'd signed.

Danny Lewicki wasn't looking to break free from this process, he just wanted a little time before he was required to live up to his end of the bargain.

The Leafs signed Lewicki to a C form in 1948 when he was 16 and a year later, when the Leafs told him he'd be moving to Toronto to play for the junior Marlboros, Lewicki requested permission to complete the five-year apprenticeship he'd begun as a machinist at a railway shop in Stratford, Ontario, where he was playing junior hockey for the Stratford Kroehlers. Lewicki reasoned he'd be 22 then, still young enough for a career in the pro game, but also armed with a fallback career choice should hockey not work out for him.

"I want to guarantee my future after my hockey days are over," Lewicki told the *Winnipeg Tribune*.

Leafs' managing director Conn Smythe, who had paid what was believed to be the largest sum ever to acquire a teenager when he purchased the rights to Lewicki's C from the AHL Providence Reds, found this demand to be completely unreasonable. Smythe told everyone that Lewicki would suit up for a pro or junior club in the Leafs system during the 1949–50 season "or he won't play at all."

George Dudley, secretary-manager of the Canadian Amateur Hockey Association, backed up Smythe. "If he refuses to sign, the pro club can suspend him and we have to honour the suspension under agreements (between the CAHA and NHL)," Dudley explained.

The wording of the C form was fairly straightforward as well. "When an amateur signs it he agrees that the contracting club within one year may call upon him to sign a standard contract and perform professionally for a specified time at terms agreed upon,"

Dudley explained. "For signing the option, he is paid a minimum of $50, usually more, and the option is renewable each year on payment of the agreed-upon sum."

The form specified that what Smythe was saying was in fact true: "During the currency of this agreement or extension thereof, the player covenants and agrees that he will play hockey only for such hockey team as may be designated by the club."

Others in hockey felt that the terms only applied to professional hockey and that while playing in the amateur ranks, NHL teams shouldn't dictate where a player can and can't skate.

"We believe the C form is only an option on a player's professional services," New York Rangers GM Frank Boucher said. "We're sure not going to insist on where a boy plays his amateur hockey."

On September 21, 1949, Smythe offered Lewicki a $4,000 per season contract for two years, plus a $2,000 signing bonus.

"I feel I'm too young to turn pro," Lewicki said. "I feel that I can still add more weight and gain more knowledge of the game."

Smythe turned the matter over to NHL president Clarence Campbell. "Lewicki already has signed an agreement with the Leafs and terms are contained in that agreement," Campbell said, referencing the C form.

On October 7, 1949, the CAHA handed Lewicki an indefinite suspension. The Stratford club hinted they might opt to challenge the C form in court.

Instead, Lewicki relented and accepted Smythe's terms. He was granted his release by the Kroehlers and reported to the junior Toronto Marlboros.

"It is all cleared up with Lewicki and it is all cleared up with me," Smythe told the *Ottawa Journal*.

In 1950–51, Lewicki was part of the Leafs team that won the Stanley Cup.

BRODA TOLD TO CUT THE FAT

With his three-time defending Stanley Cup champions mired in an 0–5–1 skid, Leafs' managing director Conn Smythe determined it was time to trim the fat.

Smythe suspended his two-time Vezina Trophy-winning goaltender Walter (Turk) Broda, ordering the portly netminder to shed seven pounds from his 197-pound frame. Defenceman Garth Boesch and forwards Harry Watson, Vic Lynn, and Sid Smith were also given the ultimatum to slim down or like Broda, be laid off work.

"We are not running a fat man's team," Smythe told *Canadian Press*. "Broda is way overweight at 197 pounds. He is off the team until he shows some common sense. He has been ordered to reduce to 190 pounds.

Boesch was told to trim from 195 pounds down to 190. Watson, at 205 pounds, was also advised to trim five pounds of fat. Lynn wasn't given specific goals other than to get slimmer.

Gil Mayer was called up from Toronto's AHL farm club in Pittsburgh and would tend goal in the Leafs' next game against Detroit. The contract of netminder Al Rollins was purchased from the AHL Cleveland Barons.

"We are starting Mayer Thursday and he'll stay in there even if the score is 500–0 against him," Smythe said. "And I don't think it will be."

Mayer, 20, allowed two first-period goals as the Leafs fell 2–0 to the Wings. Regardless, Smythe found a sympathetic ear toward his cause in former Leafs' coach Dick Irvin, now the bench boss of the Montreal Canadiens.

"I don't blame Smythe," Irvin told writer Dink Carroll. "Broda was overweight and so were those other guys. They get fat on those fat paycheques they're drawing."

Irvin put the blame for Toronto's fat-cat status squarely on the Leafs' trio of Cup triumphs.

"They think all they have to do is lie back and play hockey in the playoffs and everything will be OK. But they're cheating the public that way, and when all is said and done, it's the public that pay their salaries."

Others questioned Smythe's motives, insisting he was trying to draw attention to his club and away from the hubbub going on over football's Grey Cup between the Montreal Alouettes and Calgary Stampeders.

Whatever his incentive, the Little Pistol, as Smythe was often called, made a direct hit. Enduring a diet of grapefruit and soft-boiled eggs, Broda trimmed down to 189 pounds, and was slated to return to the net December 4.

"There's no greater sportsman than the Turkey," Smythe said prior to the game. "If the Rangers score on him tonight, I'll go out and get him a malted milk, just to show that I'm not trying to starve him to death."

Blocking 22 shots, Broda blanked the New York Rangers 2–0, launching a four-game winning streak in which he allowed a meagre three goals against.

HIS GOOSE WAS COOKED

Leafs' forward John McCormack's long neck earned him the nickname "Goose" but in the winter of 1951, you could say that McCormack cooked his own goose in terms of his career with the team.

For McCormack, wedded bliss proved to be more of a wedded miss. The day after he was betrothed to the former Margaret Gordon on January 31, 1951, McCormack was shipped to Toronto's American Hockey League farm club, the Pittsburgh Hornets.

"I guess it must be because I got married without first talking it over with Leafs management," McCormack explained in an interview with the Hockey Hall of Fame. "I wasn't even aware that that wasn't normal."

It turned out that the wedding was a no-no as far as Leafs' managing director Conn Smythe was concerned. Players were forbidden from getting married during the hockey season.

McCormack had little choice. They'd found out Gordon was pregnant, so waiting for a summer wedding wasn't going to work out for them.

A couple of weeks after his demotion, on February 14—Valentine's Day of all days—the Leafs brought the lovelorn McCormack, a sensational checker and penalty killer, back to Toronto with some puzzling words from GM Hap Day. "Johnny may not fit too well into the Pittsburgh system and probably is of more value to the Leafs," Day suggested.

The honeymoon was short lived, though, and Toronto returned McCormack to the Hornets in early March. The reason for his recall was simply that for McCormack to be eligible for the Stanley Cup playoffs, he needed to be on the NHL roster on February 15.

McCormack was also involved in a brouhaha prior to that spring's AHL playoffs. The St. Louis Flyers, who missed the playoffs, finishing a point behind Pittsburgh, protested that McCormack was an ineligible player since he was acquired following the February 15 deadline and AHL president Maurice Podoloff upheld their protest and disqualified the Hornets from the playoffs.

Pittsburgh appealed the decision to the AHL board of governors, who reinstated the Hornets following a marathon nine-hour hearing during which the Hornets pleaded that McCormack was only in Toronto to undergo treatment for a shoulder injury.

The Hornets rolled all the way to the Calder Cup final before succumbing to the Cleveland Barons, but even though he was banished to the minors, McCormack's name was still inscribed on the Stanley Cup when the Leafs beat the Montreal Canadiens in the 1950–51 final series.

"We were in Cleveland that night (the Leafs won the Cup)," McCormack said. "We lost that night and they (Toronto) won that night with Billy (Barilko) scoring the goal."

Regardless, McCormack and the Leafs were headed for divorce. Smythe dealt him to the Canadiens in the off-season.

KING OF NOTHING

After retiring from the Leafs in 1936, King Clancy served part of the 1937–38 NHL season as coach of the Montreal Maroons and later worked as an NHL referee, though he was considered perhaps the most lenient game official in league history.

"Refereeing was a good life," Clancy told Rex MacLeod of the *Toronto Star*. "I had more fun as a referee than I ever did as a player. Sure, I let a lot of things go, but only so far. If someone took a cheap shot and the other guy went back at him I would tell them, 'OK, now you're even. Don't start something or you're gone.' Usually, they listened. They knew how far they could go with me.

"I called only one match penalty all the time I was refereeing. That was the time (Detroit's) Jimmy Orlando and Gaye Stewart got into a bloody stick fight in Maple Leaf Gardens."

In 1951, when he was done officiating, Leafs' managing director Conn Smythe brought Clancy back into the Toronto organization.

Clancy coached in the minors for a few seasons, and then coached the Leafs for a few seasons, but stayed around until his death in 1986 mainly working as a goodwill ambassador for the franchise.

"What is it you do around here?" Smythe once asked him.

"Not a damn thing," Clancy retorted.

"Just keep on doing it," Smythe advised.

BRING IT BACK TO LIFE

In an article entitled "Puck's Bad Boy," Leafs' managing director Conn Smythe complained to *Life Magazine* in 1951 that the NHL he knew was growing too soft.

"Penalties?" Smythe grumbled. "What do they matter? We just write them off as mistakes.

"No man ever became a millionaire who didn't make mistakes."

Smythe felt that the league had lost its way and eliminated the individualism of its stars with a style of hockey that was too much clutch and grab, and that skill had been replaced by frenzy.

He blamed this for the decline in attendance that was evident in the four American NHL cities.

Smythe saw only one player in the league capable of lifting the fans out of their seats, and that was Montreal Canadiens' right-winger Maurice Richard. He described Richard as "a home run hitter" and believed it was up to those who ran the game to find and foster more talents like that in order to get the fans back in the rinks.

"You can't fool the public forever," Smythe said. "They're trying to take the colour out of the game.

"We're trying to put it back."

Repeating his famous phrase, "If you can't beat them out in the alley, you can't beat them in here on the ice," Smythe admitted in the piece that as a boss he drove his players hard, a fact that was confirmed by former Leaf Charlie Conacher.

"When I quit hockey I'd like to travel, and I'd like to take Conn Smythe along as companion and valet," Conacher said. "I'd show him how to be a real Simon Legree."

BAH HUMBUG

Conn Smythe scoffed at reports out of Saint John, New Brunswick, in December of 1952 that Leafs goalie Turk Broda was headed to play senior hockey for the Saint John Beavers and replace Phil Hughes as the team's goalie.

"There's a better chance Santa Claus will play goal for the Beavers," Smythe cackled.

Instead, Smythe announced that the Leafs were preparing to bring Broda back into their fold.

Broda was feted by the Leafs with $7,000 in gifts during Turk Broda Night and the goalie who'd backstopped the Leafs into nine Stanley Cup finals and six titles during his 13 seasons was honoured with non-stop applause from the 12,472 fans in attendance at Maple Leaf Gardens.

While a band played "For He's a Jolly Good Fellow," among the graft presented to Broda were a new car, an eight-piece dining room set, a 89-piece set of sterling silver flatware, a silver tea service, a 56-piece dish set, a chesterfield, a grandfather's clock, and a five-day vacation in Nelson, British Columbia.

But perhaps the most shocking gift of all came from Smythe. Pointing out to the audience that Broda had appeared in 625 regular season and 99 playoff games as a Leaf, Smythe added a kicker to end his speech.

"If we make the playoffs again this year, you'll see Turk back in there again to make it an even 100," Smythe proclaimed, a pronouncement that must have come as a shock to Leaf goalie Al Rollins.

Broda began practicing with the Leafs almost immediately afterward and appeared in exhibition games as he sought to shake the weight a half-season in retirement had added to his already-portly frame.

He finally saw game action in Toronto's final regular-season tilt March 23, 1952, at Boston, getting the start and surrendering three goals in 30 minutes work during a 4–2 loss to the Bruins.

Rollins started the opener of the Leafs' semi-final series against Detroit, but when the Red Wings took a 3–0 decision, the Leafs made a bold decision.

Smythe decided to start Broda in Game 2, and the old warhorse almost came up with a Hollywood ending. Broda blocked 24 shots, allowing only a first-period goal by Johnny Wilson, who jammed home the rebound of an Alex Delvecchio shot, but that was enough to give Detroit a 1–0 victory.

"I thought I had the winning goal blocked," Broda explained to *Associated Press*. "After Delvecchio's shot I thought I had the puck under me. That's the reason I didn't move, but it had skidded off my pad behind me and was loose for Wilson to knock in."

Who would be in goal for Game 3? Leafs' coach Joe Primeau was honest about who ran the team in his answer to that question.

"You'll have to check with Mr. Smythe," Primeau told reporters.

The Leafs stuck with Broda for Game 3, but the magic wore off and the Wings were runaway 6–2 winners. Despite the loss, the 14,402 gathered at Maple Leaf Gardens cheered every save the Fabulous Fat Man made in the Toronto net, perhaps recognizing it would be the last chance they'd get to do so.

Returning to Rollins for Game 4, the Leafs fell 3–1 and the defending Stanley Cup champs were swept from the playoffs.

The decision to go to Broda brought Smythe plenty of criticism.

"No matter how you look at it, the Toronto Maple Leafs did a disservice to 38-year-old Turk Broda when they yanked him out of semi-retirement for the Stanley Cup playoffs," wrote syndicated columnist Jim Coleman. "Watching those six goals whiz past him last Saturday night was reminiscent of seeing old Joe Louis being kayoed by the relatively unknown Rocky Marciano.

"And can you imagine what must have happened to Al Rollins' ego as he was yanked summarily from the Toronto nets and replaced by that nice stout pappy guy?"

Coleman went on to point out rumours that the Leafs were seeking to land Harry Lumley from Chicago and in the off-season that would become reality. Rollins went to the Blackhawks in a deal that brought Lumley to Toronto.

Broda, meanwhile, retired again, this time for good.

TEE TIME OR PUCK DROP?

There was a time when Conn Smythe loved the work of Bill Ezinicki.

Wild Bill, as he was known, was considered hockey's toughest body checker—just the kind of player Smythe sought for his Leafs.

"We're not playing for the Lady Byng Trophy, you know," Smythe said. "If any of my guys win the Lady Byng Trophy he can be sure he'll be sold or traded.

"I don't want any such characters."

Ezinicki, who led the NHL in penalty minutes in 1948–49 and again in 1949–50 was no such character. His detractors went as far as to suggest he was dirty and this accusation bothered Ezinicki.

"It was hard to take because in my heart I felt I had never been vicious," Ezinicki told the *Ottawa Journal.* "Robust yet, and perhaps a hard hitter. But cruel or deliberately dirty, never.

"I'm human enough to prefer friendliness to hate. There's nobody in hockey for whom I have any but the kindliest feelings."

While Smythe was passionate about Ezinicki's play on the ice, it was his summer playing pursuit that didn't sit well with the major domo of the Maple Leafs.

Ezinicki was a pro golfer and a pretty fair one at that, qualifying to play in nine U.S. Opens. But Smythe sought to get the hard-hitting winger to limit his stick work to when he was on the ice.

"Would you rather play hockey or golf?" Smythe asked Ezinicki as they dickered over a new contract valued at $7,000 a season prior to the 1950–51 campaign, an amount that was less than what Ezinicki had earned the previous campaign.

"I'd rather play golf," answered Ezinicki, who almost immediately afterward found himself playing hockey in the American League for Toronto's Pittsburgh farm club.

A month later, he was dealt to the Boston Bruins and was an immediate hit.

"I've seen guys with courage, but this Ezinicki beats them all," Bruins GM Art Ross told the *Boston Herald*. "I've never seen a guy with such an uncomplaining attitude."

Soon, though, Ross was feuding with Ezinicki over golf, especially after discovering he'd played 36 holes on the day of a 1951 playoff game with Toronto.

He was traded back to the Leafs in 1952, but Smythe vowed of Ezinicki "he'll never play for the Maple Leafs again." And he didn't, languishing in the minors until he resurfaced in the NHL with the New York Rangers in 1954–55.

CLARENCE AND FRANCIS FALL FLAT

They were better known by their nicknames—Hap Day and King Clancy—but mom and dad knew them as Clarence Day and Francis Clancy. Leaf fans knew them as defencemen on the first Maple Leafs Stanley Cup winner in 1931–32.

In 1953, Leafs' managing director Conn Smythe was certain he had assembled a winning combination when he installed Clancy as his coach and Day as his GM.

"I have come up with an unbeatable combination," Smythe bragged to the *Boston American*. "An Orangeman and an Irishman—Day and Clancy. Direct current. Get it?"

"It can't miss," Smythe guaranteed.

Day had coached the Leafs to Stanley Cups in 1941–42, 1944–45, 1946–47, 1947–48, and 1948–49, and Smythe's fondness for Clancy was well known.

"The King did not build the Maple Leaf Gardens," Smythe said. "But he sure as hell helped pay for it."

Smythe believed he was on to a sure thing.

"It can't miss," he said.

But as often is the case with sure things, it didn't pay off. The Leafs failed to win a single playoff series with these two in charge.

Clancy relinquished his coaching duties in 1956 and Day was dismissed as GM in 1957.

CONN GAME FOR COMMUNISTS

When the Soviet national team stunned the East York Lyndhursts 7–2 to win the world hockey title in 1954, Canada as a nation was stunned.

Conn Smythe was out for revenge.

The managing director of the Maple Leafs was frothing with anger, vowing to show who the real world hockey power was by packing the Leafs up at the conclusion of the NHL season and taking them to Russia for a series of exhibition games to show the Russians how Canadians really play the game.

"We're only interested in one thing—to keep the old flag flying," Smythe told *Canadian Press*. "The Leafs will go anywhere.

"I would like very much to see Canada regain her lost prestige in world hockey."

Smythe felt the Leafs would be up for the challenge.

"This club is one of the youngest we have ever had and their enthusiasm for such a trip, I think, would be unbounded."

Almost immediately, a self-appointed committee of Leaf fans set in motion plans to raise $50,000 they supposed the club would require to fund the trip. Toronto mayor Allan Lamport offered up $5,000 toward the kitty.

Toronto GM Hap Day was sceptical about the idea.

"Don't worry," Boston Bruins' GM Lynn Patrick suggested. "Hap will go to Moscow or Siberia if Conn Smythe gives him the word."

Pavel Korotkov, chief of the ice hockey branch of the Soviet committee for sports and recreation, indicated to *United Press* that there was an appetite for a visit to Russia by either the Leafs or Montreal Canadiens for a hockey series against the Soviet national squad.

"I don't care whether they are professional or amateur as long as they are the best Canada can send us," Korotkov said. "What we want is a club with a first-class reputation," indicating that Russia would "lay down the red carpet" for the Leafs or Canadiens.

However, the offer put forth by Smythe to play in the spring was quickly quashed by the Soviets, who were without artificial ice surfaces at the time. "Thanks for proposal," Korotkov said via telegram. "Sorry that match in May is impossible. Agree to discuss questions at beginning of next year."

Smythe sent a telegram to the Russian ambassador in Ottawa expressing his desire to bring his team to the country, but they countered with a note that the Russians were more interested in arranging a Canadian tour for their national team.

In the midst of the Cold War, some hockey people felt it was best that they keep Smythe far away from such a volatile political landscape.

"If Canada wants to take responsibility for starting World War III, I can see no surer way than by sending Connie Smythe to Moscow with a hockey team," New York Rangers' GM Frank Boucher said.

"Perhaps a better way would be to have the Russians send a team to Canada. They could decide after watching a game between the Maple Leafs and another National League team whether they would like to take them on.

"Perhaps that would put an end to Russian claims that they have invented hockey."

Others felt it was a brilliant idea to ship Smythe and the Leafs off to the Russia and the sooner the better.

"I hope Smythe takes a team over there—and is sent to Siberia," Boston GM Art Ross told the *Boston Record American*. "It might be a good way to get rid of him."

Nearly a decade later, in 1963, sick and tired of hearing of how good European hockey was and how Canada was shrinking as a hockey power and was no longer a serious threat for the world title, Leafs coach Punch Imlach also offered to take his team across the pond to straighten matters out.

"If Canadians are worried that Canada is losing prestige in the eyes of the rest of the hockey world I'd be glad to take the Toronto Maple Leafs over there and play them," Imlach told sportscaster Johnny Esaw. "We'll play any country any time under NHL rules and we'll see whether Canada still has the best hockey players in the world."

Then Imlach proceeded to outline the remainder of his conditions.

"If Canada will put up $50,000 and plane fare, or if the Europeans will put up $50,000 and plane fare, I'll take the Maple Leafs over there for a series," Imlach said. "They can call the series whatever they want, but we'll go.

"It would be a bargain for these countries to put up the money and the Toronto Maple Leafs will go and get that prestige for them and in no uncertain terms."

In 1968, members of the Leafs and Canadiens organization met with International Ice Hockey Federation officials proposing that the world amateur hockey championship be changed to an open tournament that could allow an NHL team to represent Canada.

J. F. Bunny Ahearne, president of the European Hockey Federation, scoffed at the notion. "What good would it do to change the rules that apply to nations just to accommodate one nation—Canada?" Ahearne told Milt Dunnell of the *Toronto Star.* "I'm not concerned about the future of hockey in Canada. Now tell me, what good would it do Canadian hockey to have Leafs, Canadiens or any other professional team represent Canada in a world amateur tournament?"

NHL president Clarence Campbell was quick to point out the league had not sanctioned any such move by either club.

"Officially as a league we're not aware of any proposals," Campbell said. "I don't know what the NHL policy would be on the matter."

SMYTHE VS. THOMSON

Defenceman Jim Thomson gave his heart and soul to the Leafs. For a dozen seasons and 717 games, he wore the blue and white, winning four Stanley Cups, earning NHL Second Team All-Star status in 1950–51 and 1951–52 and serving as team captain in 1956–57, which would turn out to be his farewell campaign in Toronto.

But it would not be a fond farewell.

When Detroit's Ted Lindsay organized the NHLPA in 1956, Thomson came on board as the Toronto player rep.

Originally, Smythe seemed okay with the union talk, suggesting "it might be a good thing" for younger players to have an organization to help them plan for the future.

Soon, though, Smythe's opinion of the NHLPA took a 180-degree turn.

As the 1956–57 season drew to a close and the Leafs missed the playoffs, Smythe ordered Thomson, a member of the NHLPA executive, benched for the final four games of the season and attacked his captain for what Smythe felt was a case of not putting the team first.

"I find it very difficult to imagine that the captain of my club should find time during the hockey season to influence young players to join an association that has no specific plans to benefit or improve hockey," Smythe told *Canadian Press*.

Thomson didn't take the criticism quietly. "I want to play hockey in the NHL again next season, but certainly not with the Leafs because I feel my loyalty has been questioned," Thomson said. "After what's happened the last six weeks I wouldn't feel right playing for the Leafs."

Thomson lobbied to be moved elsewhere if Smythe no longer had any use for him. "Smythe holds my contract," Thomson said. "If I can't do justice to the Maple Leafs, the next move is up to the man who holds my contract."

That move came quickly, albeit quietly. Asked about Thomson's status in late April following an NHLPA meeting, Smythe scoffed. "Thomson is no longer our player," Smythe explained. "He was waived out of the league at the end of the season and his contract was transferred to Rochester (of the American Hockey League)."

Thomson admitted that this was the case. "Smythe sent me a contract two weeks ago to play in Rochester and I guess he offered me a major league salary," Thomson said. "I sent it back to him and told him I didn't want to sign that contract at any time.

"I won't go to Rochester. I just won't go."

On August 6, 1957, the Leafs sold Thomson's contract to the Chicago Blackhawks for $15,000. A year later, the Blackhawks returned Thomson to the Leafs, but he retired rather than play again for them.

VERBAL VOLLEYS

The bad blood that developed between Conn Smythe, when he served as president of Maple Leaf Gardens, and his son Stafford, who was the chairman of the committee of seven that ran the Maple Leafs, often revolved around Leafs' coach-GM Punch Imlach.

During the 1959 Stanley Cup playoffs, after the Leafs won Game 3 of their best-of-seven set with the Boston Bruins, Conn Smythe announced that Imlach, who had ousted Billy Reay as coach of the Leafs earlier in the season, would continue to coach the team the following season.

"We have a coach and we want to keep him," Smythe told *Canadian Press*. "We don't need a manager in this set up. I look after league matters. Staff (Conn's son Stafford Smythe) takes care of team problems. Bob Davidson does the scouting. King Clancy takes the heat off Punch in public relations, and we have an extremely efficient office staff.

"Getting Punch was a godsend to us. He's a coach and a good one. I like the way he works with his players. He has patience. If he brought in another coach for next season it could set us back five years. We've got to build this team up to championship calibre."

Stafford Smythe immediately labeled this proclamation as "ill timed," and complained about his father "mixing too much" with the team.

"When Imlach became general manager in November his duties included that of coach," Stafford Smythe explained. "It is entirely up to him if he wants to bring in a new coach. The decision that he will be coach next year is off because the decision belongs to Punch."

THE WORST SEATS IN THE HOUSE

Appalled by the poor quality of seats allotted to visiting Leafs' fans at the Montreal Forum for the opening two games of the 1960 Stanley Cup final, Leafs' managing director Conn Smythe brought in the carpenters prior to Games 3 and 4 at Maple Leaf Gardens.

Workmen hurriedly installed 50 new seats behind the grays and just under the roof girders of the rink. Smythe indicated these seats would be reserved for Canadiens' fans as retaliation for the "nose-bleed alley" seating afforded Leafs' fans in Montreal.

Smythe complained to NHL president Clarence Campbell about the woeful quality of seating offered Toronto fans in Montreal, but when Campbell did nothing to accommodate his concerns, the Leafs' boss took action.

Under NHL rules governing Stanley Cup final seating, the visiting team was entitled to 120 seats. Previously, the Leafs offered the Canadiens 20 box seats, 50 in the blues and 50 in the greens. The new seats replaced the 50 blue seats, which were some of the best spots to watch a game at the Gardens.

CONN'S CREDO

Conn Smythe offered a simple recipe for success to his players during the time he ran the Maple Leafs.

"I've never seen an athlete get any better through smoking, drinking, sex, or lying," Smythe would explain. "Any young Canadian athlete who believes in his God, his Queen, and his country will have a happy life."

Smythe stood by these principles and in 1961, when his son Stafford and business partner Harold Ballard opened a beer lounge in the Gardens, Smythe stepped down as president and sold his shares in the building to the two men for $2 million.

In 1966, his son and Ballard booked a heavyweight title bout featuring Muhammad Ali, who Smythe viewed as a draft dodger for his refusal to be drafted in the U.S. Army to fight the war in Vietnam. In protest, Smythe resigned from the Gardens' board of directors.

"The Gardens was founded by men—sportsmen—who fought for their country," Smythe said. "It is no place for those who want to evade conscription in their own country."

SMYTHE VS. THE CANADIAN FLAG

Conn Smythe was adamantly opposed to the introduction of the maple leaf flag as Canada's flag, determined that the red ensign flag should be maintained as Canada's flag.

Smythe made his feelings known in a letter he wrote to Canadian Prime Minister Lester B. Pearson, among more than 300 letters he penned to Canadian Members of Parliament on the subject.

He also let Leafs' centre Red Kelly, the Liberal Member for York, know how he felt on the matter.

"I had three or four meetings with Mr. Conn Smythe," Kelly told Paul Hunter of the *Toronto Star*. "He wrote every member in the House because he wanted the Ensign. He told me that he fought over there … he got wounded and he fought for the Red Ensign—Canada—and he didn't want that changed.

"When I'd go to the House, I'd hear all the stories of how the Canadian soldiers were recognized by the maple leaf on their lapel. So I'd come back and have another meeting with Mr. Smythe and I'd give him all the arguments that I'd heard in caucus. He listened. He didn't have a rebuttal. Then a week or so later, I'd get a note to go see him and he'd have new arguments."

"He was a tough character but at least he listened to what I had to say."

Although the new Canadian flag flew at Maple Leaf Gardens toward the end of the 1963–64 season, it was removed to begin the 1964–65 campaign on orders from team management and replaced by the Ontario flag. The next day, the Maple Leaf Gardens' switchboard lit up with complaints from Leafs' fans who'd attended the game.

Even after the new flag became the official Canadian flag on February 15, 1965, the Red Ensign continued to fly at Maple Leaf Gardens.

"Because we're winning," insisted Gardens' executive vice-president Harold Ballard. "There's nothing wrong with the new flag. I think it's great.

"We're going to fly it right after we win the Stanley Cup. But we're not changing anything, even flags, while we're winning."

The whole debate seemed to be politically fuelled. Gardens' chairman of the board John Bassett was publisher of the *Toronto Telegram* and his newspaper was supporting Conservative John Diefenbaker in the upcoming Canadian federal election and the Torys were anti-maple-leaf flag.

The season before, when the maple leaf flag flew at the Gardens, the *Telegram* had come out in support of Lester Pearson and the Liberal party, the group responsible for the introduction of the new flag.

The *Brandon Sun* jokingly suggested in an editorial that the team should be renamed the Toronto Red Ensigns.

Eventually, the Leafs gave in and hung the red maple leaf flag, Ballard insisting that calls from patrons were 3–1 in favour of the maple leaf.

OF STANLEY AND OTHER MUGS

Along the way, the Leafs have won virtually every NHL award. No really, they have.

HAVE A CIGAR

As of the start of the 1940–41 NHL season, no Maple Leafs' goalie had ever won the Vezina Trophy. To end that run Toronto goalie Turk Broda would need some help.

He was one goal behind Johnny Mowers of the Detroit Red Wings and was in the Boston Garden crowd the night of March 18, 1941, along with the rest of the Maple Leafs, to see the Bruins battle the Wings.

Published reports indicated that Broda was in line for a $1,000 bonus if he won the Vezina, so he was as tense as if he were in the net himself as the game got underway. Not even the sight of Toronto defenceman Wally Stanowski, who showed up for the game wearing dark horned-rimmed glasses compete with giant nose and fake moustache and an oversized stogie dangling from his mouth, could get a grin out of the normally amiable Broda.

Boston forward Bill Cowley had just the ticket to make Broda smile, though. Cowley fired a puck into the net past Mowers barely a minute into the game, and Broda cracked a wide smile. He was practically delirious with joy when Cowley netted his second of the night in the third period, guaranteeing the Vezina would got to the pudgy Toronto netminder.

Never let it be said that Broda wasn't one to repay those who helped him out. "Early this morning, before the first edition of

The (Boston) Traveler hit the streets, a burly young man, broad of beam and with a broad, beaming smile, trudged to the Hotel Brunswick with a package under his arm," wrote Arthur Siegel. "The broad-beamed body was that of beautiful Turk Broda, bearing a gift of cigars for Bill Cowley, who had personally given Broda undisputed possession of the Georges Vezina Trophy, the cup which goes to the least-scored-upon goaltender in the National Hockey League."

FROM MASCOT TO MAIN MAN

When Toronto won its first Stanley Cup as the Maple Leafs in 1931–32, a highlight of game nights at Maple Leaf Gardens were the twirling turns on the ice taken during intermissions by young Billy Taylor, the club's 11-year-old mascot.

A decade would pass before the Leafs would again lift Lord Stanley's mug, and one of those doing the heavy lifting for Toronto was Taylor.

After winning the 1938–39 Memorial Cup with the Oshawa Generals, Taylor turned pro in 1939–40 and quickly advanced into the Leafs' line-up. In the 1942 playoffs, Taylor collected 10 points in 13 games as Toronto rallied from a 3–0 series deficit in the Stanley Cup final against Detroit to oust the Red Wings in seven games.

When they trailed the set 3–0, it was the cocky Taylor who boasted, "We'll just win four in a row."

He shared the Leafs' scoring lead with 60 points in 1942–43, and Toronto coach Hap Day was enamoured with Taylor's work.

"I wouldn't trade him for any centre in the league, not even (Boston's two-time Hart Trophy winner) Bill Cowley, because Billy has his best years ahead," proclaimed Day. "Taylor is the smartest stickhandler in the business."

HOW'D YOU SPEND YOUR WEEKEND?

It may be the most common question posed in high-school hallways on Monday mornings.

"What did you do on the weekend?"

Everyone answers this query at some point during their teenage years, but it's doubtful anyone ever had a better response than the one Gaye Stewart was able to deliver on Monday, April 20, 1942.

Stewart was 18, and had spent the winter skating for the junior Toronto Marlboros and attending to his Grade 12 studies at Toronto's Northern Secondary School.

In the spring, he'd find himself in the midst of an oddity that would end with his name inscribed on the Stanley Cup.

"When the Marlboros were eliminated from the playoffs, the Leafs turned me pro and sent me to play with Hershey in the American League," recalled Stewart, who suited up for five regular-season and ten playoff games with the AHL Bears.

"When Hershey was eliminated from the playoffs, they brought me back to Toronto and I practiced with the Leafs."

Facing the Detroit Red Wings in the Stanley Cup final, the favoured Leafs stumbled and lost the first three games of the best-of-seven set. Heading into Game 4, Toronto coach Hap Day shuffled his line-up. He sat slow-footed veterans Bucko McDonald and Gordie Drillon, the latter the 1937–38 NHL scoring champion, and inserted youth in the form of Don Metz, Hank Goldup, and Stewart.

"I remember there was no panic in the dressing room (prior to Game 4)," Stewart recalled. "Everyone went about their business as usual. (Managing director) Conn Smythe came in and said a few words to us right before we took the ice."

The Leafs edged the Wings 4–3 to stay alive. In Game 5, they handed Detroit a 9–3 shellacking, and then posted a 3–0 shutout to take Game 6.

Playing for all the marbles in Game 7 on Saturday, April 18, at Maple Leaf Gardens, Toronto rallied for a 3–1 victory, becoming the first and only team to ever win a Stanley Cup final after falling behind 3–0 in the series.

Stewart celebrated the win with his new teammates, and got to extol the tale to his classmates two days later.

"First thing Monday morning, I was back in class," Stewart said, armed with the best 'what did you do on the weekend' story in high-school history.

THREE TIMES TWO

The Leafs were the first NHL team to threepeat as Stanley Cup champions and they were also the first to do it twice.

Toronto won Stanley Cups in 1946–47, 1947–48 and 1948–49, the latter championship coming despite nearly missing the playoffs with a dismal 22–25–13 record. The Leafs joined the 1937–38 Chicago Blackhawks—who beat the Leafs in that spring's final—as the only teams in NHL history to win the Stanley Cup despite a losing regular-season record.

Nearly two decades later, they did it again. Toronto upset defending champion Chicago to win the 1961–62 Cup and then took back-to-back titles at the expense of the Detroit Red Wings.

As was the case with the previous trio, the third one in 1963–64 proved the toughest. Toronto finished third in the standings and won a hard-fought seven game series from first-place Montreal, getting a hat trick from Dave Keon in a 3–1 win at the Forum in Game 7.

It took another seven-game series victory and a rally from a 3–2 series deficit over the Wings to capture the Cup. Game 6 was won at Detroit on a goal scored in overtime by defenceman Bobby Baun, who was playing despite a hairline fracture in his ankle.

The Leafs drubbed Detroit 4–0 on home ice in Game 7, Johnny Bower posting the shutout and Andy Bathgate, acquired in a blockbuster trade with the New York Rangers earlier in the season, netting the Cup winner.

It was the first and only Cup win of Bathgate's Hall-of-Fame career. "I've been around a long time waiting for something like this," Bathgate told *Canadian Press*. "I didn't know it would take a trade to get me to the Cup celebration, but I couldn't be happier."

The celebration in the Toronto dressing room was something to witness. Forward Ed Litzenberger playfully opened beers on his skate blades. Defenceman Carl Brewer slumped against the back wall, smiling and belting out the words to "The Maple Leaf Forever."

Normally gruff Leaf coach Punch Imlach was lavish in praise of his team. "Three of them went out there with their legs frozen,"

Imlach said. "Bob Baun, Carl Brewer and Red Kelly all had needles to deaden the pain of their leg injuries and then they all told me they wanted to play.

"What more can I say? What more could I ask?"

PARALLELS BETWEEN 1947–49 LEAFS AND 1962–64 LEAFS

Beyond the fact that both groups won three successive Stanley Cups, these two Toronto Maple Leafs dynasties shared numerous common traits:

1947-49	**1962-64**
Captain Syl Apps wore No. 10	Captain George Armstrong wore No. 10
First win came against defending champs (Montreal)	First win came against defending champs (Chicago)
Last two wins came against Detroit	Last two wins came against Detroit
Acquired Max Bentley in five-for-two trade	Acquired Andy Bathgate in five-for-two trade
1947-48 Leafs finished first overall	1962-63 Leafs finished first overall
1948-49 Leafs lost 25 games	1963-64 Leafs lost 25 games
Howie Meeker won the Calder Trophy in 1946-47	Kent Douglas won the Calder Trophy in 1962-63

WHERE'S STANLEY?

With seven rookies in their line-up, part of a rebuilding job after missing the 1945–46 playoffs, the Leafs shocked the hockey world by copping the Stanley Cup in a six-game final series win over the defending champion Montreal Canadiens. With an average age of 24.05 years, the 1946–47 Leafs were the youngest team to win the Stanley Cup.

Certainly, they caught the Habs by surprise. "How did they even make the playoffs?" Canadiens' goalie Bill Durnan wondered aloud following Montreal's decisive 6–0 verdict in the series opener.

After the Leafs captured the Cup on Teeder Kennedy's goal during a 2–1 Game 6 triumph, a joyous gathering of 14,565 at Maple Leaf Gardens remained standing for ten minutes, chanting "We want the Cup," in unison.

Finally, they began heading for the exits when it was announced that the Stanley Cup was not in the building.

The overconfident Canadiens had left Lord Stanley's mug behind in Montreal.

THEIR BEST FINISH EVER

When it comes to fantastic finishes, nothing will top what the Leafs accomplished on the final weekend of the 1947–48 season.

Entering the weekend, the Leafs were atop the standings with 73 points, one more than the second-place Detroit Red Wings, whom they would face in a home-and-home set to close out the regular season.

Meanwhile, Toronto's Turk Broda and Detroit's Harry Lumley were in a chase for the Vezina Trophy. Both had allowed 138 goals entering the final two games of the campaign.

At Maple Leaf Gardens on March 20, 1948, the Leafs got two goals from Teeder Kennedy and edged the Wings 5–3 to clinch first overall in the NHL standings for the first time since the 1934–35 season.

The next night at Olympia Stadium, captain Syl Apps, who was playing his farewell NHL season, fired a hat-trick as the Leafs dumped the Wings 5–2 and locked up the Vezina for Broda. It was also a milestone moment for Apps, who finished his NHL career with 201 goals, surpassing Charlie Conacher (200) to become the Leafs' all-time goal-scoring leader.

The fun was just beginning for the Leafs. They would sweep the Wings in the Stanley Cup final, marking the first season in team history in which Toronto won both the regular-season and Stanley Cup titles.

RECORD SETTERS

Hard as it may be to believe today, there was a time when the Leafs were the scourge of the NHL.

When Toronto swept the Detroit Red Wings to win the 1949 Stanley Cup final, that victory established a number of NHL firsts for the franchise.

First team to win three consecutive Stanley Cups.

First team to win seven Stanley Cups overall.

First team to win the Stanley Cup five times in an eight-season span.

The Leafs also set a mark by winning 11 consecutive Stanley Cup final games, a mark that they would extend to 12 games with a victory over the Montreal Canadiens in Game 1 of the 1951 Cup final series.

TYING ONE ON

For a game that ultimately didn't count, a heck of a lot went down.

Hurting after a 2–0 loss on home ice in the opener of their 1951 Stanley Cup semi-final series, the Leafs headed into Game 2 against the Boston Bruins at Maple Leaf Gardens on Saturday, March 31, looking for revenge.

In the end, they didn't get the result they were seeking, but the Leafs also didn't suffer a setback, the last time in the history of the tournament for Lord Stanley's mug that a game was played and no one came out a winner.

The contest was barely four minutes old when Leafs' defenceman Bill Barilko beat Bruins' goalie Jack Gelineau with the first shot on goal of the game, and it stayed that way until midway through the second period, when Boston's Johnny Peirson got the puck past Toronto's Turk Broda to even the count.

Little did anyone know at the time that the scoring was done for the night.

The two teams headed to overtime deadlocked at 1–1 and played through the first 20-minute extra period without deciding an outcome. But the game was about to be brought to an end regardless.

New York Rangers' GM Frank Boucher, the NHL representative at the game, determined that there would be only time for one period of overtime play and if the game weren't decided in that frame, it would be called a draw, since it was too close to midnight and Sunday sports were not permitted in Toronto except between the hours of 1:30–6 p.m.

It was the first tie game in Stanley Cup play since 1935, when the league still utilized a two-game, total goals series, and it is also the last tie game in Stanley Cup history.

If the series were to go the distance, announced NHL publicity director Ken McKenzie, an eighth game would be played in Toronto and the tie would not count toward the outcome of the set.

Fans, once they realized they were the victims of a cruel April Fool's Day prank, wondered whether they'd be given rain checks like at a baseball game that isn't played to a conclusion.

Even though they didn't see a winner determined, the 14,056 at Maple Leaf Gardens would have been hard pressed to claim they didn't get their money's worth.

The rugged tilt featured no less than seven fights, some of them were world-class tilts. Captain Teeder Kennedy was cut over the eye by his Boston counterpart Milt Schmidt, a wound that required eight stitches: the game was halted while they scraped Kennedy's blood off the ice.

Boston's Dunc Fisher was carted off on a stretcher, cut for a dozen stitches by a check from Barilko. Peirson was taken to hospital with a fractured cheekbone after a hard check from Toronto defenceman Jim Thomson.

Bruins' forward Pete Horeck required 10 stitches over his eyebrow, and it took three stitches to repair a wound to teammate Murray Henderson, also above the eye.

Bruins' coach Lynn Patrick threw a punch in the direction of a Leaf player during one altercation. W. A. H. O'Brien, chairman of the board for the Leafs, left his seat in the royal box next to the Viscount Alexander of Tunis, Canadian governor-general, to go to ice level and berate referee Red Storey.

Leafs' manager Conn Smythe was also on the move, dashing to where Boucher and NHL referee-in-chief Carl Voss were sitting to voice his displeasure over the charging major assessed Barilko in overtime for his hit on Peirson. Fans nearby encouraged Smythe with applause and as he made his way back through the crowd, held out their programs seeking an autograph.

Ever the showman, Smythe happily obliged.

After the game was called, the players hustled to Union Station to catch the train to Boston for Sunday's third game of the series. The Leafs won that one 3–0 and took the next three afterward.

Although the series is recorded in the annals of Stanley Cup lore as 4–1 Toronto verdict, it will always be remembered that it took the Leafs six games to win it in five.

PRIMEAU'S TRIPLE PLAY

Joe Primeau was a Hall-of-Famer on the ice and a one-of-a-kind coach behind the bench.

He's the only bench boss in hockey history to lead teams to Memorial, Allan, and Stanley Cup victories.

His unique trio began in 1945, when Primeau guided the St. Michael Majors to a Memorial Cup win over the Moose Jaw Canucks.

Four years later, Primeau guided the Toronto Marlboros to the Allan Cup crown over the Calgary Stampeders, and was hired to coach the Leafs when Hap Day was promoted to GM.

In his first season as an NHL coach, Primeau guided the Leafs to the Stanley Cup title over the Montreal Canadiens.

"It was the most thrilling game I've been through," Primeau said of their 3–2 Cup-clinching overtime win over the Habs. The Leafs tied the game on Tod Sloan's goal with Toronto goalie Al Rollins on the bench for an extra attacker and won on Bill Barilko's goal 2:53 into overtime.

Interestingly, seven members of that Leafs' team were part of Primeau's other Cup wins as a coach.

Defencemen Jim Thomson and Gus Mortson and forward Sloan played for St. Michael's while forwards Danny Lewicki and Bob Hassard and defenceman Hugh Bolton won with the Marlies. Forward John McCormack was an ever-present on Primeau title teams, skating for all three of his title-winning clubs.

THE MIRACLE RALLY

The Leafs entered the stretch drive for the 1958–59 NHL regular season stumbling. Sitting in fifth spot, out of a playoff position, they'd lost two in a row, gone 2–4–1 in their last seven and 4–8–2 over their previous 14 games.

Entering a weekend home-and-home series March 13–14 against the fourth-place New York Rangers, even the most optimistic of Leafs' fans couldn't imagine that a miracle was in the works.

The Rangers, with 62 points, stood seven ahead of the Leafs, but had opened the door a crack by losing two in a row.

The Leafs quickly ran New York's losing skid to four games. In the first meeting at Maple Leaf Gardens, Johnny Bower blocked 31 shots for his third shutout of the season while Dick Duff and Frank Mahovlich each scored twice in a 5–0 rout.

The next night's tilt at Madison Square Garden was much closer. The Leafs squandered 4–2 and 5–4 leads and needed Bob Pulford's goal with 2:06 to play to grab a 6–5 decision.

Toronto was within three points of a playoff spot and the race was on.

While the Rangers lost 5–3 to the Boston Bruins, the Leafs were heading to Montreal, where they took advantage of Canadiens' back-up goalie Claude Pronovost for a 6–3 victory over the defending Stanley Cup champions at the Forum.

Entering the final weekend of the season, New York's advantage was down to a scant point.

On March 21, the Leafs hammered the Chicago Blackhawks 5–1, but the Rangers found some life and defeated the Detroit Red Wings 5–2.

It would all come down to the final night of the regular season—the Rangers at home to face the Habs, while the Leafs travelled to Detroit.

Harry Howell gave the Rangers the lead, but after that it was all Montreal. Jean Beliveau collected two goals and an assist, while Dickie Moore counted a goal and an assist to set an NHL scoring record with 96 points in Montreal's 4–2 victory.

"No comment," barked Rangers' coach Phil Watson as reporters came up to him afterward. He also barred the door to his team's dressing room.

New York finished the season on a 1–6 slide and all they could do now was wait.

At first, it appeared hopeful. Two future Leafs—Norm Ullman and Marcel Pronovost—gave Detroit a first-period lead. After Larry Regan and Bob Baun scored to tie it, Ullman put the Wings back in front.

Carl Brewer and Regan gave Toronto the lead for the first time, but Pronovost knotted the count and it was 4–4 after 40 minutes.

The third period was all Leafs. Dick Duff gave Toronto the lead and Billy Harris added an insurance marker. The 6–4 final put the Leafs in the playoffs for the first time since the spring of 1956.

"We did it the hard way," assistant GM King Clancy told *UPI*.

Emboldened by their rally, coach Punch Imlach predicted a bold future for his Leafs.

"We've got the confidence and the team spirit to go all the way," Imlach told the *Boston Herald* prior to the Leafs' semi-final series with the Bruins. "It was a long time coming.

"We had to eliminate a defeatist complex that had built up over the last two years but now we're rolling."

The Leafs toppled the Bruins in a hard-fought seven-game set to reach the Stanley Cup final for the first time since 1951, but fell in five games to the Habs.

"They're going to be well worth watching in the near future," Montreal coach Toe Blake said of the Leafs.

"Toronto could be a major power for a number of years if we get the farm system working right," added Imlach.

Toronto would return to the final in 1960, losing again to the Canadiens, but would win three straight Stanley Cups between 1962–64.

BOOMER'S BIG BREAK

The Leafs were in trouble in Game 6 of their 1963–64 Stanley Cup final series against the Detroit Red Wings at Olympia Stadium.

Losers by a 2–1 count in Game 5 at Maple Leaf Gardens, Toronto's hope for the third straight Stanley Cup title required a win in Detroit to bring both teams back to Maple Leaf Gardens for a winner-take-all seventh game scenario.

A goal from Billy Harris pulled Toronto even, sending Game 6 to overtime. Looking at times like they didn't have a leg to stand on, the Leafs were seeking a hero, and one would arrive who could barely stand on one leg.

Defenceman Bob Baun left the game in the third period after being struck in the ankle by a shot from Detroit superstar Gordie

Howe. He returned for overtime and early in the frame, Baun's point shot banked off Red Wings' defenceman Bill Gadsby and past Terry Sawchuk for the game winner.

Back in Toronto, Baun stayed away from doctors and suited up for the final game of the series, surviving on guts and pain killers. Likewise, centre Red Kelly, playing in his record 142nd Stanley Cup game, persevered despite a knee so painful he required a wheelchair to make it home following Game 6.

Kelly not only scored one of Toronto's goals in the Leafs' 4–0 Game 7 triumph, he also kept Howe in check.

"When guys like Kelly and Baun come into the room demanding that they play, and kept coming back to be shot up with anaesthetic, it was more than enough in the way of inspiration for our team," Leafs' coach Punch Imlach told the *Ottawa Journal*. "From a coach's standpoint this was enough to have a lot going for me. It was real ammunition.

"I never saw a team of mine much higher before a game. They clumped around on their skates before they left the room. They saw Kelly with his knee and Baun with his ankle, shot up and ready to go. It did more for the rest of the club than anything I could say or anybody else could do."

Vanquished Detroit coach Sid Abel couldn't believe how well Baun played on what would be determined to be a hairline fracture of his right fibula. "He'd better be in a cast tomorrow to prove he was really hurt in Detroit," Abel groused. "All those Leafs played a whale of a game."

Abel got all the evidence he'd need the next day during the Leafs' Stanley Cup parade. As he got into the car that was to drive him to Toronto City Hall, Baun stumbled and reinjured the leg. Forced to go back to hospital, he missed the parade.

THE THREE BIGGEST GAMES OF THE 1967 PLAYOFFS

In every Stanley Cup run, there are turning points, moments when it either all comes together or all falls apart.

For the 1966–67 Leafs, the last Toronto team to win the Stanley Cup, these were those moments:

APRIL 15, 1967

Deadlocked 2–2 in their semi-final series with the favoured Chicago Blackhawks, Toronto coach Punch Imlach made a bold decision prior to Game 5 at Chicago Stadium, opting to go with Johnny Bower in goal over Terry Sawchuk, who'd started the first four games of the series.

In his first game back since fracturing a finger, Bower struggled to find his groove and after one period with the scored tied 2–2, Bower sought out Imlach during the intermission.

"I told Punch that I guess I was a bit shaky and wasn't feeling just right," Bower recalled. "I said maybe you better put in Ukey (Sawchuk). This is an important game to the guys, a lot depends on it. Ukey is real hot."

Imlach appreciated Bower's forthrightness, listened to his veteran netminder and made the switch.

"Bower's a very honest guy," Imlach told *Canadian Press*. "I asked him if he wanted to go on and he said he'd rather not."

Right from the faceoff to begin the second period, Chicago superstar Bobby Hull got loose down the left wing and unloaded one of his howitzers toward the Toronto net. It went off Sawchuk's left shoulder and into the crowd and Sawchuk slumped to the ice as if a sniper had picked him off.

"I was afraid that I'd hit him in the neck or throat," Hull said. But after some attention from trainer Bobby Haggert, Sawchuk rose to his feet and continued.

Boy did he continue.

Sawchuk turned in one of the most famous relief performances in Stanley Cup history. "Sawchuk did everything," wrote *CP*'s David Miller. "He leaped, sprawled, twisted, jumped, sprang, fell, kicked and probably prayed."

As for his save on Hull, Sawchuk shrugged off any talk of a brilliant stop.

"Are you kidding?" Sawchuk retorted. "All you do is hope that it hits you, especially when Bobby Hull is the guy at the other end. There's no skill in that."

In all, he made 37 saves and the Leafs posted a 4–2 victory. "It's the best game Sawchuk has played here," Chicago coach Billy

Reay said. "I'm satisfied with the way we played—we had lots of chances—but he beat us."

Three nights later, a 3–1 win at Maple Leaf Gardens put Toronto into the Cup final against the defending champion Montreal Canadiens.

April 25, 1967

To a generation of Leafs' fans, Nikolai Borschevsky's Game 7 overtime winner against Detroit in the opening round of the 1993 playoffs is the biggest Toronto goal they've witnessed.

For another generation, it's Lanny McDonald's Game 7 winner versus the New York Islanders in the 1978 quarter-finals.

In reality, Bill Barilko scored the most famous OT winner in Leafs' history when he potted the Cup winner against Montreal in 1951. But on a long night in Toronto, Bob Pulford netted the second-most important OT winner in franchise history.

Coming home from Montreal with a 1–1 split at the Forum, Game 3 would be a pivotal moment in the set.

Some hockey people were of the opinion that Imlach drove his veteran team too hard with his long, tough practices. There were no such things as maintenance days in Punch's world. The only way to stay sharp was to stay on the ice.

When the Leafs pulled out a 3–2 double-overtime victory over the Canadiens to take a 2–1 series lead, Imlach viewed it as evidence that all that hard work paid off.

"We trained all year for this," Imlach told *CP*.

Imlach's players, especially the grizzled veterans, agreed with his assessment. "Us old war horses are better in a long race," reasoned defenceman Marcel Pronovost.

"You always keep going," added captain George Armstrong. "Afterwards you feel tired."

"The team seemed to pick up momentum as the overtime progressed," suggested left-winger Frank Mahovlich.

Leafs' goalie Johnny Bower, at 42 the oldest player on the ice, was also the busiest, blocking 60 shots. Pulford finally ended the evening at 8:26 of the second overtime period, taking a cross-crease pass from Jim Pappin and slamming the puck past Montreal netminder Rogatien Vachon.

"I'd have to say it was the greatest goal of my life," Pulford said.

Considering Montreal won Game 4 by a 6–2 count and would have taken a 3–1 series advantage home had the Habs found that OT winner in Game 3, certainly Pulford's tally was Toronto's biggest goal of the 1967 playoffs.

April 29, 1967

On the off day prior to Game 4 of the series, Imlach called Sawchuk into his office and informed him he intended to ride Bower's hot hand for the remainder of the series.

According to lore, Sawchuk, figuring he was off the hook, went on a bender that night at a Toronto bar and was still hung over when he arrived at Maple Leaf Gardens the morning of the fourth game of the final series.

Expecting to occupy a comfortable seat at the end of the Leafs' bench, instead Sawchuk found himself back on the hot seat when Bower pulled a hamstring in the pre-game warm-up.

Whether it was rust or a persistent headache from his alleged rousing night before, Sawchuk wasn't himself and the Habs rolled to an easy 6–2 triumph.

It was a joyous bunch of Canadiens who headed confidently home for Game 5. "We heard in the dressing room that Bower had been injured and he had been murder to us in the last two games," Montreal coach Toe Blake said.

Instead, they would run into a brick wall. Sawchuk, sobered up and fortified, blocked 37 shots and the Leafs cruised to a 4–1 victory.

"Sawchuk played a great game," said Imlach, who also had praise for his other players.

"They aren't the most talented hockey club in the world, but when they get together they can really go out there."

On May 2, via a 3–1 victory, those Leafs went out there and did something that no Toronto team has done since.

They won the Stanley Cup.

HOCKEY'S MOST FAMOUS EMPTY-NET GOAL

When Leaf fans remember the goals the led the team to its most recent Stanley Cup win in 1967, the one that always seems to resonate the most was actually shot into an empty net.

It was the final goal of the Cup final series win over Montreal, sent home from the neutral zone by Leafs' captain George Armstrong to clinch a 3–1 win in Game 6 and a 4–2 decision in the best-of-seven series.

With Canadiens' goalie Gump Worsley on the bench in favour of an extra attacker, Leafs' coach Punch Imlach sent Armstrong, Bob Pulford, Allan Stanley, Tim Horton, and Red Kelly over the boards for a faceoff in the Toronto zone in front of goalie Terry Sawchuk.

Stanley won the draw from Montreal captain Jean Beliveau and sent the puck back to Red Kelly, who fed Pulford. Pulford backhanded it ahead to Armstrong, who whipped a shot into the vacated cage from just outside the Canadiens' blue line with 47 seconds left in the period.

"I just flipped it over (Montreal defenceman Jacques) Laperriere's stick and it coasted down the ice to the net," Armstrong explained of his famous tally.

The captain of all four of Toronto's Stanley Cup winners in the 1960s, more than any Leaf captain in franchise history, Armstrong, who set up Dick Duff's winner for Toronto's Cup winner in 1962, the Leafs' first title in 11 years, still recalls the 1967 triumph with the most fondness among the quartet.

"It was a great mesh of young and old and great goaltending," Armstrong said. "The old fellows kept us in the games and the young fellows came along and gave us the extra edge.

"We had all the fight and desire."

In the Cup decider, Ron Ellis, 22, and Jim Pappin, 27, who led all playoff scorers with 7–8–15 totals, tallied the first two Leaf goals. Meanwhile, Sawchuk, 37, made 40 saves for the win.

Of all the Toronto players on board for the victory, Armstrong was the longest-serving wearer of the Leaf, first debuting with the team at 19 in 1949–50.

Armstrong was named captain by Leafs' managing director Conn Smythe during a March 23, 1957 *Hockey Night In Canada* broadcast and continued to wear the C through 1969, making him the longest-serving captain in franchise history.

Armstrong's easy-going style of leadership was a hit with his teammates. Tied 4–4 at Detroit after two periods of their last regular-season game of 1958–59 season and needing a win to qualify for the playoffs, Armstrong calmly reassured coach Punch Imlach that all was under control. "Don't worry Punch," Armstrong told Imlach as the Leafs headed out for the final frame. "We'll get this one."

Toronto scored twice for a 6–4 victory.

So important was Armstrong to the Leafs' cause that four times the team lured him back into action from retirement—first in 1967 and again in 1968, 1969, and 1970.

Armstrong finally retired for good in 1971. "It took them 20 years to find out I can't play hockey," Armstrong joked.

THE ANONYMOUS LEAFS

Imagine a member of the 1967 Stanley-Cup-winning Leafs waltzing into a Toronto establishment in the midst of their magical Cup run and going completely unnoticed.

Defenceman Aut Erickson and forward Milan Marcetta could pull it off. And, as a matter of fact, they did.

They were the mystery men of Toronto's last Cup-winning team, both recalled from Victoria of the Western Hockey League as support players and then pressed into action when some of the ancient warriors who wore the Leaf uniform that spring were sidelined by injury.

"To get a break like that after all those years, it was probably the biggest thrill of my life for sure," Marcetta told the *Toronto Star*. "How many guys play years and years and years and never win a Stanley Cup? I come out of the blue and get called up and get to be on the winning team."

Marcetta suited up for three playoff games, including the May 2, 1967 Cup-clinching 3–1 win over the Montreal Canadiens at

Maple Leaf Gardens. Erickson saw action in Game 5 of Toronto's semi-final series with the Chicago Blackhawks, a 4–2 win at Chicago Stadium when Leafs' coach Punch Imlach opted to dress six defencemen for the contest.

During the playoffs, the team put up Marcetta and Erickson at Toronto's Westbury Hotel, and despite their role in Stanley Cup glory they stayed well off the radar of rabid Leaf fans.

"Nobody had any idea who we were," Marcetta said. "Nobody was asking for autographs. You could sit in a restaurant and listen to people talking about the game.

"Some would say, 'They're going to do it.' Others would say, 'They're a bunch of old guys. They ain't going to do nothing.'

"Everybody was talking about the Leafs. It was nuts. The atmosphere was unbelievable."

Neither player ever saw duty in a regular-season game for the Leafs. Both moved to expansion teams for the 1967–68 season—Marcetta with the Minnesota North Stars and Erickson with the Oakland Seals.

THE HILLMAN HEX

When the Leafs won the 1966–67 Stanley Cup, one of the unsung heroes was Larry Hillman, who played stalwart defence alongside Marcel Pronovost. During 12 playoff games that spring, the duo was victimized for just one five-on-five goal.

After the season, Hillman, who'd yo-yoed up and down between the Leafs and the AHL throughout his Toronto tenure, thought he'd capitalize on his success and seek an increase in salary from $15,000 to $20,000 per season.

Leafs' coach-GM Punch Imlach refused, offering only $19,000, and Hillman held out for the extra $1,000. Imlach bumped his offer to $19,500, but vowed to fine Hillman $100 for every day he held out.

Hillman finally caved after 24 days out of work and was fined $2,400.

Afterward, Hillman claimed he was so angered that he inflicted a curse on the Leafs so that they would never again win the Stanley Cup.

"Yes, it's still there," Hillman told the *Toronto Star* in 2016. "It seems to have worked.

"I've left it on because they didn't pay me the $2,400, with interest," Hillman said. "It would have been a lot cheaper to pay that than signing all those million-dollar players."

Time heals all wounds, though, and Hillman has decided that 50 years is enough suffering.

In 2017, he has promised to lift the curse.

TORONTO'S TROPHY DROUGHTS

Mention the year 1967 to a Leafs' fan and they might recall it fondly, or they could cringe in despair. Usually it depends on which half of the half-century their age tends to fall.

Of course, that was the last time the Leafs won the Stanley Cup and yes, it's been awhile, but compared to Toronto's dry spell when it comes to the NHL's other major awards, things aren't so bad.

The only trophy of note won by the team was the 2002–03 Lady Byng Trophy awarded to forward Alexander Mogilny. But talk to almost any current NHLer and they'll tell you they want their name on the Lady Byng like they want their name on a plane ticket to their club's minor-league affiliate.

Since the league expanded from six to twelve teams in 1967, the Stanley Cup isn't the only award that's eluded the Leafs. From a team standpoint, they haven't finished first overall in the NHL since 1962–63. From an individual point of view, Toronto's trophy case is relatively vacant.

Hart Trophy:

Last Leaf Winner: Teeder Kennedy, 1954–55

They called him the heart of the Leafs, so it was only appropriate when Ted (Teeder) Kennedy was voted the Hart Trophy winner in 1954–55, his final full NHL season, as Kennedy and Leafs' goalie Harry Lumley ran first and second in Hart balloting.

"He's the greatest player in hockey," Leafs' managing director Conn Smythe told *Canadian Press*. "You can have your Richards, Howes, Schmidts, and Abels. I'll take Kennedy."

Leafs legend Joe Primeau, who coached the team to the Stanley Cup in 1950–51, thought it difficult to find fault with Kennedy. "I can't think of but two weaknesses that fellow has," Primeau said. "First, he's crazy about horses.

"Second, he is the most reluctant player about getting off the ice and letting somebody else take over I ever saw.

"He works too hard."

Art Ross

Last Leaf Winner: None

The trophy that goes annually to the NHL's leading scorer wasn't donated until the 1947–48 season, a decade after Gord Drillon was the most recent Leaf to top the league's scoring race.

Viewed as an enigma, a scorer who refused to back check, Drillon was booed out of Toronto in 1942, four years after he won the scoring title, after he was benched in the midst of that spring's Stanley Cup final against Detroit and the Leafs' fans turned on their former hero.

"One of the toughest touches came when a bunch of hoodlums appeared at our apartment house about midnight, tossed stones at the windows and put on a wild hooting demonstration," Drillon told Vern DeGeer of the *Globe & Mail*. "Even the kids in the neighbourhood got to booing me as I walked down the street. And only a few weeks previously I had been a pal to them.

"I had been dreaming about winning that Stanley Cup ever since I was a kid. It grew and grew in my mind each season. But when the series was finished out and I wasn't even on the bench, that Cup grew smaller. Just a shattered dream, I guess."

Considering how much Leafs' managing director Conn Smythe despised Boston GM Art Ross, perhaps he didn't mind that no Leaf was ever inscribed in the trophy during his lifetime.

Vezina

Last Leaf Winner: Johnny Bower/Terry Sawchuk, 1964–65

When Toronto coach Punch Imlach claimed Sawchuk from the Detroit Red Wings in the 1964 NHL Intra-League draft, he envisioned a scenario where veterans Sawchuk and Bower would be able to spell each other and the rest would allow both not only to play longer, but to excel in the short term.

"At the start of the season, we shook hands and I said, 'Terry, no matter what happens, if I win the grand Vezina myself, I'll split the prize money with you,'" Bower relayed in his book, *The China Wall*. "He said, 'OK, likewise.'"

After the season, Bower and Sawchuk used their $1,000 prize money to throw a party for their teammates.

Norris

Last Leaf Winner: None

Five times, Leafs defencemen have finished runner-up in the Norris voting, most recently Borje Salming in 1979–80. Salming also finished second in the 1976–77 balloting, as did Tim Horton (1963–64, 1968–69), Carl Brewer (1962–63), and Allan Stanley (1959–60).

Brewer came the closest to winning, edged 98–81 in the balloting by Chicago's Pierre Pilote, a future Leaf. Brewer's teammate Horton (37 points) was third in the voting.

In 1977, Robinson defeated Salming by a 186–157 margin.

Kelly, the first winner of the Norris, played centre in Toronto after he was traded to the Leafs in 1960.

Conn Smythe

Last Leaf Winner: Dave Keon, 1966–67

Not only is Keon the last Leaf to win the award named for the man who founded the Leafs, he's also the only one.

"Dave Keon is the best player in the National League," Leafs' coach Punch Imlach said at the time. "He does everything. I wouldn't trade him for anybody, not even Gordie Howe."

Had there been a Conn Smythe Trophy in 1964, Keon might have won it that spring. He scored a hat trick in Toronto's Game 7 semi-final triumph at Montreal and was Toronto's top goal scorer in the Cup final series against Detroit with four.

The season before, Keon likely would have also contended were there a Smythe. He set a Stanley Cup record with two shorthanded goals in the same game and led Leaf scorers with 4–2–6 numbers as they beat the Wings in a five-game final series.

A HARD HAB-IT TO BREAK

Long-time Leaf Bob Nevin called Toronto-Montreal the team's "traditional rivalry."

Hall-of-Famer Red Horner suggested that the games he played against the Canadiens were the most enjoyable of his Leaf career.

"I liked playing against the Montreal Canadiens best of all," Horner said. "They were the class of the league. Howie Morenz played for them and he was the finest player in the league."

When the Stanley Cup dreams of long-suffering Leaf supporters were dashed in the spring of 1993 after their Game 7 home-ice loss to the Los Angeles Kings in the Western Conference final, naturally there was extreme sadness throughout Toronto.

Surprisingly, there were also pangs of disappointment felt in La Belle Province, where fans of the Montreal Canadiens, who would go on to beat the Kings in the Cup final series, were looking forward to a Stanley Cup showdown with their long-time rivals from Ontario.

"It was kind of a different feeling around here," *Hockey Night In Canada* broadcaster Dick Irvin recalled.

Since it was the 100th year of competition for Lord Stanley's mug, traditionalists were hoping for a Montreal-Toronto final.

Yes, even those traditionalists who lived in Montreal.

An editorial cartoon in a Montreal French-language daily captured the unexpected feeling which overwhelmed Canadiens' fans.

It pictured three Habs fans, decked out in their blue, white and red Montreal sweaters, sipping their favourite brand of beverage and rooting for the likes of Doug Gilmour and Wendel Clark.

"Imagine us cheering for the Toronto Maple Leafs," the caption read.

"It was amazing how many people in this city were talking about a Leafs-Canadiens final," Irvin remembered. "People were really looking forward to it.

"There were a lot of disappointed people when it was L.A. It was a bit of a letdown."

For both teams, no doubt, because one fact that's been a certainty throughout NHL history—when the Leafs and Habs face each other in the playoffs, the survivor almost always skates off with the Stanley Cup.

Naturally, that's been the case in each of the five Stanley Cup final series in which they've met—Toronto wins in 1946–47, 1950–51, and 1966–67, and Montreal triumphs in 1958–59 and 1959–60.

Toronto also won the Cup after eliminating Montreal from the 1917–18, 1944–45, 1962–63, and 1963–64 playoffs. Meanwhile, the Canadiens went on to capture the title after early-round playoff series victories over Toronto in 1943–44, 1964–65, 1965–66, 1977–78, and 1978–79.

The lone exception to the rule came in 1924–25. The Habs defeated Toronto in the NHL final that spring but lost the Stanley Cup final to the Western Canada Hockey League's Victoria Cougars—the last time a team from outside the NHL captured Lord Stanley's mug.

JOHNNY BOWER'S CHAMPAGNE WISHES

On the shelf of the bar in the basement of his Mississauga, Ontario home, Johnny Bower keeps a prized possession, a link to the Toronto Maple Leafs' greatness of decades gone by.

There sits a bottle of champagne, pilfered from the dressing room the night of May 2, 1967, when the Leafs defeated the Montreal Canadiens to capture the Stanley Cup, Toronto's last Stanley Cup title.

Nearly 50 years later, the bottle remains filled with the drink of champions, while Toronto's dreams of another Stanley Cup parade remain unfulfilled.

"When the Maple Leafs won the Stanley Cup in 1967, I grabbed two bottles of champagne," Bower recalled. "They were left in the dressing room, so I took them and hid them behind my bench."

When Bower and his wife Nancy celebrated their 50th wedding anniversary on November 3, 1998, they popped the cork on one of the bottles. The other was put aside, to be saved for another special occasion.

"Nancy marked on the label, 'Do not open until the Leafs win the next Stanley Cup,'" Bower said.

Anyone know the relative shelf life of champagne?

Toronto's last Stanley Cup win came in the last campaign of the so-called Original Six era.

The League grew in size to 12 teams the following season and today, the NHL is 30 deep in teams.

While they've had a few close calls—Toronto was one win away from going to the Cup final in the spring of 1993, which would have led to a rematch with the Canadiens, and there's also been final four appearances by the club in 1977–78, 1993–94, 1998–99, and 2001–02—for the most part, the Leafs just seem to grow further away from contender status.

The question all of the ex-Leafs hear from Leafs' fans remains the same—when will the team win it all again?

"We get that a lot," admitted Mike Pelyk, a Leafs' defenceman from 1967–74 and again from 1976–78. "The reality is, when you look at the Stanley Cup since 1967, it's hard to win."

No one has to tell a Leafs' fan that.

"I get asked all the time, 'When are the Leafs going to win the Cup?'" Bower said. "I always say, 'They've got some young kids, give them time.' And the response I've been getting lately is 'Time? For crying out loud, it's been nearly 50 years.'

"I don't really have an answer for that one."

THEM'S FIGHTIN' WORDS

Conn Smythe said 'if you can't beat them in the alley, you can't beat them on the ice.' Often, the Leafs took his words to heart.

FRIEND AND FOE

Even during the heat of action, it wasn't out of character for King Clancy to lend a helping hand to an opponent.

Fierce foes in the 1930s, when the Leafs welcomed the Montreal Maroons to Maple Leaf Gardens on February 13, 1932, it might have been the eve of Valentine's Day, but there was no love lost between these two teams.

"All the pent-up bitterness of eight years of intense rivalry, eight years of robust, hard-checking hockey, of hot tempers smouldering from a series of rib-cracking games this season broke out into the fiercest fist fight the National League has seen in recent years as a spectacular climax to an ordinary struggle in which Toronto Leafs scored a one-sided 6–0 victory over the Maroons," the *Montreal Gazette's* L. B. Shapiro wrote.

As the final seconds of the third period wound down and the clock neared zero, Toronto's Busher Jackson jabbed the butt end of his stick into the ribs of Montreal defenceman Lionel Conacher. Conacher dropped his gloves and the bout was on, with one second showing to be played.

Quickly, everyone on the ice found a partner. Toronto's Alex Levinsky paired off with Nels Stewart. Montreal's Hal Starr waded into King Clancy and Starr, a pro grappler in the off-season, caught Clancy with a flying mare, a wrestling manoeuvre where one opponent is lifted vertically over the other's head with his feet facing upwards, and then tossed down on the canvas—or in this case, the ice—upon his back.

Leafs' captain Hap Day and Montreal's Archie Wilcox tangled. Maroons' forward Hooley Smith darted from the penalty box, where he'd been serving a minor infraction, and tore into Leafs' centre Joe Primeau. Bill Phillips bolted from the Montreal bench seeking to get in on the action.

While all this was going on, Toronto goalie Benny Grant and Flat Walsh, his Montreal counterpart, entertained themselves by passing the puck back and forth to each other from one end of the rink to the other.

From amidst the pile of flailing fists, Stewart emerged in obvious pain, grasping his hand and displaying a dislocated thumb. He skated to the bench seeking first aid, but then reconsidered, realizing that he was leaving his team a man shy on the ice, and turned to wade back into the brawl.

Clancy and Stewart came together and Stewart held out his damaged hand. Analyzing the situation, Dr. Clancy diagnosed the injury. Grasping Stewart's arm firmly, he pulled the thumb back into place. Flexing his hand, the pain faded from Stewart's face and he smiled—just as he took a punch in the face from Clancy, and fists were flying again with unabated vigour.

When referees Cooper Smeaton and Mike Rodden finished tabulating the punishment they'd administered nine major penalties, a new NHL record for a single game. Starr, Wilcox, Phillips, Clancy, and Day were each fined $25 by the NHL, but that wasn't the worst of the carnage.

Stewart would have been wiser to rely on professional medical treatment than to attend Clancy's on-ice clinic. Taken to hospital for X-rays, it was revealed that Stewart had suffered a broken thumb and he'd be out of action for several weeks.

After the game, two of the combatants, Clancy and Starr, who were close friends from Ottawa, came face-to-face as they emerged from their respective dressing rooms and headed down a Maple Leaf Gardens' hallway. There was a pause for a split second while the two men stared each other down.

Then they smiled and shook hands.

"We're just a couple of saps," Starr said.

"And the worst brand of all," replied Clancy. "Irish saps."

BREAKING BAD

Red Horner was the bad man of the NHL. He led the league in penalty minutes for eight straight seasons and in one of those campaigns, the 1935–36 season, Horner was especially truculent. Twenty-five games in, he was already the runaway leader with 123 penalty minutes, an average of 4.92 minutes per game.

As if they were almost seeking to emphasize Horner's penchant for foul play, the *Ottawa Citizen* listed him as leading the NHL's International Division with two hours and three minutes in penalties. At the same time, Detroit's Ebbie Goodfellow topped the American Division with a meagre 48 minutes.

Toronto coach Dick Irvin chastised his veteran defenceman, asking him to slow down his steady parade to the sin bin, and Horner bet his boss he could quit the foul game cold turkey.

Horner bet Irvin that he could go four straight games without incurring a single infraction of the rules.

He skated through a 6–1 win January 25 without an infraction and followed with clean sheets on January 30 in a 3–0 loss to the Canadiens at Montreal and in a 3–2 overtime decision over the Chicago Blackhawks February 1 at Maple Leaf Gardens.

Through two periods of the next night's game at Chicago, Horner was again on his best behaviour, but in the third period, referees Billy Bell and Odie Cleghorn called him for a pair of minor penalties and Horner came up less than 20 minutes short of his payday from Irvin.

Horner led the NHL in penalty minutes seven out of eight seasons between 1932–40, and his 167 PIM in 43 games in 1935–36 stood as the NHL single-season record for two decades but even those who sent him to the sin bin later suggested that for all his miscreant deeds, he wasn't a bad fellow.

Speaking at a charity dinner, NHL referee-in-chief Cooper Smeaton sought to downplay the image of Horner as the bad man of the league.

"The big redhead was just a hard-hitting hockey player who wouldn't hurt anybody," Smeaton claimed, a statement that caused an immediate reaction from one of the night's other speakers, Leafs' managing director Conn Smythe.

"If that's the case," Smythe wondered, "then why did you penalize him so much?"

IN THE STEW

Riotous occurrences in Leaf games at Boston were never a surprise but what was shocking about the outburst during a February 4, 1936 Toronto 3–0 win at Boston Garden was that Conn Smythe had nothing to do with it.

Generally at the epicentre of any altercation, Smythe didn't make the trip to Beantown for this meeting with the Bruins. Instead, it was Leafs' coach Dick Irvin who sparked the trouble.

Unhappy with a penalty assessed to Leafs' forward Andy Blair by referee Bill Stewart, Irvin reached out and grabbed Stewart by the sweater as he skated past the Toronto bench, spinning the official right around.

"We've been getting it rubbed into us all winter and I'm going to punch you on the jaw," Irvin told Stewart.

Stewart whipped open the gate to the Leafs' bench and set out in pursuit of Irvin, who raced up an aisle near the bench while Leafs' forward Busher Jackson impeded Stewart's progress.

Boston GM Art Ross arrived on the scene to serve as peacemaker and quelled the uprising.

Stewart advised both Leafs that he would settle things with them after the game. Instead, Stewart reported the incident to NHL president Frank Calder.

"If Irvin isn't fined," Stewart said. "I'll never work another Toronto game. It's about time they did something to stop managers from attacking referees.

"Irvin certainly had no complaint, for he was leading 2–0 and Blair's penalty was deserved. Just because a team is in a losing streak is no reason to attack a referee."

A few minutes after this episode, a Boston fan near the Toronto bench took a punch at Irvin, who retaliated and Boston police, stationed nearby following the first incident, acted quickly to restore the peace.

Nothing came of Stewart's complaint and he continued to officiate games for another year until he was hired to coach the Chicago Blackhawks.

Stewart had the last laugh in 1938, when his Blackhawks delivered the knockout blow to Irvin's Leafs in the Stanley Cup final.

BROTHERS IN ARMS

It was difficult to determine the highlight of the February 27, 1937 brawl between the Leafs and Montreal Maroons.

Maybe it was when the combatants finally made their way to the Maple Leaf Gardens' penalty box and found Leafs' managing director Conn Smythe waiting for them. It could have been the knock-down, drag-out scrap between Leafs' tough guy Red Horner and the Big Train of the Maroons, Lionel Conacher, that continued in the sin bin, where Conacher slugged Horner so hard he knocked him clear through the open gate and back out on the ice.

That brought the Toronto police on the scene and was the cue for both benches to empty and jump into the ruckus.

Really, though, when you're talking unique moments, it probably happened not long after the first punch was thrown.

The trouble all started in the third period when Horner cross-checked Gus Marker and Lionel Conacher rushed to his aid. That brought Leafs' right-winger and Lionel's younger brother Charlie Conacher into the action. He grabbed his sibling and pulled him out of the pile and two brothers set to tangling.

"The only time I recall them clashing was one night when we were playing the Leafs," former Maroons goalie Bill Beveridge recounted to the *Ottawa Journal*. "The two brothers got mad, but it wound up in a wrestling match and no harm done."

Well, maybe some harm done, but not for long. Soon the Conachers found a common enemy. When the police got involved in the tussle and two of them grabbed Lionel Conacher to pull him off Horner, Charlie proved that blood is thicker than the colour of your hockey sweater and both Conachers turned on the gendarmes and began trading punches with the cops.

In the final moment of the game, Charlie fired a hard, low shot that struck his brother in the ankle. When Lionel was unable to continue, his brother was the one who helped him off the ice to a huge ovation from the Toronto crowd.

It may have been the only time the brothers fought, but there were other interesting moments when the Conachers crossed paths.

In a December 10, 1933 game while Lionel was with the Chicago Blackhawks, a shot by Charlie deflected off Lionel and past Blackhawks' netminder Chuck Gardiner for the only goal of the game.

Early in a November 18, 1930 contest, Lionel, then in his first stint with the Maroons, hit Charlie across the back with his stick and was penalized.

In the second period of Toronto's 3–0 win, Charlie scored and had Lionel to thank for it. He took a shot at Maroons' goalie Flat Walsh. Lionel dove in a vain effort to block his brother's effort and as he went down, lost his stick and it flew into the path of the puck. Referee Bert Corbeau immediately signalled automatic goal, as was called for by the rules of the day.

Charlie gave Lionel the raspberry as he skated past him back to centre ice for faceoff.

"I just forget all about he's my brother when I go into the game," Charlie claimed.

THE HOCKEY FIGHT OF THE CENTURY

The March 29, 1940 *Windsor Daily Star* headline said it all: "Greatest Brawl in History Climaxes Wings' Elimination."

The Leafs and Wings had wrapped up their Stanley Cup semi-final series with a wham-bang conclusion—a bench-clearing brawl in the final minute of the third period.

Reporter Doug Vaughan noted it as a final chapter of, "Unreasoning hysteria, written with flailing fists and punctuated with blood, black eyes, busted noggins, and bruised bones."

Ooh, tell me more.

"The 12,447 fans were privileged to have ringside seats for the wildest player free-for-all in the annals of major league history."

The undercard started in the second period. Detroit's Alex Motter and Toronto's Red Horner tangled on the ice and picked up where they left off in the penalty box, Horner flattening Motter with a right hand in the sin bin. Motter was sporting a swollen left eye and this did not sit well with a Detroit fan of the fairer sex, who leaned into the penalty box and took a swing at Horner. The sorrel-topped Toronto enforcer was all set for another fistic encounter when he realized his newest opponent was a woman and opted to pull his punch.

Early in the third period, Detroit's Don Grosso thumped Leafs' forward Hank Goldup so hard with a bodycheck it sent Goldup clear over the boards and into the laps of some unsuspecting spectators.

The main event was still to come though, and featured all 28 skaters, as well as both goaltenders, with sticks down and gloves off, scrapping for all they were worth.

It started when Toronto's Gus Marker and Detroit's Sid Abel began mixing it up at the Toronto blue line. While they were entangled, the remaining players on the ice also dropped their gloves and set off in pursuit of dance partners.

Players quickly streamed from both benches to get in on the fun. "In the space of 30 seconds the ice was littered from one end to the other with sticks, gloves and tussling figures," Vaughan noted. "No three-ring circus ever offered such a show. It was here a fight, there a fight, everywhere a fight."

In the middle of the ice, Detroit tough guy Jimmy Orlando and Toronto's Syl Apps stood toe-to-toe trading punches for a full five minutes. Detroit goalie Tiny Thompson pummelled Toronto forward Pete Langelle to the ice. Done with Sid Abel, Marker set off after Syd Howe. Leafs' netminder Turk Broda scored a hat trick of scraps, trading blows with Ebbie Goodfellow, Ken Kilrea, and Jack Stewart. After winning a clear-cut decision over Apps, Orlando was left to deal with Horner, who'd departed the penalty box to get in on the action. They fought, separated, found each other a second time and had at it again.

Referee Teddy Graham and linesman Donnie McFadyen were helpless as they tried to separate the combatants. "In the ensuing 15 minutes they refereed more fights than the busiest Gold Gloves official that ever lived," Vaughan suggested.

By the ten-minute mark of the donnybrook, just three fights were still ongoing. But any thought of just giving peace a chance soon passed. Orlando and Horner, two of the toughest customers in the league, came together a third time and were still trading punches a good minute after exhaustion finally overcame all the other combatants.

"I used to hate the games I played in the NHL against the Detroit Red Wings," Horner lamented years later. "I'd be taking on four or five guys every time we played them."

When all was said and done that fateful night in Detroit, each player was fined $25 and Toronto skated away with a 3–1 victory and a 2–0 sweep of the best-of-three series.

BEANTOWN BEAT DOWN

It wasn't unusual for things to get rough and even out of hand when the Leafs visited Boston Garden, so perhaps the events of March 30, 1948, shouldn't have come as a surprise to anyone.

The Leafs dominated the Bruins 5–1 on the scoreboard, but took a severe beating from some unruly Boston fans.

"Thugs attack Leafs stars, coach after Bruins lose," announced the front-page headline in the *Boston Herald*.

Toronto defenceman Wally Stanowski was slow to leave the bench at the conclusion of the contest and was swarmed by Boston fans. Teammates Teeder Kennedy and Garth Boesch and Toronto coach Hap Day rushed to Stanowski's rescue.

Boesch was sucker-punched behind the ear and rendered unconscious. Kennedy's gloves were pilfered in the melee, as were Stanowski's stick and Day's hat. Only some fast action by another group of Boston fans who pushed back the troublemakers saved the Leafs from a further pounding.

The trouble had started much earlier.

During the first period of play, Boston captain Milt Schmidt took Toronto defenceman Bill Barilko hard into the boards and as he pinned Barilko to the fence, a fan took the opportunity to throw several punches his way.

The Leafs complained about this to referee George Gravel and he ordered the ejection of the fan, though curiously, none of Boston's finest could be found to carry out his orders.

Soon, Bruins' owner Weston Adams was on the scene and in Gravel's face.

"Go on, drop the puck," Adams growled at Gravel, according to reports in the *Boston Herald*, jabbing his index finger into Gravel's sweater. "There are 13,000 people here tonight waiting to see a hockey game. Don't stop to deal with an individual."

Boesch was left groggy after his assault and couldn't remember the final score of the game. The Leafs insisted the ringleader of the post-game fracas was the same fan who punched Barilko earlier and who was protected by Adams from ejection.

"It was a positive disgrace," Smythe told *Canadian Press*. "It could never happen in Toronto. The police did nothing.

"Why doesn't Adams stop being a fan and a cry baby and conduct his games in major league fashion? When the fans jump us and we don't get any protection we'll protect ourselves with our sticks and fists."

Adams was quick to counter. "It seems to me Smythe is doing all the crying and the Bruins have all the injuries," he said.

Adams was referring to Boston forward Murray Henderson, whose nose was broken in a fight with Leafs forward Harry Watson.

Adams and Smythe engaged in a heated argument in the Leafs dressing room after the game. Adams was brusquely ejected from the room.

Smythe was already drawing up plans for the Leafs' next visit to Beantown. "Maybe after this we'll have to use military formations to leave the ice," he said. "Put holding parties out on the flanks and move the main forces down the middle."

THE BRAWL TO END ALL BRAWLS

It started out about getting even, but when it ended, all involved were much poorer for their participation.

The Leafs were playing host to the Chicago Blackhawks on December 7, 1963, and leading 3–0 late in the game when Chicago tough guy Reggie Fleming speared Toronto's Eddie Shack, apparently retaliating for taking Shack's stick to the jaw earlier in the game.

Almost immediately both benches emptied. With Shack doubled over in pain, teammate Bob Baun jumped in to defend his honour against Fleming. Murray Balfour paired off with Toronto's Larry Hillman, Chicago's Stan Mikita tangled with Ron Stewart and Chico Maki got into it with Leafs' defenceman Carl Brewer.

As the slugfest waged on, Balfour ended up in a scrap with Brewer, the two of them falling through an open gate into the Leafs' bench. When the two men arose, Balfour came up with a cut over his right eye and some cutting accusations.

Balfour claimed that while he was raining punches down upon Brewer, either Leafs' coach Punch Imlach or trainer Bob Haggert had sucker-punched him, opening the four-stitch gash over his eye

"Brewer never hit me," Balfour told *Canadian Press*. "I drove him into the bench and was beating the hell out of him.

"He started yelling 'Bobby, Bobby, Bobby'—then Haggert and Imlach landed on me. I don't know which one of them hit me, but it was one of them, they were both there."

Haggert claimed the sucker-punch came from a fan in the Maple Leaf Gardens' crowd, while Imlach had a few accusations of his own to make, blaming Chicago coach Billy Reay for deliberately instigating the donnybrook.

"He sent Fleming out there," Imlach growled. "He knew what would happen when he sent that guy out there and it did. We can't afford that kind of thing."

With a national television audience tuned in on *Hockey Night In Canada* on Saturday night, NHL president Clarence Campbell seemed to agree with Imlach on that last point.

After a week-long investigation, Campbell issued an NHL-record $4,925 in fines to the two teams, saving most of his vitriol for the rival coaches, hammering each of them with $1,000 stipends.

"In my opinion there was no real control exercised by coaches Billy Reay (Chicago) and George Imlach (Toronto) over their players on the bench and there was no indication of any effort being made by either of them to bring them under control after the outbreak," Campbell noted in the statement that accompanied his meting out of the punishment.

"In taking this severe action it is hoped that this type of conduct will be stamped out for good."

SCRAPPY STEWIE

Leafs' forward Ron Stewart was in a fighting mood as Toronto tangled with the Montreal Canadiens in Game 4 of their Stanley Cup semi-final series on April 2, 1964, a 5–3 Toronto triumph.

The game was barely four minutes old when Stewart dropped the mitts and traded punches with Montreal forward Dave Balon. Balon had rode roughshod over the Leafs in Game 3 of the set and Stewart decided that the Habs' winger needed some straightening out.

The outcome of the game no longer in doubt, with five seconds left in the third period, Montreal tough guy John Ferguson set off in pursuit of Stewart, perhaps to exact revenge for Stewart's beat-down on Balon, and the gloves came off again.

NHL rules called for an automatic misconduct and $25 fine to be assessed to Stewart for his second fight of the game.

Seeing as Stewart felt he held his own against NHL heavyweight champion Ferguson—"I had a little trouble getting my footing after the initial crash, but once I got my hands free I think he felt it," he said—and since there were paydays to be had in fighting, Stewart contemplated a move up in class.

"I'm going after (world heavyweight boxing champion) Cassius Clay next," Stewart proclaimed to *Canadian Press*. "I can't resist the lure of all that easy money."

THE NIGHT THE TEAM DIED

The defending Stanley Cup champion Leafs were off to a solid 7–4 to start the 1967–68 NHL season when they rolled into Boston Garden for a Sunday encounter with the Bruins.

By the time the game was done, so were the Leafs.

Early in the second period, Toronto forward Brian Conacher was ragging the puck to kill a penalty, when he saw Bruins' defenceman Bobby Orr lining him up for a bodycheck. Conacher dumped the puck down the ice and to protect himself, brought his stick up, catching Orr across the nose with the blade and cutting him open.

Orr jumped back up to his skates and raced 50 feet to get after Conacher, dropping the gloves and attacking the Leaf player, who'd already been knocked to the ice by Boston forward John McKenzie. One punch struck Conacher in the eye and his contact lens cut into the eye, leaving him with blurred vision and unable to defend himself.

"He's a tough kid and he can handle himself," Toronto coach Punch Imlach said. "He just couldn't see."

Both benches soon emptied, but no Leaf came to Conacher's aid. When he finally regained his footing, Conacher was assaulted again, this time by Boston's Ken Hodge.

Afterward, Conacher's words said it all. "I just covered up," he said. "There was no sense fighting 15 Bruins."

Years later, Conacher recounted the fear he felt when he came back to the ice that night following repairs for injuries he'd suffered during the brawl.

"When I stepped back on the ice, the roar was deafening as the fans screamed for my blood," Conacher wrote in his book *Hockey In Canada: The Way It Is*.

"I was no sooner on the bench when Punch came down and told me he was going to send me right back on the ice. As much as I did not want to go I knew that he was right and that I had to show them I was not afraid. I was, though."

Word of Toronto's lack of aggressiveness spread quickly throughout the league and teams took to roughing up the Leafs, especially away from Maple Leaf Gardens, where Toronto went 7–20–5 the rest of the way. After a 3–1 win January 28, 1968, at Chicago, the Leafs went 13 road games without tasting victory until a 5–2 win March 21, at Detroit.

By then the Leafs were eliminated from post-season play. missing the playoffs for the first time since the 1957–58 season.

"We were just not good enough," Imlach lamented to the *Windsor Star*'s Jack Dulmage. "We couldn't even beat the expansion teams. Every time we met one, they would outskate us."

DOREY WAS A JIM DANDY

As he sat in the Leafs' dressing room, ejected from their October 16, 1968 game at Maple Leaf Gardens against the Pittsburgh Penguins, Jim Dorey figured his second NHL game might be his last one.

Dorey, a 21-year-old rookie, set two NHL records in the contest, but they weren't the kind a newcomer to the league wanted to add to his resume. Dorey established new NHL marks for penalties (eight) and penalty minutes (38) in a game.

It started innocently enough. Dorey was assessed two minors in the first period and a third just past the midway mark of the second frame.

Late in the period, Dorey got called for high sticking veteran Pittsburgh forward Ken Schinkel, who Dorey felt had taken a dive to embellish the call. When Schinkel came up smiling, Dorey punched him in the face.

Dorey then got into a scrap with Pittsburgh's John Arbour. Curiously, Dorey and Arbour had been roommates along with future NHLers Derek Sanderson and Bill Goldsworthy during their junior days with the Niagara Falls Flyers, and battling each other was nothing new to them.

"I don't know what caused it, but it seemed that every time we got back to our boarding house a fight would break out among us," Dorey explained. "We were always belting each other.

"Never at the rink, just at home. It was a shambles. It was also the way we settled our differences."

As Dorey was being escorted to the penalty box after fighting Arbour, Pittsburgh's Keith McCreary chirped him from the bench.

"He said something like, 'Enjoy your trip back to the minors, rookie,'" Dorey recalled. "And I lost it."

Dorey dove into the Pittsburgh bench to get at McCreary and ended up touching off a bench-clearing brawl. When all was said and done, Dorey was assessed a high-sticking minor, two fighting majors, a ten-minute misconduct, and a game misconduct.

As he sat alone with his thoughts in the Toronto dressing room, those thoughts turned dark. Deep down, Dorey figured McCreary might be right and that his days as an NHLer, which had barely begun, were over.

"I was staring at the floor, feeling sorry for myself when I see a pair of feet in front of me," Dorey recalled.

It was Toronto assistant GM King Clancy. The Leafs had been pushed around by other teams during the 1967–68 season and were clearly seeking to toughen up their squad.

"Wow kid, that was really something," an excited Clancy bellowed. "It's just what this team needed."

Leafs' coach Punch Imlach soon joined them, pulling a wad of bills from his pocket and handing them to Dorey.

"Great job kid," Imlach said. "Now get yourself lost for the weekend."

Trailing 1–0 after two periods, the Leafs rallied that night for a 2–2 tie.

Dorey shattered Reg Fleming's NHL mark of 37 penalty minutes in a game and the single-game penalty standard of seven previously shared by Georges Boucher of the Ottawa Senators and Ted Green of the Boston Bruins. He was also hit with a $125 fine by the league.

He finished the season with a club-record 200 penalty minutes in 61 games, fighting 11 times, five of them against the Boston Bruins and three of those tilts versus ex-Leaf Eddie Shack.

FORBES' FLAILING FAREWELL

When the Leafs acquired rugged centre Forbes Kennedy from the Philadelphia Flyers late in the 1968–69 season, Toronto coach Punch Imlach predicted that Kennedy would "stir things up when he was on the ice."

In his first playoff game as a Leaf, Kennedy touched off one of the wildest brawls in Stanley Cup history. During the third period of a 10–0 drubbing handed Toronto by the Boston Bruins, Kennedy scrapped with Boston goalie Gerry Cheevers and forward John McKenzie, and when linesman George Ashley sought to break up the latter bout, Kennedy also decked him. He was assessed two majors for fighting, an automatic misconduct for the pair of fistic encounters and a game misconduct for striking Ashley.

"(Leaf coach) Punch (Imlach) had called me over late in the third period and said, 'Forbie, I want you in there,'" Kennedy recalled to writer Shawna Richer in 1998. "Well, I knew he wasn't sending me in there to tie the score. It was 10–0.

"So I went out and I got chopped by Gerry Cheevers and I thought it was a good time to get something going. Well, away she went. They were coming from everywhere. I got hit with a beer from a fan. The Boston players were joking that when they fired the beer I opened up my mouth.

"It went for about 45 minutes. Boy, I was tired at the end."

Kennedy finished the night with seven penalties, tying the Stanley Cup record set by Boston's Eddie Shore on April 4, 1927. His five third-period penalties shattered the mark of four Shore set on the same night. Kennedy's 24 third-period penalty minutes were a minute shy of the Stanley Cup standard established by Montreal's Marcel Bonin.

All total, the 36 penalties handed to both teams broke the mark of 35 set by the Leafs and Habs on April 14, 1966.

"I went to the dressing room and into the shower and Punch came in and he said. 'Geez, I sent you out to get something going, not to start the Third World War,'" Kennedy remembered.

Kennedy was handed an indefinite suspension for striking an official and slated for a hearing with NHL president Clarence Campbell. Toronto assistant GM King Clancy accompanied Kennedy to the hearing and as they sat waiting to enter Campbell's hotel suite, sought to soothe Kennedy.

"Don't worry about a thing," Clancy told Kennedy. "I'll take care of this. You've got nothing to worry about.

"Just let me do all the talking."

The pair was finally invited into Campbell's quarters and seated directly in front of his desk. There was a long silence as Campbell perused referee John Ashley's report of the incident, broken only by occasional scowls from Campbell as he looked up at Kennedy.

"Son," Campbell finally said as he locked his gaze on Kennedy, "you are in serious trouble."

With that, Clancy leapt to his feet, Kennedy assuming he was about to launch into his defence plea. Instead, Clancy beat a hasty retreat.

"Well kid," Clancy said, slapping Kennedy on the back, "you're on your own. I'm out of here." And he left the room.

Kennedy was suspended four games and fined $1,000, a hefty sum for someone earning just $19,000 a season.

"Oh geez, it was something, that riot," Kennedy said. "I was so tired at the end of it. We all just went for beers. Then in the middle of the night, there was a knock at my door and I opened it and a hundred flash bulbs went off.

"It was some big story."

Campbell pointed to photos and film of the incident that clearly displayed Kennedy "launching a right hand punch to linesman (George) Ashley's head, knocking him down to the ice.

"Ashley was straight in front of Kennedy," the official statement indicated, "and there was no Boston player within ten feet of him. Ashley was not physically restraining Kennedy in any way and afforded no provocation for such a blow.

"In these circumstances the only rational conclusion is that Kennedy intentionally struck the official. This is a very serious offence which calls for exemplary punishment. Assaulting an official cannot be condoned at any time and Kennedy's record of misconduct over the past two seasons does not entitle him to leniency. It is intended that this decision will serve as a deterrent to others who may be similarly inclined."

In his defence, Kennedy insisted he wasn't certain that he'd struck Ashley. "I don't know if I hit him or not but I pushed him and all of a sudden I saw him on the ice. I was not seeing very well because of the water in my eyes caused by the blow on the nose (from McKenzie)."

The following month, the Leafs sold Kennedy's contract to the Pittsburgh Penguins, but the nine-season veteran would never play another NHL game.

At least he went out winner. Kennedy's 219 penalty minutes led the NHL in 1968–69, the last time a centre would do so until Sean Avery of the Los Angeles Kings in 2003–04.

WEAKENED WITHOUT BERNIE?

In the Stanley Cup playoffs during the 1960s and 1970s, it just wasn't considered a series until both benches emptied.

Bench-clearing brawls were the norm, but when the Leafs and New York Rangers got down to it in Game 2 of their quarter-final series April 8, 1971, at Madison Square Garden, gloves weren't all that was flying.

Early in the third period, Rangers forward Vic Hadfield and Toronto centre Jim Harrison set to scrapping for the second time of the night and when things started to go south for Harrison in the battle, Leafs' goalie Bernie Parent sought to help a brother out, racing from his net to jump on Hadfield's back.

That was the cue for both teams to come spilling over the boards. In the ensuing melee, Parent's fiberglass mask was sent sailing over the glass and disappeared into the raucous New York crowd.

The finger of blame was quickly pointed in Hadfield's direction.

"We don't know that for sure," Hadfield claimed in an interview with *The Hockey News*. "King Clancy's the only one who knows for sure who threw it, and he's been dead for years, so I guess we'll never know."

Or maybe we do. Ultimately, Hadfield acknowledged his guilt.

"It was an intense game and in the heat of the moment, you do things," Hadfield explained. "When Parent jumped on me, I turned on him and grabbed his mask.

"I tossed it, but it wasn't my intention to toss it in the crowd."

Parent doesn't buy Hadfield's innocent act. "He was all over Harrison, so I jumped him," Parent admitted. "Then Hadfield ripped off my mask and threw it into the crowd."

Toronto assistant GM Clancy waded into enemy territory, scouring the crowd in search of Parent's facial protection, to no avail. Quickly realizing the error of his ways, Clancy hollered over the glass to one of the Leafs' players to give him a stick for protection purposes.

"I looked around and didn't see anyone I knew, so I showed them I'm a pretty good sprinter," Clancy told Dick Beddoes of the *Globe & Mail.*

When the game resumed, Parent could not continue. "It was the only mask I had with me, so I couldn't play anymore," Parent said.

Jacques Plante, Toronto's back-up that night and the owner of the company that designed both his and Parent's mask, took over and played the rest of the way as the Leafs won 4–1. Afterward, he put in a rush order for a new mask to be made for Parent.

As the series moved to Maple Leaf Gardens, Toronto GM Jim Gregory offered a reward of two tickets to the game and free transportation to Toronto for anyone who returned Parent's mask to the team.

NHL president Clarence Campbell was also talking money, but his stipend was in the form of punishment. He fined the two clubs a record $16,650, including $5,000 fines to both teams, which was also a new standard.

Rangers' defenceman Brad Park and Leafs' centre Darryl Sittler were each fined $450. New York goalie Ed Giacomin and Toronto defenceman Mike Pelyk drew $400 fines, while Hadfield was docked $250. All the other players on both teams were forced to cough up $200 apiece.

"In view of the deplorable spectacle they produced, the automatic fines provided in the playing rules are not adequate for their offences," Campbell said.

The Rangers went on to win the series in six games and a few days following the conclusion of the series, a box wrapped in plain brown paper with no return address was delivered to the Leafs offices. When they opened it up, the package contained Parent's mask.

Parent would have the last laugh on Hadfield. Playing with the Philadelphia Flyers in the 1974 Stanley Cup semi-finals, Parent was the winning goalie as the Flyers beat Hadfield's Rangers in a seven-game series en route to their eventual Cup final win over the Boston Bruins.

During a 16-season NHL career, Hadfield would never win the Stanley Cup.

A TIGER'S TALE

Dave (Tiger) Williams offered a unique perspective as to why trouble so often found him on the ice.

"I skate in straight lines," Williams explained. "If you're going to cross a pasture, you're going to get shit on your boots."

No one got into more shit in NHL history than Williams, who finished as the league's all-time penalty-minute leader with 3,966, of which 1,670 were garnered in 407 games as a Leaf.

Williams set a club record with 299 penalty minutes in 1975–76, topped that with a league-leading 338 PIM in 1976–77, and bettered it one more time with a vengeance, garnering 351 PIM in 1977–78.

The Tiger also topped the NHL in sin bin time with 298 minutes in 1978–79.

Williams also went to court in 1977, charged with assault after hitting Dennis Owchar over the head with his stick and opening a 46-stitch cut on the Pittsburgh Penguins defenceman's head during an October 20, 1976 game.

He was found not guilty and left unrepentant.

"I'm a conveyor belt," Williams said. "Nothing fancy. I just do the same thing day after day. I play hard. I throw everything into it.

"On the ice, I like to call a guy's bluff. Some guys go out there and bluff all the time. But they're only tough when the situation is best for them.

"I'm out there doing my job, and I'm not making excuses."

Even on February 18, 1980, the day the Tiger's time in Toronto came to an end after the Leafs traded him and Jerry Butler to the Vancouver Canucks for Rick Vaive and Bill Derlago, Williams couldn't muster up any bitter feelings.

"Over the years, Toronto has been awfully good to me," Williams said.

In recent years, the NHL has steadily moved away from employing players in the role of enforcer, and Williams believes that it is a catastrophic error in judgement.

"Here's my question to everyone in the hockey world: Can that guy you keep (instead of an enforcer) change the game?" Williams queried to the *Toronto Star*. "Can that guy tell his teammates, 'I've got your back, no matter what?' I don't think so.

"To me, it's an arsenal you need."

It's also a payload that the Tiger delivered throughout his Leafs career.

TIE-ING ONE ON

No Leaf spent more time in the penalty box than Tie Domi, who sat out 2,265 minutes, the equivalent of nearly 38 games, in the sin bin.

No Leaf dropped the gloves with greater frequency than Domi, who fought 333 times during his NHL career, 251 of those bouts coming as a Maple Leaf.

No wonder Domi was beloved by Leaf Nation.

"Having the most fights in NHL history, I didn't really talk about it," Domi said. "I wasn't really counting."

To much of the NHL, Domi will be remembered for his foolish acts—sucker-punching Ulf Samuelsson, taunting opponents with WWE antics, and riding his stick down the ice after scoring a goal.

Most of all, he'll be recalled as the player who turned perhaps the best NHL game he ever played—a sensational performance against New Jersey in the 2001 Stanley Cup playoffs—into a disaster when Domi's cheap shot in the dying seconds left Devils' defenceman Scott Niedermayer lying unconscious on the ice. Domi was suspended for the remainder of the playoffs.

In retrospect, even Domi knows the incident will remain a black mark.

"I've got this whole building chanting my name and I'm getting ready to be first star on *Hockey Night In Canada* with Ron (MacLean) and Don (Cherry)," Domi said. "That was probably the stupidest thing I've ever done in my life and the biggest regret I have in my career."

You have to give Domi credit. He took a limited skill package, found a niche within the game at which he could excel and marketed the product successfully, becoming so popular that he was feted in Wayne Gretzky-like fashion during ceremonies at the Air

Canada Centre in 2006 upon playing his 1,000th game, a decision that was looked upon as ridiculous in hockey circles beyond Leaf nation.

The truth is, Domi didn't have to fight. He was a better-than-average skater who possessed enough skill to produce a career high 15 goals with the Leafs in 2002–03, one of three times during his career than he reached double digits.

"I had most of the fights for my teammates and that was part of my job, protecting my teammates," Domi said. "There's no rear-view mirrors in hockey.

"It was a big part of my life, but it wasn't my life."

PUNCH'S DUTY

Toronto coach Punch Imlach ruled over his successful empire with an iron fist.

BY GEORGE, IT'S PUNCH

He arrived at Windsor Arena on November 4, 1938, known simply as George Imlach, but by George, by the end of that night, he'd head back to Toronto with the handle that would make him famous within the hockey world.

Punch Imlach put the punch in four Stanley Cup wins as coach of the Toronto Maple Leafs during the 1960s, including the club's most recent title in 1966–67. But it was Windsor Arena that put the Punch in Imlach.

He was a shifty centre with the Toronto Goodyears in the Ontario Hockey Association senior series, a squad that travelled to southwestern Ontario for a pre-season tilt against the Windsor Chryslers of the Michigan-Ontario League.

Imlach's teammates included future National Hockey League players Hank Goldup and John (Peanuts) O'Flaherty, while Art Herchenratter, later a Detroit Red Wing, was part of the Windsor line-up.

A curious crowd of 2,900 showed up at the old barn to check out the heralded Toronto visitors and they were given an early reason to cheer when Windsor's Herb Jones converted Bert Tooke's feed 6:10 into the game with Johnny Inglis in the penalty box for the Goodyears.

It was a short-lived celebration, however. Wilfred (Blondy) Sutcliffe tied it for Toronto, and then Imlach and Goldup made it

3–1 Goodyears by the end of the opening frame. Inglis upped it to 4–1 in the second period, and then O'Flaherty and Windsor's Gordie Anderson traded third-period goals in a 5–2 Goodyears victory.

Shortly after O'Flaherty tallied what would be the game's final goal just 2:45 into the final period, fireworks broke out on the ice. Windsor's Norval Fitzgerald tangled with Toronto's Eddie King and was barely out of the penalty box when he set his bombsights on Imlach.

"(Fitzgerald) thudded into the boards with George Imlach and uncorked a swing as the Toronto player went to the ice," wrote *The Windsor Star*'s Doug Vaughan. "Fitzgerald drew a major and Imlach, who was knocked out in the collision, had to be assisted from the ice."

In his 1969 book *Hockey Is A Battle*, which he penned with Scott Young, Imlach picks up the story. "I'd always been just plain George Imlach up until then," Imlach wrote. "But there was this game in Windsor. I was going along the boards and this fellow took me into the boards hard and gave me the elbow and the foot thing at the same time. Up in the air I went and down I came and hit my head on the ice. I was knocked cold.

"When I came to, I guess the only thing I knew was that someone had done this to me, so I came up swinging. And who was I swinging at but Bill Smith, our trainer."

Concussed, Imlach's teammates announced he was punch drunk. The Toronto media covering the game picked up on this and he became known in the papers as Punchy Imlach. "Until some kindly typesetter got fed up with putting the last letter on and just left it at Punch," Imlach noted.

Just like that, a legend was born.

LIVING UP TO HIS NAME

Amidst rumours in the spring of 1959 that the Leafs were about to acquire centre Alex Delvecchio from the Detroit Red Wings, Punch Imlach launched into a tirade at the nonsense of it all, insisting that Delvecchio, who'd recently been awarded the Lady Byng Trophy, simply wasn't his sort of player.

"I don't want any Lady Byng winners on my club," Imlach growled to *Associated Press.* "I'll fine any player who wins the Lady Byng Trophy."

Not surprisingly, the trophy that annually goes to the NHL player exhibiting the best combination of sportsmanship and playing ability was of little interest to a man known as Punch.

"Is Delvecchio that good?" Imlach asked. "He didn't score 20 goals and he didn't get more than a couple of penalties. So what was the guy doing?

"My only conclusion is that Delvecchio was doing nothing. I don't care who it is, no player in this league can go through 70 games and get only a couple of penalties if he is checking. He's bound to trip or board someone."

Imlach would soon change his tune, and maybe even dine on some crow.

Less than a year later, he dealt with the Wings to acquire defenceman Red Kelly, a three-time Lady Byng Trophy winner with Detroit as a defenceman. Converted to centre by Imlach, Kelly won the Lady Byng Trophy in 1960–61, his first full season as a Leaf, launching a run on Lady Byngs by Toronto players.

Centre Dave Keon would win the award in 1961–62 and 1962–63, as the Leafs won the Stanley Cup both seasons, by which time Imlach had certainly changed his tune regarding Lady Byng winners.

"He is the most valuable player in the NHL, the best centre and the most consistent guy in the business," Imlach said of Keon.

The following season, Imlach traded to acquire forward Don McKenney, the 1959–60 Lady Byng winner, from the New York Rangers, giving Toronto three different Byng-winning players in the line-up as the Leafs won a third consecutive Stanley Cup in 1963–64.

NOT A FAN

Defenceman Kent Douglas won three Stanley Cups under Punch Imlach as a Leaf, but he was always of the opinion that the Leafs won in spite of Imlach.

"The only reason he was successful was because of the guys that were in the room," Douglas said. "It had nothing to do with him. He didn't know a damn thing about hockey.

"His coaching ability was very limited. 'Next line,' was pretty much what it was.

"He and I never got along, not from day one. It was just his attitude. I played for (Eddie) Shore (with Springfield of the AHL), who certainly was pretty damn good as far as being a hockey player, and very good as a coach."

"Imlach was at the bottom of my list, in terms of ability (as a coach)."

Douglas felt Imlach was more self-promoter than leader.

"It was always 'me, me, me.'" Douglas said. "It was the team that lost, and he was the greatest coach in the world when we won. But if you've got the horses, you win the race. It's simple.

"We knew we could win if we worked at it. That was the thing that we had, the work ethic. We weren't one of those fancy teams. We moved the puck, put it in the other team's end, banged it at the net, and if it didn't go in, someone might get a rebound and knock it in."

A regular with the Leafs from 1962–63, when he won the Calder Trophy as the NHL's top rookie and the first of three straight Stanley Cups, Douglas was sent to the minors after playing 39 regular-season games for the Leafs in 1966–67, and wasn't recalled from the minors for the playoffs as the Leafs won another Cup.

The Oakland Seals claimed Douglas in the 1967 NHL expansion draft.

NO TIME FOR TOURISM

The Dearborn, Michigan chamber of commerce likely didn't approach Leafs' coach Punch Imlach to do any ads in order to promote tourism in the area.

As the Leafs did battle with the Detroit Red Wings during the 1963 Stanley Cup final, Imlach secreted his team away to a Dearborn hotel to keep them from the hustle and bustle of the Motor City.

Holding a press conference in their home away from home at the Leland Hotel, directly across the road from the world-famous Henry Ford Museum, Imlach was questioned as to whether he'd investigated any of the automotive history that was a stone's throw away.

"I've never been in the Ford Museum," Imlach growled. "I'm not a bit interested about the past. It doesn't concern me at all.

"I'm only interested in the present and the future."

NO GOOD DEED GOES UNPUNISHED

It isn't often that a goaltender riding a hot streak gets benched, but that's what happened to Johnny Bower in 1964 when the veteran Leafs' netminder raised the ire of coach Punch Imlach.

Bower's crime? Showing compassion for a fellow human.

OK, so it was Montreal Canadiens' tough guy John Ferguson, quite possibly the most hated opponent in the eyes of Leaf fans.

Here's what happened: During a 6–1 rout of the Canadiens on January 8, 1964 at Maple Leaf Gardens, Ferguson, a constant thorn in Bower's side, crashed through his crease. Bower used his stick to spill Ferguson. But when Ferguson fell headlong into the boards and looked to be hurt, Bower skated over to the Montreal forward to ensure that he was okay.

Bower's concern infuriated Imlach. "I don't know what Bower said to him but I don't like it," Imlach told *Canadian Press*. "We are here for one thing only—to win.

"We are not running a kindergarten."

In his last nine games, Bower was 6–1–2 with three shutouts and a 1.33 goals-against average. So when Imlach informed him late in the next day's practice that he was being sat down in favour of back-up Don Simmons, Bower stormed into the dressing room, angrily took off his gear and headed home.

The official spin from the Leafs was that Bower was dealing with a nagging hand injury and that the team wanted him to take some time off to allow the ailment to clear up.

"I have seen this about three times in the last three weeks and it has not improved," Leafs' team physician Dr. Jim Murray said. "I think it will become chronic if he doesn't have a period of rest."

Simmons played the next six games, going 2–4, before Bower returned for a 1–1 tie with the New York Rangers.

The Leafs would go on to win their third straight Stanley Cup, beating the Detroit Red Wings in a seven-game final series. Bower posted a 4–0 shutout in the deciding game.

POSITIVE PUNCH

Opening the 1964 Stanley Cup semi-finals by suffering a 2–0 loss at Montreal to the Canadiens—the fourth time during the season that Habs goalie Charlie Hodge had shut out the Leafs—and another setback in Game 3 on home ice to fall behind 2–1, coach Punch Imlach took his team out for a night at the movies.

A devotee of Dr. Norman Vincent Peale, the man behind the power of positive thinking, Imlach took his players to see the film "One Man's Way," Hollywood's take on Dr. Peale's life.

Coincidence or not, the Leafs came out breathing fire in Game 4 of the series. Frank Mahovlich figured in all five goals of a 5–3 triumph, scoring twice and assisting on three others.

The Leafs would win the set in seven games and take their third straight Stanley Cup via a seven-game decision over Detroit in the final series.

IT SUITS HIM

During the 1964 playoffs, Leafs' coach Punch Imlach, a noted clotheshorse, purchased a new suit on every road trip to Montreal. A superstitious sort, when the Leafs bounced the first-place Canadiens in the Stanley Cup semi-finals, Imlach figured he was on to something.

He was especially certain of that when early into the 1964–65 campaign, he failed to pick out some new clothes while in Montreal and the Leafs lost to the Habs.

Imlach immediately went back to his old ways.

"I bought a new suit on our last trip here and we won," Imlach told *CP* after a 5–2 win at Montreal on February 4, 1965. "I did the same thing this time and we beat Montreal again.

"I'm gonna keep buying new suits the rest of the season and I don't care how much it costs me."

It wasn't the only strange item on Imlach's agenda. He sent five defenceman out as his starting line-up—Allan Stanley, Tim Horton, and Kent Douglas on his forward line and Bob Baun and Carl Brewer along the blue line—and the resulting confusion it caused the Canadiens paid dividends when Horton scored ten seconds after the opening faceoff.

"That was just to set the pace and it worked," Imlach said.

Imlach's suit plan didn't prove to be his strong suit. Montreal dumped the Leafs out of the playoffs in a six-game semi-final series, ending Toronto's three-year reign as Stanley Cup champions.

PUNCHING BACK

Acquired from the New York Rangers late in the 1963–64 season, Andy Bathgate netted the Cup-winning goal as the Leafs earned their third straight Stanley Cup that spring. But within a year, Bathgate was in Punch Imlach's doghouse and he blasted the Toronto coach after Toronto's reign ended with a playoff loss to the Montreal Canadiens in the 1965 semi-finals.

Bathgate was of the opinion that Imlach's long, hard practices had simply drained the veteran Leafs of their life.

"Many (players) didn't get along with the coach," Bathgate told the *Brampton Times*. "Even (Ron) Ellis and (Pete) Stemkowski, the rookies, complained of overwork, but Punch paid no attention.

"This season we played some of our best games in practice."

Hampered by injuries, Bathgate was limited to 55 games and 16 goals, as both he and left-winger Frank Mahovlich fell into disfavour with Imlach.

"We are athletes, not machines," Bathgate said. "And Frank is the type who needs some encouragement.

"I won't play next season if I'm kept only as a utility man."

Bathgate needn't have worried. He was traded to the Detroit Red Wings about a month after his public outburst.

PUNCH AND CARL

Appearing at the Ottawa YMCA on May 6, 1965, Carl Brewer spoke of the inspiration he drew from veteran Leafs teammates Johnny Bower and George Armstrong.

"It makes me think I might be able to put in another 18 years in the league," Brewer said.

A few months later, Brewer changed his mind and left it all behind.

Brewer shocked hockey when he walked out of Leafs' training camp in Peterborough, Ontario and announced his retirement from the game on October 18, 1965, at the age of 26.

When the Leafs won three consecutive Stanley Cups from 1962–64, Brewer was an integral part of the bedrock of that success.

Brewer was an NHL First All-Star Selection in 1962–63 and a Second Team choice in 1961–62 and 1964–65. His strengths were his skating and puck movement, but Brewer also brought an edge to the ice, twice leading the NHL in penalty minutes with 150 in 1959–60 and 177 in 1964–65, though Brewer downplayed this accomplishment.

"If they didn't count holding I would probably win the Lady Byng Trophy," Brewer said.

Brewer wasn't the only hockey man who scoffed at his toughness. "Hit him once and he won't bother you," Montreal Canadiens GM Frank Selke suggested. "He'll back off the puck and you can go right by him."

Brewer cited "personal reasons" for leaving hockey.

"I hated to fly," Brewer explained. He also didn't like the way the Leafs were treating defensive partner Bobby Baun, a holdout from camp locked in a contract dispute with the team.

He also didn't think much of Leafs' coach Punch Imlach, citing a 1964 contract squabble over $100 as cause for the animosity.

"Money wasn't the basic cause of the explosion," Brewer explained. "It was the way I was treated—as if I was a washed-up player."

For Imlach, the feeling was mutual.

"If he walked into camp today and said he wanted to sign a contract, I would ask him which of the other five National Hockey League teams he wanted to play for," Imlach told *Canadian Press* in 1966. "Then I'd attempt to make a deal for him."

Brewer, who had previously walked away from the Leafs in 1960 and 1964 only to return after brief breaks from hockey, was different than most NHLers of his era. He quoted from Ernest Hemingway. He lived for a time in Paris. In the off-season, he pursued higher education, studying at the University of Toronto.

"I know a lot of people think I'm a mixed-up person and don't know what I want," Brewer explained to writer Maurice Smith in 1967. "I was never cut out to be a hockey player.

"It put me in a position where I was in the public eye. Consequently I have not been permitted to have a private life like the average human being and that I can't stand."

After a meeting between Brewer and Imlach, the Leafs agreed to permit Brewer to regain his amateur status and in 1967, he played for Canada in the world championship.

"This summer he walked into my office and offered me a contract," Imlach said. "Then I offered him one.

"Next I read in the paper that he had decided to play for Canada's national team."

Brewer was named outstanding defenceman at the world tourney in Vienna. He played the 1968–69 season with HIFK Helsinki in Finland.

"Helsinki is the biggest little city in the world," Brewer told writer Andy O'Brien. "Until you attend a showing of *Fiddler On The Roof* with dialogue in Finnish, you haven't lived."

The Leafs dealt Brewer's rights to the Detroit Red Wings in 1968 and in 1969, free from the tyrannical Imlach, he shocked everyone again by announcing he was returning to the NHL.

Reunited with Baun on the Wings' blue line, Brewer's astonishing return ended in a selection to the NHL's Second All-Star Team. But he left again after the season, insisting the Wings had refused to honour performance bonus clauses in his contract. Traded to the St. Louis Blues, Brewer joined them in February 1971 and then retired again in 1972, only to return a year later with the WHA's Toronto Toros.

When Brewer hung his blades up again in 1974, it appeared that this one would stick, and it did—for almost six years.

Then Imlach, of all people, came up with a brilliant idea. Hired in 1979 as GM of the Leafs, Imlach lured Brewer out of retirement to make yet another comeback.

His team was struggling and in turmoil, so the last person you'd think Imlach would turn to would be a guy who'd given him so many fits during the 1960s.

"We think Brewer can help us," Imlach said. "He was one of the best skaters who ever played for me."

Brewer went to Toronto's New Brunswick Hawks farm club on a tryout basis, playing three AHL games, and was called up to the big club on Christmas Eve. "I feel that I'm ready," Brewer told *United Press Canada*. "The legs are in good shape.

"I am apprehensive (about playing) in some ways, but I'm looking forward to it."

In his Leafs debut redux on Boxing Day 1979, Brewer started the game paired with Borje Salming on the game's opening shift, and 51 seconds in was in the penalty box for hooking, the start of a long night for the Leafs, who lost 8–2 to the Washington Capitals at Maple Leaf Gardens.

"I wasn't disappointed," Brewer said of his first NHL game since 1972.

Brewer was ostracized within the Leafs' dressing room by teammates who felt he was nothing more than an Imlach spy, a curious accusation considering the long-running acrimony between the two men.

"I don't think Brewer can help this team but that's only my opinion," Leafs' defenceman Dave Hutchison told *CP*. "Obviously some people don't agree with me.

"A lot of guys in this league would rather play 80 games against Brewer than one against me."

The biggest impact Brewer made during his second tour as a Leaf was on a goalpost in practice when he struck his head and required 30 stitches to close a wound to his scalp.

Brewer finished with five assists in 20 games and retired again. But he would make one more comeback before he was finished, and this one would come to haunt the NHL owners and managers, who he was certain were taking advantage of the players.

Convinced that NHLPA head Alan Eagleson and NHL owners were in cahoots and funnelling off some of the pension money owed to players, Brewer spearheaded a class-action suit against the league. After a three-year court battle, the players won a $40 million settlement from the NHL.

"The alumnus owes a lot to him," former Leaf teammate Frank Mahovlich said.

WON'T LET THE CAT OUT OF THE BAG

When Emile (The Cat) Francis was named general manager and coach of the New York Rangers in 1965, one of the first messages he got was from Punch Imlach, his counterpart with the Toronto Maple Leafs. But it wasn't a note of congratulations.

Imlach wanted to remind Francis, the former NHL netminder who'd given up playing goal in 1960, that he still remained on Toronto's reserve list.

"A couple of years ago," Francis told the *Brandon Sun* in 1968, "he sent me a letter telling me to report to training camp and saying he'd fine me $50 for every day I was late and $50 more for every pound I was overweight."

Finally, late in the 1967–68 season, Imlach relented and issued Francis his unconditional release.

"I'm available," Francis laughed. "But I'll be tough to sign."

OLD-TIME HOCKEY

Punch Imlach's fondness for veteran players was well documented and he never shied away from offering up his reasoning for this philosophy.

"I don't believe in age," Imlach explained to the *Montreal Gazette* in 1965. "Ability is what counts with me. Age doesn't mean a thing.

"I don't care how old a player is. I'm only interested in talent. How can you really tell when a hockey player is too old?

"I'm only interested in results and so far I've been getting them from the experience of veterans in the playoffs."

It had nothing to do with sentiment. Like all coaches, Imlach sought the players who could most help his team win, and in his opinion, it was the old hands who did this.

"Youth has nothing to do with ability," Imlach argued. "If an older man can do the job best, he deserves it. And I'm paid to win now, not in the future."

It was hard to argue with Imlach's logic in the spring of 1967, when the Leafs won their most recent Stanley Cup while suiting up 10 players 30 or older and two—defenceman Allan Stanley (40) and goalie Johnny Bower (42)—who proved that there was life in hockey after 40.

Imlach cited Bower as Exhibit A that age was irrelevant. "As long as his eyesight and reflexes are okay, he can be my goalie until he's 60, as far as I'm concerned," Imlach said.

Though Bower did not agree with his boss on much, he echoed his sentiments on old-school talent. "Too many fellows around 35 or 36 decide to retire when they should have good years ahead," Bower reasoned.

PUNCH'S CHEESY MOVE

On the eve of the June 9, 1965 NHL Intra-League Draft, Leafs' goalie Johnny Bower was discussing the future.

"I expect Gerry Cheevers to make the Toronto club this fall after his fine year with (AHL) Rochester last season," Bower said. "He'll have to fight me and Terry Sawchuk for the number one job."

There's just one problem with that math—three into two won't go. Leafs' coach Punch Imlach could only protect two goalies, and opted to go with his cagey veterans, Bower and Sawchuk, though he did his best to try and squirrel Cheevers away for the future.

Cheevers had played some forward while a junior with Toronto St. Michael's, so Imlach sneakily tried to list him under the Toronto forwards left unprotected for the draft. NHL president Clarence Campbell immediately stepped in and ruled that the Leafs couldn't do that. The league's board of governors also turned down a Leaf proposal to increase the goaltenders' reserve list from two to three.

On draft day, Boston GM Hap Emms quickly pounced on Cheevers.

"Cheevers was a tremendous junior," Emms told the *Boston Herald*. "He is young and if he becomes the great goalkeeper we think he will, he will be in the Boston nets for 10 years."

Limited to two games with the Leafs during the 1961–62 season—a 6–4 win over Chicago December 2, 1961, and a 3–1 loss at Detroit the next day—Cheevers would make his Bruins debut October 27, 1965, against the Leafs, making 33 saves but losing 2–1 to Sawchuk.

"Sure I thought about protecting Cheevers," Imlach told *Associated Press*. "But you know, goalies are like wine. They improve with age."

In the short term, it was hard to argue with Imlach's logic. Bower and Sawchuk combined to win Toronto the 1966–67 Stanley Cup. But the following season, Boston would make the playoffs for the first time since 1960 and in the spring of 1969 the Bruins would win their first playoff series since 1958 as Cheevers backstopped them to a quarter-final sweep of the Leafs.

Boston won the Stanley Cup in 1969–70 and 1971–72 and Cheevers also got the Bruins to the Cup final series in 1976–77 and 1977–78, long after Bower and Sawchuk were gone from the NHL scene.

PUNCH'S TRIPLE PLAY

In Toronto, Leafs goalies weren't the only ones adept at playing all the angles. A team of lawyers couldn't have exploited arcane loopholes any more brilliantly than Punch Imlach had when he was in charge of the team.

Exhibit A—Toronto's regular season-ending game on April 3, 1966, against the Red Wings at Detroit's Olympia Stadium.

Imlach became the first coach in NHL history to dress and use three goaltenders in a league game.

Johnny Bower started the game with Terry Sawchuk on the bench as his back-up, and parried all ten shots aimed his way, while Brit Selby and Pete Stemkowski scored to spot the Leafs a 2–0 lead.

Sawchuk entered the fray in the second period, making seven saves, allowing a goal by Norm Ullman after Eddie Shack spotted the Leafs a 3–0 lead.

By the time the third period began, Bruce Gamble had suited up and was now between the pipes, Bower was behind the bench coaching the team, and Imlach was in the stands back of the Toronto bench.

Val Fonteyne and Bruce MacGregor put pucks past Gamble as Detroit rallied for a 3–3 tie, giving Gamble the decision and Bower an unofficial draw in the only period he served as an NHL coach.

Imlach pulled Bower from the game, claiming he was overcome with an undisclosed illness. Then he invoked the NHL's emergency goalie rule after the second period to utilize Gamble.

"Sawchuk tells me that he hurt himself when Detroit scored in the second period and so I declared a state of emergency and brought in Gamble to play the third period," Imlach told the *Windsor Star*'s Jack Dulmage. "What's wrong with that I'd like to know?"

Detroit coach Sid Abel indicated he would have kicked up a fuss had the game mattered in the standings but felt that referee John Ashley was too lenient with Imlach's bending of the rules.

"How the heck can they use three goalies when it's obvious there wasn't much wrong with the other two?" Abel wondered.

"Of course it was a nothing game but I thought Ashley let them fool around too much. We'd have raised a stink if the game had been important, you can bet."

Ashley had no idea about Imlach's plans prior to their implementation.

"Notify him?" Imlach growled. "What do I need to notify him for? I'm running this club.

"I said there was an emergency. I don't know whether he heard me or not and I don't care."

Imlach and Bower often feuded, so Imlach likely took some sort of perverse pleasure installing his netminder as a quasi-coach.

"I wanted him to see what it was like," Imlach said. "It might do him some good.

"Some of these guys think all there is to it is swinging the gate."

Imlach stated that he planned to carry all three goalies for Toronto's upcoming playoff series against the reigning Stanley Cup champion Montreal Canadiens, mainly because he wasn't certain which two of his three netminders he planned to dress.

Maybe Imlach should have used all three goalies at once against the Habs, who swept the Leafs aside in four games en route to their second straight Stanley Cup win.

PUNCH'S PLAY

Not much went right for the Leafs during their 1965–66 Stanley Cup semi-final series. They were rapidly swept aside by the eventual champion Montreal Canadiens, and coach Punch Imlach didn't pull any punches.

"They're a bunch of bums," Imlach said of his team. "But they're my bums."

The fiery coach was prepared to put his money where his mouth was, and nearly took to the ice in defence of his boys when a brawl saw the Leafs and Habs establish a new Stanley Cup record with a combined 130 penalty minutes.

Imlach was certain that referee Art Skov had screwed up and wasn't going to give his team what he felt was a deserved power play from the fray, so he raced back into the Toronto dressing room and laced up his skates.

"I was going out after the referee," Imlach explained. "They were going to have us shorthanded and I wasn't going to go for that. I had to have two minutes advantage coming to me someplace. Things were bad enough without me getting a hosing.

"It was going to cost me $100 in fines to go out on the ice, so I wasn't going to go out there and chase him with just my shoes on."

His counterpart, Montreal coach Toe Blake, blaming Imlach for the brawling, invited him to don his blades and come out fighting.

"Who the heck does Imlach think he is sending men out to play hockey that way?" Blake asked. "If Imlach feels that way about hockey, why doesn't he come right out on the ice and throw punches?

"I'd take a punch at him right now if he was here."

Fortunately for all involved, the sight of a coach on skates chasing a referee around the rink, not to mention two coaches trading blows at centre ice, was avoided when Leafs' assistant coach-GM King Clancy walked around the rink to the penalty box area and got things sorted out.

"I sent Clancy over to straighten it out," Imlach said. "They just lost track of the penalties for a minute, that was all."

HE MISSED THE POINT

King Clancy was adept at giving the needle.

Taking the needle was an entirely different story.

With coach Punch Imlach felled by influenza, Clancy was left to work the bench for Game 2 of the Leafs' 1966 Stanley Cup semi-final series at the Montreal Forum against the reigning Cup champion Canadiens.

The Leafs lost 2–0 to fall behind in the series by the same count, but long before the game, Clancy lost his lunch.

On the afternoon of the game, as he walked the hallways of the Leafs' Montreal hotel, Clancy was suddenly overcome with a woozy sensation. He was sick to his stomach and left temporarily without his false teeth.

"I staggered back to my room and just made it to my bed and who's there (but his roommate) Imlach," Clancy explained to *Canadian Press*. "Up came the team physician, Dr. (Hugh) Smythe, and he opened his bag. The next thing I knew he gave the needle to Punch and when I saw that, I ran out of the room.

"If I had had that needle, too, I wouldn't have been able to coach."

SHACK ATTACK

The Leaf world was shaken in August 1966 when Leafs' coach Punch Imlach announced that forward Eddie Shack, third on the team in goals during the 1965–66 season with 26, had been demoted to Victoria of the Western Hockey League.

"I discovered there is a clique of three or four players who created trouble in the team," Imlach told *Canadian Press*. "I have enough proof and now I'll have to act."

Imlach felt for the good of the club he was left with no choice but to make some tough decisions regarding his personnel.

"In cases like this you have to act radically," Imlach said. "Shack was only one player doing things he shouldn't have done. There are others and I'm prepared to trade them if I can get the right man in exchange."

Imlach refused to name any of the other players involved in this so-called clique.

"All I'll say is anybody on my hockey team who won't comply with club rules or will try to create trouble will either be traded or sent to the minors."

Shack's punishment was only a paper one. He made it back to the Leafs before the start of the 1966–67 season and was part of Toronto's most recent Stanley Cup winner.

LOSING STREAK PULLS PUNCH

Though the 1966–67 season certainly ended well for the Toronto Maple Leafs, it also nearly brought an end to coach Punch Imlach.

A ten-game losing streak, the longest in franchise history, nearly derailed Toronto's magical Stanley Cup run before it began and was responsible for putting Imlach in the hospital.

The skid started January 15, 1967, the same day that the Green Bay Packers beat the Kansas City Chiefs 35–10 in Super Bowl I. At the beginning of the day, Toronto sat third in the NHL with 42 points, 13 ahead of the fifth-place Detroit Red Wings.

Dropping a 4–0 decision that night at Chicago, the Leafs didn't just keeping losing—they completely lost it. Over the next ten games, they were outscored 47–15. Seven of the ten setbacks were by three or more goals and there was just a solitary one-goal loss during the streak.

"The team has gone sour," Imlach complained to the *Montreal Gazette*, blaming it on his stars, people like Dave Keon, Frank Mahovlich, and Bob Pulford. "They're getting the big money after all. I have a right to expect something more from them.

"Never mind knocking the fringe players. These are the guys who are supposed to produce for us."

The tenth straight setback, a 5–2 home-ice loss to the Detroit Red Wings, in which future Leaf Norm Ullman fired a hat trick, moved the Wings one point ahead of Toronto for the fourth and final playoff spot.

The skid finally ended not with a roar, but a whimper and a February 11, 4–4 tie with Chicago. The next night, the Leafs finally got back on the winning track, getting a third-period goal from Jim Pappin to defeat Boston 2–1.

The Leafs won again, 6–0 over the New York Rangers on February 15, but it wasn't enough to help Imlach. He was hospitalized February 17 due to exhaustion and King Clancy took over behind the bench, running off five more victories to get the Leafs back in the playoff hunt.

The Leafs went 8–1–1 under Clancy. Imlach returned March 12 for a 5–0 loss at Chicago.

"They gave me these pills and tell me to take it easy," Imlach said. "But how do you take it easy running a hockey team with all this noise and excitement?"

GOODBYE LARRY

Punch Imlach once saved Larry Regan from a minor league fate. Midway through the 1958–59 season, his first as coach-GM of the Leafs, Imlach claimed Regan, the 1956–57 Calder Trophy winner as the NHL's top rookie, on waivers from the Boston Bruins.

"Regan should give us the edge we have been looking for," Imlach explained. Regan helped the Leafs eliminate the Bruins in the 1959 Stanley Cup semi-finals as Toronto reached the Cup final series for the first time since 1951.

Nearly a decade later, Regan, no longer a player, landed the job as the first GM of the expansion Los Angeles Kings in 1967, and Imlach gave him the bum's rush.

All too familiar with Imlach's hard-driving workouts, Regan was watching the Leafs practice on an off day prior to the start of the 1967 Stanley Cup final against Montreal when he began heckling his old coach and advising the players that they'd already worked hard enough and deserved a break.

Imlach summoned security and had Regan escorted from Maple Leaf Gardens.

"I was only kidding," Regan told *Canadian Press*.

"So was I—but on the square," countered Imlach. "It's tough enough getting my guys to keep their minds on the workout without Larry heckling from the sidelines."

BATTLE OF THE SIDEBURNS

The Leafs were early into training camp in the fall of 1968 when coach Punch Imlach called long-haired rookie defenceman Brad Selwood over for a conversation.

"Do you know how to shave?" Imlach asked Selwood.

"Yes sir," Selwood answered.

"Do you have any blades?" the Leaf coach queried.

"Yes," Selwood said sheepishly.

"Then use them," growled Imlach.

"I'm going to get a haircut tonight," Selwood vowed.

Leafs' trainer Joe Sgro was threatened by Imlach with a $25 fine if he didn't get his sideburns removed immediately. Goalie Bruce Gamble and centre Wayne Carleton trimmed their sideburns, but defenceman Mike Pelyk's grooming was substandard.

"Get some more off, or else no cheque," Imlach threatened.

By the next day, Imlach proudly reported that the Leafs were living in a sideburn-free existence.

DID SHAKEY PUNCH PUNCH'S TICKET OUT OF TORONTO?

Leafs centre Mike Walton, in a dispute with coach Punch Imlach over ice time that had gone on for six weeks, finally decided he couldn't take it anymore and quit the team.

When Walton—known to his teammates as Shakey—didn't show up to make the trip to Montreal for a 2–1 loss February 20, 1969, Imlach immediately suspended his petulant forward.

He might have also signed his own ticket out of Toronto at the same time.

"I haven't heard from Walton," Imlach told *Canadian Press*. "The question I'm asking is, 'Is Walton here to play for the Maple Leafs tonight?'"

Alan Eagleson, counsel to the NHLPA, provided the answer as to why Walton wasn't there.

"Mike wants to pursue his career in hockey, but he feels he isn't getting enough playing time," Eagleson stated.

At first, the frequently bombastic Imlach tried to bite his tongue.

"I find it very hard to keep my policy of not speaking badly about anybody in a situation like this, but if you have nothing good to say, you should keep your mouth shut and that's all the comment I'm going to make."

It wasn't the first time that Walton and Imlach had butted heads. In October of 1966, Walton walked out in a contract dispute with Toronto's AHL farm club in Rochester and indicated he'd only come back to play pro hockey if it was with the Leafs. In 1968, he was one of the Leafs singled out by Imlach when he instituted a no sideburns policy on the team.

There was speculation that the Leafs had offered Walton to the Philadelphia Flyers. Flyers' GM Keith Allen admitted he "would dearly love" to acquire Walton, acknowledging that there had been discussions which would have sent goalie Doug Favell to the Leafs for Walton.

"He'll be traded," Imlach said. "I've been through this before. He'll be traded when the right offer is made."

Imlach pointed to the phone on his desk.

"That thing hasn't been ringing off the hook. I've heard that other teams are interested. Where are they? Why aren't they getting in touch with me?

"The phone hasn't rung all day from anybody looking for a trade."

Imlach also felt it a tad selfish that Walton walked out on the team right after one of the Leafs' most significant victories of the season, a 5–1 triumph over the defending Stanley Cup champion Canadiens.

"Can you imagine anyone complaining of being benched after we win a big game?" Imlach asked. "Wouldn't you think a player, if he placed the team's interest first, would be a little pleased?"

Imlach also scoffed at Walton's claim he wasn't playing enough.

"As for ice time, our records show he was on the ice as long as Henri Richard was for the Canadiens," Imlach pointed out. "I haven't heard that Richard quit."

Six days later, it appeared the two sides had patched up their differences when Walton rejoined the Leafs.

"Mike phoned me and asked if he could play tonight," Imlach explained. "I suggested he come down and we could talk it over, and he did. It's only fair if he feels that he can help the team that we should take him back.

"Everything happens for the best and I hope that this helps Mike along."

It had been a rough year for Imlach. In December, the hockey committee of Maple Leaf Gardens called him on the carpet when the team was floundering in the basement of the NHL's East Division. Imlach vowed at the time Toronto would make the playoffs, which they did, but moments after the Leafs were swept in the opening post-season round by the Boston Bruins, Leafs' co-owner Stafford Smythe bounded into the press room at Maple Leaf Gardens and proclaimed, "He's through altogether."

He being Imlach.

"I told him two minutes ago," Smythe said. "I said, 'It's the end of the Imlach era."

In his book *Hockey Is A Battle*, Imlach allowed that he had a deal lined up with Boston to send Walton there for forwards Eddie Shack and Jim Lorentz, but it was scuttled.

He speculated that Smythe might have been the one to kill the trade and encourage Walton to come back to the Leafs because Smythe knew he was going to fire Imlach at season's end.

Smythe had good reason to be close to Walton. Walton's wife Candace was Smythe's niece and the granddaughter of his father, long-time Leafs' managing director Conn Smythe.

THREE INTO TWO

Third game. Third goalie.

Punch Imlach figured he was onto something that was genius.

In 1964, Imlach picked up veteran Terry Sawchuk from Detroit in the NHL Intra-League Draft and alternated the veteran with fellow grizzled legend Johnny Bower and they won the Vezina Trophy.

Four years later, Imlach redid the math.

"I was the first one to use the two-goalie system," Imlach chortled. "Now I'll be the first with the three-goalie system."

Imlach opened the 1968–9 NHL season by playing rookie Al Smith in goal for the first four games. He then went to the veteran Bower, 44, who promptly blanked the Boston Bruins 2–0 in his season debut.

Instead of riding the hot hand, Imlach went back to the bullpen, starting Bruce Gamble, who beat the New York Rangers 5–3.

"We have a special situation with a guy like Bower," Imlach explained. "It's an exceptional situation. You just don't know how long he can go on.

"Three-goalie system," Imlach added. "Sounds interesting, huh?"

THANKS PUNCH

On April 9, 1969, three days after he was fired as coach-GM the Leafs, Toronto city council announced plans to hold a reception and dinner in honour of all Punch Imlach did for the city.

"We should do something for Punch so that the city of Toronto will remain a great city instead of being a sourpuss just because he lost one Stanley Cup series," controller Allan Lamport said.

HE HAD A HEART

There were those outside of hockey, and maybe even a few within the game, who might have been a little taken aback when Punch Imlach was felled by heart trouble in 1972.

There were many who thought Imlach heartless when he served as coach and GM of the Leafs.

John Andersen, who worked alongside Imlach with the Leafs and later for the Buffalo Sabres, delivered a counter punch to the popular opinion of Punch.

"To the outsider, Punch appears tough," Andersen wrote in a 1972 piece for the *Toronto Sun*. "Yes, Punch is tough. Tough on his players, but even more so, tough on himself."

Then Andersen proceeded to relay of couple of tales of how Imlach showed he had a heart.

The first was in 1967, shortly after the Leafs won their most recent Stanley Cup. Imlach was preparing his protected list for the upcoming

NHL expansion draft and realized he couldn't keep all of his loyal soldiers who'd been with him for four Stanley Cup titles in the 1960s.

After much soul-searching, he decided veteran defenceman Allan Stanley would have to remain unprotected. He opted to tell Stanley face-to-face.

"I was with Punch when he met Stanley to give Stanley the news in person," Andersen recalled. "Stanley took the news like the great pro that he was. He understood Punch's decision and told him so but it was not an easy meeting for Imlach.

"It lasted longer than planned and it was anything but a tough, cold general manager that went home that day not too pleased with himself for having done what had to be done."

Anderson recalled another touching story from the 1967–68 season when rookie centre Bill Masterton of the first-year Minnesota North Stars died tragically after striking his head on the ice during a game against the Oakland Seals.

"Imlach is hockey 24 hours a day," Andersen wrote. "His team comes first. The NHL comes second.

"When Minnesota North Stars lost Bill Masterton in a tragic accident in 1968, they desperately needed a centre. (Minnesota GM) Wren Blair phoned Imlach and the two arranged to have (former NHL all-star) Bronco Horvath sold by the Leaf organization to Minnesota.

"The NHL by-laws stipulated that deals between two NHL clubs must be final, so Punch had no guarantee that Horvath could be returned to Toronto after the season. Punch went ahead anyway.

"He reasoned that Horvath, who was then with Toronto's (AHL) farm team in Rochester, deserved another chance in the NHL and could help the North Stars. In other words, it would be good for hockey and the NHL.

"Life is a two way street. Hockey has been good to Punch and he is good for the sport."

COME BACK PUNCH

Early in the 1975–76 NHL season, Harold Ballard surprised everyone when the Leafs' owner announced a standing offer to Punch Imlach to return to the Leafs at any time.

"Staff Smythe (Leafs' president at the time) fired Punch (in 1969), not me," Ballard insisted to the *Brandon Sun*.

"My wife became sick during that last game Punch coached (in the 1968–69 Stanley Cup playoffs against Boston). I took her home at the end of the second period.

"Just as I pulled in my driveway a bulletin flashed over the car radio—Punch Imlach had been fired. I damned near had a fit."

In 1979, out of work after being fired as GM of the Buffalo Sabres, Imlach took Ballard up on his offer and returned as GM of the Leafs.

PAL HAL

Love him or loathe him, Harold Ballard always made for entertaining copy.

BALLARD GIVES BEATLES A HARD DAY'S NIGHT

When Harold Ballard booked the Beatles to play a Labour Day, 1964 show at Maple Leaf Gardens, he didn't bother to tell the Fab Four that he was planning to double down on his investment.

Tickets to the show sold out in an hour, so Ballard simply began selling tickets for a second show the same day without bothering to first clear the plan with the Beatles.

After an argument between Ballard and Brian Epstein, the band's manager, the Beatles knew Ballard had them over a barrel. If they reneged on performing the second show, they'd come off looking like the bad guys.

Not satisfied with putting one over on the hottest band in rock and roll, Ballard ordered thermostats inside Maple Leaf Gardens to be cranked up on what was an unseasonably warm Labour Day in Toronto. Then he instructed his concessionaires to sell only large drinks.

While the Beatles made out fine—drawing 70 per cent of the gross ticket sales from the first show and 60 per cent of the second show—Ballard also made a fortune in beverage sales.

A PENNY SAVED

The Leafs under the ownership of Harold Ballard and Stafford Smythe were nothing if not frugal.

Toronto missed the playoffs during the 1967–68 season, but had already printed up playoff tickets for that spring. So they were simply filed away, saved for future use.

When Toronto fans picked up their ducats for the 1969 playoffs, the front of the ticket read "Stanley Cup playoffs '68."

Printing a new set inscribed with the correct year would have cost the Leafs $1,250.

WHAT IF THEY'D HELD FIRM?

Following the annual meeting of the Leafs' board of directors on June 26, 1969, some major changes were made.

Listing the reasoning as "differences of opinion on administrative matters," the board announced the firing of president Stafford Smythe and executive vice-president Harold Ballard. Both men were asked to resign their positions and when they refused, were removed. John Bassett, chairman of the board, was the driving force behind the changes.

George Mara was named president, amidst an ongoing investigation of the Gardens' books by Revenue Canada and the RCMP.

Smythe and Ballard maintained their seats on the board and between them, still controlled nearly 50 per cent of Maple Leaf Gardens stock. In November of 1969, the two men waged a proxy war and were reinstated to their positions. Bassett opted to get out and sold his shares to Smythe and Ballard in September of 1971.

Six weeks later, Smythe died of a bleeding ulcer just before he was to go on trial for tax evasion. Ballard purchased Smythe's shares for $7.5 million in February 1972. Since he now controlled 60 per cent of Gardens' stock, Ballard installed himself as president and chairman of the board, as well as governor for the Leafs.

CALLING DR. BALLARD

In real life, Dr. Hugh Smythe, brother of team president Stafford Smythe and son of managing director Conn Smythe, was the Leafs team physician.

On film it was co-owner Harold Ballard.

The 1971 Canadian film *Face Off*, once described to writer Lance Hornby by Art Hindle as "a perfect time capsule of Toronto and the Maple Leafs in the early '70s," may have featured Canadian actor Hindle in its lead role, but the true stars of the film were the Leafs.

Reportedly the first movie in Canadian film history with a $1 million budget, Hindle played Billy Duke, a rookie sensation for the Leafs. His body double in the film and in game action was Leafs' defenceman Jim McKenny, and all of the other 1970–71 Leafs are also featured in the film, some of them, like long-time captain George Armstrong, with speaking roles.

"George was actually a pretty good actor for a hockey player," Hindle said. "He didn't try to push it. People could critique him, but I thought he was pretty good."

Beyond the Leafs, stars from other NHL teams such as Derek Sanderson, Pete Mahovlich, Ed Giacomin, and Rod Seiling appear on screen and actual NHL game footage is spliced in to give the movie a more authentic feel.

Joe Sgro filled his regular role as Leafs trainer while some Toronto sports personalities such as George Gross, Ken McKee, Fergie Olver, and Scott Young, father of Neil and upon whose novel the film was based, also had roles, as did Ballard.

Only seen on screen briefly during a scene in the Leafs dressing room, in the film's credits, Ballard was simply listed as "Leaf Doctor."

TAKE A HIKE

Hockey Night In Canada not airing on the CBC?

Late in the 1971–72 season, as the Leafs scrambled to secure a playoff spot, Harold Ballard sought to make it so.

Angered by a CBC technicians' strike that was preventing his team's games from being aired on the network, Ballard put his team's broadcast up for grabs.

"I am offering the telecasts of the Toronto Maple Leafs commencing this Saturday to whatever station or group of stations will guarantee coverage of the Leafs' stretch run for a playoff position," Ballard told *Canadian Press* on March 6, 1972.

Ballard was especially perturbed that a Leafs-Los Angeles Kings telecast the previous Saturday was pulled from the air after just seven seconds of play.

"Last Saturday's disgraceful action by the CBC technicians left hockey fans across the country frustrated and represented an action in our building that I will not permit the CBC to allow to happen again.

"These people are through. The next time they come into the Gardens they will buy their own tickets—if they can get them. Leaf fans must be ensured coverage of our fight to get into the playoffs. The fans deserve it, the players deserve it and so do the sponsors."

Ultimately, the Leafs qualified for the playoffs and the NHL followed Ballard's lead. All broadcasts for the remainder of the regular season and playoffs were switched to the rival CTV network.

DID WHA COST THE LEAFS A CUP?

Rick Ley never regretted becoming a New England Whaler. He won championships there, had his number retired.

Still, there was always a lingering doubt. What if he had stayed? What if they had kept that Maple Leafs team together?

How far could the Leafs have gone?

All the way, perhaps?

"I certainly think so," Ley said. "You can never tell for sure, you just don't know what the chemistry would have been like, but I would have been willing to bet that would have been a team that had a chance to contend."

A chance that was torpedoed by the emergence of the World Hockey Association in 1972.

"Toronto by far was hardest hit (by the WHA raiders)," suggested Ron Ward, another ex-Leaf who ended up in the new league. "It cost them a Cup."

The Leafs had lost in the quarter-finals of the 1972 Stanley Cup playoffs to the eventual champion Boston Bruins. A young team, in a rebuilding mode since their roster of ancient warriors captured Lord Stanley's mug in 1967, the Leafs appeared headed in the right direction.

In goal they had a budding superstar in Bernie Parent. A kiddie corps of defencemen included Ley, Brad Selwood, Jim McKenny, Mike Pelyk, and Brian Glennie. Up front, veterans Ron Ellis, Dave Keon, Paul Henderson, and Norm Ullman were meshing with youngsters Darryl Sittler, Jim Harrison, Guy Trottier, and Rick Kehoe.

The future looked bright. Then, in the summer of 1972, Toronto's fortunes took a dramatic U-turn.

Five players jumped to the new league. Ley and Selwood ended up in New England. Trottier went to Quebec, Harrison to Edmonton. Worst of all, Parent bolted to the Miami Screaming Eagles.

"(Leafs' owner) Harold (Ballard) didn't believe the WHA was going to work, I guess," Ley said. "He didn't want to pay anybody. To tell the truth, they didn't really even try.

"That was the shame of it. If they had tried, I probably would have stayed for a lot less money.

"Toronto lost a pretty good nucleus of their hockey team that year."

In the long term, the Leafs lost a lot more.

The ship now listing, Toronto missed the playoffs the following season. Henderson, Pelyk, Ullman, and Keon jumped overboard to the WHA over the course of the next two seasons.

In the meantime, the Leafs had done extremely well at the draft table. With Sittler already in place, they added Lanny McDonald, Errol Thompson, Bob Neely, Ian Turnbull, Dave (Tiger) Williams, and signed as a free agent a slick Swedish defenceman by the name of Borje Salming.

"You think about some of the additions to the hockey club in the next few years," Ley said. "You wonder where that would have taken us in the future."

When Parent jumped back to the NHL, the Leafs traded Parent's rights to the Philadelphia Flyers and he backstopped them to consecutive Stanley Cups in 1973–74 and 1974–75, a time frame in which there can be no doubt he was the game's most significant player.

Could the Flyers have won either Cup without Parent? No chance. Could the Leafs have won a Cup with Parent?

Ley would have liked their chances.

"I played junior with Bernie (in Niagara Falls)," Ley said. "He was a great goalie. I'd still say he was as good as any of them in the game today."

After 26 years, Ley came back to the Toronto organization as an assistant coach, helping the club reach the Stanley Cup final four in 1998–99.

He admits he's considered what could've been had he, had everybody, stayed put.

"I guess I've thought about it," Ley said. "Not at great length, but I've thought about it. We had the opportunity to become a real good hockey team."

Good enough to cop a Cup? Maybe.

HULL OF AN IDEA

Harold Ballard was no fan of the WHA, but he sure enjoyed sticking it to the Russians.

Perhaps then it should have come as a surprise that Ballard was a rare NHL voice in favour of including Bobby Hull as part of the Team Canada roster for the 1972 Summit Series against the Soviet Union.

Originally part of the squad, Hull was removed from the team when he jumped from the Chicago Blackhawks and signed with the WHA's Winnipeg Jets, since the Canadian Amateur Hockey Association had no working agreement with the fledgling league.

There was a public outcry to include Hull on the team and appeals were made to Canadian Prime Minister Pierre Trudeau to step in and mediate some sort of resolution.

Even Ballard, one of the harshest critics of the WHA after he'd lost several players to the rival loop, came out strongly, if not diplomatically, in favour of Hull being a member of Team Canada.

"I don't give a damn if Hull signed with a team in China," Ballard barked. "He's a Canadian and he should be on the Canadian team."

No one listened, though, and Hull was left off the team as Canada edged the Russians 4–3–1 in the eight-game series.

PAL HAL IN A CELL

For someone about to be sentenced to prison time, Harold Ballard was in a jovial mood as he arrived at a crowded Toronto courtroom the morning of October 20, 1972.

"We should have sold tickets," Ballard, 69, joked as he looked at the overflow crowd.

Ballard's lawyer, J. J. Robinette, was stopped in the hallway outside the courtroom by another barrister. "I'll bet there are more bets and pools on the outcome of this than on the Stanley Cup," the lawyer remarked.

Among those who spoke on behalf of Ballard's character prior to sentencing was *Hockey Night In Canada* broadcaster Jack Dennett.

Accused of 47 counts of theft and fraud charges totalling $205,000, the court heard testimony during the six-week trial that Ballard utilized Maple Leaf Gardens funds to pay for construction on his suburban Etobicoke home, that he purchased two motorcycles for his sons with Gardens corporate cheques and paid for a limousine for his daughter's wedding with a Gardens cheque.

Records showed he spent $82,000 of Gardens money on home renovations and gifts for his children. But Ballard claimed he knew nothing of this. Citing a "clear pattern of fraud," Judge Harry Deyman wasn't buying it.

"I simply cannot understand a businessman of Mr. Ballard's stature seeing thousands of dollars of improvement without making sure he knew what the cause was," Judge Deyman said.

"I find it completely incredible that a businessman of Mr. Ballard's acumen could have goods and services of such variety and cost furnished to him to his knowledge without expecting to pay for them."

Sentenced to concurrent three-year terms, Ballard was transferred to Kingston's Millhaven Penitentiary, in the minimum-security wing. Free on a three-day pass in the summer of 1973 after serving eight months, Ballard mocked the Canadian penal system, insisting he was looking forward to getting back to his jail cell.

"In some ways it's more like a motel than a penal institution," Ballard told *Canadian Press*. "A typical meal is tenderloin steak, garden peas, baked potato, apple pie and ice cream.

"I imagine prisoners eat much better than the average Canadian."

Ballard also stated that he felt no remorse for the criminal activity that led to his prison stay.

"Any infinitesimal guilt I felt disappeared when I signed the cheque paying back the money to the Gardens," Ballard explained.

Ballard's words did not sit well with Canadian solicitor-general Warren Allmand. "Mr. Ballard is in for a few surprises because his conditions may change a little," Allmand said.

For instance, that Ballard was doing business and holding a press conference during a pass granted to allow him to visit family was abusing his temporary-absence privilege and a second request for another three-day pass by Ballard was rejected.

Eventually moved to a Toronto halfway house, Ballard was paroled October 19, 1973, after serving barely one-third of his sentence.

HAL NO PAL OF WHA

Tired of their long battle with the World Hockey Association, NHL owners began developing a framework for a merger with the rival league in 1977, but Leafs owner Harold Ballard was dead set against the idea.

"I have been quite disturbed about this thing they call amalgamation or expansion," Ballard told *Canadian Press*. "It's not amalgamation, it's expansion. The survey that I've made, there are seven (NHL owners) that are definitely not interested in the WHA."

Ballard was still bitter with the WHA for driving up player salaries and gutting what was an up-and-coming Leafs team in the early 1970s.

"You don't go into business with people who have tried to torpedo you," Ballard said. "They stole 18 of our players. They took our junior players from the (Toronto) Marlboros (which Ballard also owned) and never compensated the club for the players they took.

"They have done that with a few of the junior teams and that leaves you with a sour taste in your mouth."

The Leafs' owner was also of the opinion that there were too many NHL teams currently struggling, so it made no sense to add more teams to the fold.

"That league is in a deplorable condition and we have enough trouble in our own league with three or four clubs," Ballard reasoned. "I would like to get them straightened out before we get involved with anybody else."

Ballard also didn't believe that there were as many NHL teams as anxious for a merger as people were led to believe and was anxious to discuss the notion with other owners.

"I would like to find out who is interested in having the WHA in with the National Hockey League," he said "At that time I would like to say to them that if they are so interested in having the WHA in the National Hockey League, why don't you go and join them?

"Those WHA clubs who want to join us are leaving their partners. That's not the kind of partners I would want."

Despite Ballard's objections, the NHL invited four WHA teams—the Hartford Whalers, Winnipeg Jets, Quebec Nordiques, and Edmonton Oilers—to join the NHL in 1979.

BLUE ON BLUE

In 1977 the NHL governors voted 13–5 mandating that the names of players be placed on the back of all sweaters over top the player's number, but Leafs' owner Harold Ballard was dead set against the idea.

Fearing that adding the names of the players to their uniforms would crush program sales, Ballard adamantly refused to adhere to the new NHL policy, taking a shot at the physical stature of NHL president John Ziegler in the process.

"Mr. Ziegler is going to have to keep his little nose out of my business," Ballard said. "It's always the smallest guy in the schoolyard who makes the most noise.

"Who does this man think he is? I'm wondering what we have here. This guy is working for us. We're not working for him. He's a president, not a commissioner, but he's starting to act like a dictator.

"He's a rookie president. We should send him to the minors. Why doesn't he keep his nose to the grindstone and start dealing with the real business of the league.

"If he fines me, I guess I might have to break his neck."

When finally ordered to comply with the governors' mandate by Ziegler late into the 1977–78 season, Ballard responded for a February 26, 1978 game at Chicago by putting the names on the back of the blue Leaf sweaters in the same blue, making them almost illegible.

"I've complied with the bylaw," Ballard told *Associated Press.* "The names are stitched on, three inches high.

"It's a pity you can't see them. I'll never make it as a colour coordinator, will I?"

Ballard frankly admitted his goal was "to make a mockery of the rule.

"I also thought about switching the sweaters, like having Ian Turnbull wear (Errol) Thompson's and having (Borje) Salming wear (Mike) Palmateer's and the like, but I checked the rules and found out I couldn't do those things," he chortled.

After he was threatened with fines of up to $5,000 per game by the league, Ballard finally relented and put the names clearly and properly displayed on the back of the team's home and away sweaters.

NO WAY COULD HE SEE

A sub-plot during Toronto's 1978 upset win over the New York Islanders in the Stanley Cup quarter-finals was the verbal battle between Leafs owner Harold Ballard and Alfonse D'Amato, the presiding supervisor for Hemstead, New York.

D'Amato was appalled that prior to the games at Maple Leaf Gardens, the Leafs played "O Canada" but not "The Star Spangled Banner" and demanded that Ballard remedy the situation immediately.

The ever-cantankerous Ballard countered that playing both anthems prior to the game would be "a waste of time" and suggested he might be willing to play the national anthem of the United States prior to games in Toronto if the opposition was willing to spot the Leafs a one-goal lead.

FOSTER FORCED OUT

When he first called a hockey game on radio in 1923, Foster Hewitt was a reluctant participant.

"At the time it didn't really mean a thing," Hewitt told the *Ottawa Journal* in 1979. "It went fairly smoothly except that two or three times, the telephone operator cut in to ask what number we were calling?

"By the time it was over, I'd had my fill."

Becoming radio director for the Leafs in 1927, Hewitt grew into the most famous voice in the NHL, calling Leafs' games on radio and television for 51 years.

"We watched games on radio," explained veteran *Toronto Star* sportswriter Frank Orr. "Kids today can't understand that, but we could picture the plays in our imagination.

"We had pictures that we sent away for so we knew what the players looked like."

But like most with a career in the sporting world, it was not left up to Hewitt to determine when the end came.

Accepting bids for radio broadcast rights for the 1978–79 NHL season, Leafs' owner Harold Ballard opted to go with CKO over Hewitt's station CKFH.

"Naturally I'm disappointed," Hewitt said. "If it was a straight question of dollars and cents, I could understand. But our bid was exactly the same, except that CKO's bid was for two years and ours was for one. Crazy thing is, we'd been trying to get a two-year deal for years, but Ballard would never go for it."

Hewitt, the man for whom the Hockey Hall of Fame's broadcasting award is named, sought an explanation from Ballard but never received one.

"I tried to contact him seven times to talk it over and each time I phoned, I made sure he was in his office when I called," Hewitt said. "Not once would he answer his phone or return my call.

"I just didn't think he was fair about it. You have to know Ballard to even begin to figure it out. But I long ago learned that if you can't say something good, well ..."

Hewitt still went to Leafs' games after he was removed from calling them, but being removed from his calling seemed to take the life out of the man.

"I guess I have to talk to enjoy it," Hewitt said. "I don't get the same kick out of it."

As far as his signature goal call, one that was adopted by almost all of his imitators—He shoots, he scores!—Hewitt laid no claim of ownership to it.

"It just seemed the shortest way to register what had happened," Hewitt said. "It just came out."

A year after removing Hewitt as the Leafs' broadcaster, Ballard tore down his famous gondola and incinerated it, even though the Hockey Hall of Fame had sought to acquire and display it.

"Hell, we're not in the historical business," Ballard said. "And that gondola wasn't so old anyway."

IT'S IN THE BAG

After a 6–4 setback February 28, 1979, against the Atlanta Flames, Leafs' coach Roger Neilson proved prophetic. "If it doesn't turn around, there'll be some kind of shake up, you can be sure of that," Neilson told *Canadian Press*. "Changes will have to be made—the players know that, we all know that."

The next day, after a 2–1 loss to the Montreal Canadiens, change did indeed take place. Neilson was fired. Leafs' owner Harold Ballard installed former coach John McLellan on an interim basis. Meanwhile, Leafs' GM Jim Gregory tried to get permission from the Chicago Blackhawks to hire Ed Johnston, who was coaching the New Brunswick Hawks at the time, the AHL farm club shared by both Chicago and Toronto. There was also speculation that Leaf scout Gerry McNamara might be named coach.

Ballard told reporters that Neilson was fired before he told Neilson. "It could have been done in a better way," Neilson said.

"I hated to do it," Ballard said. "But it was something that had to be done. You couldn't meet a nicer guy than Roger, but some players were not playing up to their abilities under his system."

Gregory admitted that he was a little surprised that he still had a job. "A lot of people have asked why I don't get fired," Gregory said. "I don't know the answer to that. I'm not the owner. Mr. Ballard is the owner."

One day later, with no coach announcement having been made, curious Leafs' fans tuned in to *Hockey Night In Canada* to see the

Leafs play host to Philadelphia Flyers, but mostly to discover who would be behind Toronto's bench.

After "O Canada" was finished and just before the puck was dropped for the opening faceoff, who should come out and take up his place behind the Leafs' bench but Neilson.

He received a 90-second ovation from the Maple Leaf Gardens crowd.

Afterward Ballard insisted he'd never dismissed Neilson.

"He wasn't fired," Ballard said. "He was just put on furlough for a day or two."

Ballard asked Neilson to come out to work that night wearing a mask and then pull it off when he took up his position behind the bench.

"We had some of those ski masks like the pro wrestlers wear," Ballard said. "And the idea was that we'd have (a scout) go out to the bench wearing one of those masks. Then Roger was going to go out and shake hands with him.

"Then (the scout) was going to retreat, and Roger was going to take his mask off behind the bench."

Neilson wouldn't do it and just shook his head at the whole scenario. "Yesterday if you would have told me this was possible, I would've said the whole thing was crazy," he said.

"There was no hoax about it. Certainly if there was, I didn't know about it and the players didn't know about it."

Leafs' players held a vote and informed Ballard they would only play for Neilson. "I voted for Roger," Leafs goalie Mike Palmateer acknowledged.

"They could have gotten anyone to coach this team," Leafs forward Lanny McDonald said. "But he's the one we wanted.

"He's the one who makes us go."

Neilson would go for good at the end of season, fired again by Ballard, who this time made the dismissal stick.

REBUKED BY PARLIAMENT

Not many NHL owners can claim that their words earned them a tongue-lashing on the floor of the House of Commons, but Harold Ballard could.

In 1979, when the bombastic Leafs' owner made disparaging comments about women to host Barbara Frum while appearing on CBC radio's "As It Happens," he drew the ire of federal sports minister Iona Campagnolo.

Ballard informed Frum that, in his opinion, "Broads belong on their backs. You know what they're good for, don't you? You let them up once in a while to put on their shoes."

Campagnolo wasn't about to take Ballards' insults lying down.

"As a woman who is up on her feet in this House, I would like to say that I consider Mr. Ballard's remarks to be a disgrace to all women in Canada."

Frum responded to Ballard with a letter. "We know that you had a very gruelling weekend. Staunch Maple Leaf fans were baying for your blood and your players did not exactly concur with your executive decision (to fire coach Roger Neilson). It's not easy for a man of your stature to admit defeat before the carping critics of the press. So when we talked … you were under great strain. We understand. There's no hard feelings."

She signed it "your favourite BROAD-caster."

When Ballard didn't respond to Frum's letter or Campagnolo's admonishment, Frum sent a second letter but for one of the few times in his life, Ballard remained silent.

Fellow CBC broadcaster Peter Gzowski ran across Ballard at a charity event a short time later. He was filling in for Frum as guest host of "As It Happens" and asked Ballard if he'd be willing to guest on the show and discuss the role of women in society.

"You can go f**k yourself," was Ballard's response.

SITTLER'S C OF TROUBLE

In his first tenure as coach and general manager of the Toronto Maple Leafs from 1958–69, Punch Imlach knew only one captain, George Armstrong.

When he began his second tenure as GM of the Leafs in 1979, it became quickly apparent that Imlach and captain Darryl Sittler didn't see eye to eye.

Right off the bat, there was trouble when the Leafs sued Sittler and Toronto goalie Mike Palmateer in a bid to prevent them from participating in *Hockey Night In Canada*'s "Showdown" program, a shootout and skills competition featuring NHL players.

Their feud came to a head in late December: a day after Imlach dealt Sittler's best friend Lanny McDonald to the lowly Colorado Rockies, Sittler tendered his resignation as captain of the Leafs on December 29, 1979.

"I told my teammates and my coach before the game that I was resigning as captain of the Toronto Maple Leafs," said Sittler in a typed prepared statement he handed out to the media following Toronto's 6–1 win over the Winnipeg Jets.

"When I was made captain, it was the happiest day of my life. I have tried to handle my duties as captain in an honest and fair manner. I took player complaints to management, and discussed management ideas with players.

"At the start of this season I was personally sued by my own hockey team management. I was told it was nothing personal. I explained my position to Mr. Imlach and (team owner Harold) Ballard at that time. I told them that I felt that a captain's role was to work with players and management, not just management.

"Mr. Ballard and Mr. Imlach made some negative comments about me and my teammates some weeks ago and I met with them to discuss it. I was told I was being too sensitive.

"I had had little or no contact with Mr. Imlach and it is clear to me that he and I have different ideas about player and management communication.

"I have recently been told that management has prevented me from appearing on *Hockey Night In Canada* telecasts.

"I am spending more and more time on player-management problems and I don't feel I am accomplishing enough for my teammates.

"The war between Mr. Imlach and (NHLPA executive director Alan) Eagleson should not overshadow the main issue—the Toronto Maple Leafs.

"I am totally loyal to the Toronto Maple Leafs. I don't want to let my teammates down. But I have to be honest with myself. I will continue to fight for players' rights, but not as captain of the team. All I want to do is give all my energy and all my ability to my team as a player."

McDonald, who was making his debut for the Rockies while Sittler was stepping down as captain of the Leafs, let go with an emotional outburst when informed of Sittler's actions.

"I am one of the fortunate ones," McDonald told *Canadian Press*. "I've been given a second chance. The Leafs are a very disorganized, disgruntled team that is going nowhere because there is no communication between the players and management and even between management and management. I feel sorry for (the players).

"I blame Mr. Imlach and I am very sad that Mr. Ballard gave him total control. It's too bad that personal feelings against myself, Mr. Eagleson and Mr. Sittler entered into it. It's sad to see a team that had so much heart go through this."

Ballard countered by lambasting Sittler, calling him "treasonous and a cancer to the team." But that fall, with GM Imlach hospitalized due to heart problems, Ballard ended his feud with Sittler, who agreed to return as captain.

"It's the happiest day of my life," Ballard claimed, taking back all of his previous harsh words for Sittler.

But much like that of Richard Burton and Elizabeth Taylor, this second honeymoon didn't last long. By November of 1981, Sittler was demanding to be traded, offering up the Minnesota North Stars and Philadelphia Flyers as destinations of which he would approve.

On January 20, 1982, Sittler's wish was granted and he was dealt to the Flyers for Rich Costello, Ken Strong, and a 1982 second round draft pick that would prove to be future Leaf Peter Ihnacak.

"I am not proud of having to leave the team like this," Sittler told *UPI*. "It would have been very nice to have retired a Maple Leaf.

"It's a sad day to leave a team you have been with your entire career. I should not be surprised at leaving like this though. I have seen it before and I have seen it happen to other Leafs."

When the end came, the normally combative and cantankerous Ballard chose to take the high road.

"I'm glad for Sittler, I'm glad for the Leafs and I'm glad as hell it's over," Ballard said. "Sittler has had a great career and I wish him success with his new team."

In 1991, one year after Ballard's death, Sittler returned to the Leafs as a consultant to GM Cliff Fletcher. He continues to work for the team as a roving goodwill ambassador.

TO RUSSIA, WITHOUT LOVE

In 1983, when a Soviet jet shot down a Korean passenger airliner, Leafs' owner Harold Ballard vowed no Russian team would ever again play hockey at Maple Leaf Gardens.

He eventually relented, but never forgot. On January 4, 1985, as the Moscow Dynamo battled the Canadian national team at Maple Leaf Gardens, Ballard ordered the following message be flashed across the scoreboard during a break in play:

"Remember Korean Airlines flight 007 shot down by the Russians. Don't cheer, just boo." It was signed, "Harold."

"I've never had much use in my life for people who are constantly on the take without returning at least their share," Ballard told the *Montreal Gazette*, explaining his dislike for the Soviets. "They come over here and take our money, our sticks, skates, practice jerseys and anything in sight."

Curiously, Ballard was a fan of Vladimir Lenin, one of the leaders of the 1917 Russian revolution. He even displayed a bust of Lenin in his office at the Gardens.

"People say he was a son of a bitch, but if you read Russian history and find out how poor the peasants were, you have to think that Lenin and (Karl) Marx had some good ideas," Ballard said.

A PERFECT 10

No NHL team had ever opened a season with 10 straight wins. The Leafs hadn't won a game at Chicago Stadium in 13 years.

In one night, both of those situations changed.

Paced by two long-suffering Leafs—Wendel Clark with two goals and Todd Gill with a pair of assists—the Leafs doubled the

Blackhawks 4–2 to improve to 10–0 on the season and to win in Chicago for the first time since December 22, 1989.

"Ten in a row. Wow. That's going to be a tough one to beat," Leafs winger Glenn Anderson told the *Toronto Star*. "I'm just speaking for myself, but there's no way I thought this team could get off to a start like this.

"It's all heart, desire and dedication that's getting us through, because the talent we have is nowhere near what some other teams have."

For those who were long-time members of the Leafs organization, the reason for the shock turnaround in the team's fortunes—the Leafs had reached the Stanley Cup final four in the spring of 1993 for the first time since 1978—was because Harold Ballard was no longer running the team.

"I hate to say it, because I always considered Harold Ballard to be a friend of mine for whom I played on the Toronto Marlboros team, but he did the Leafs a lot of harm," former Maple Leaf Gardens' president Paul Mara told George Gross of the *Toronto Sun*. "Over the years he was responsible for them, the Leafs swayed from what they used to be—a class act.

"The basic problem of those unhappy years was at the top. After Harold departed the scene, the new ownership was determined to bring top hockey men back to the organization as managers and coaches."

New owner Steve Stavro brought in Stanley Cup winner Cliff Fletcher to serve as Leafs' GM and Fletcher hired Pat Burns, who'd guided the Montreal Canadiens to the 1989 Stanley Cup final, to be his coach.

Deals added the likes of Doug Gilmour and Dave Andreychuk and the draft brought in goalie Felix Potvin, who made 46 saves in their 10th win in a row.

"Steve Stavro realized what had to be done to bring back pride into the organization," Mara said. "He instilled quickly the much needed esprit de corps by bringing back old players and executives, hanging up banners demonstrating the glorious past of the club and recreating the Maple Leaf family spirit as we once knew it."

Minus Ballard, the Leafs were a perfect ten.

THE LEAFS YOU SHOULD KNOW

Some of the more fascinating, intriguing and unusual players who've worn the blue and white.

APPS THE BEST EVER

Forget about Howie Morenz. According to no less a source than Detroit Red Wings' coach Jack Adams, the greatest NHL player he'd ever seen was Leafs' centre Syl Apps.

Adams made this revelation to the *Winnipeg Tribune* in 1939.

"He's the best player who ever had skates on," Adams said. "Syl Apps is a greater hockey player than Howie Morenz ever was."

Adams cited Apps for his terrific speed, an uncanny ability to follow the puck, and an unfailing sense of opportunism.

Two years earlier, Canadian sportswriters agreed with Adams, selecting Apps as the Canadian athlete of the year.

The 1936–37 season was his first NHL campaign and skating on a line with Busher Jackson and Gordie Drillon, Apps posted 45 points for the Leafs to win the Calder Trophy as the league's top rookie and finish one point behind NHL scoring champion Sweeney Schriner of the New York Americans. But Apps was more than a hockey player.

At Hamilton's McMaster University, he starred in hockey, football, and track and field. In 1934, Apps was British Empire Games pole vault champion and earned the right to represent Canada at the 1936 Summer Games in Berlin when he won the Canadian Olympic trials with a vault of 13 feet, ½ inch. Apps just missed at 13 feet, four inches in a bid to better Vic Pickering's Canadian mark of 13 feet, 5/8 inches.

He finished sixth in the pole vault at the Summer Olympics.

THE STANOWSKI SPINORAMA

When Wally Stanowski skated with the puck, hockey people compared him to Eddie Shore.

When Stanowski skated without the puck, people compared him to Dick Button.

A remarkably powerful yet elegant skater, Stanowski wowed everyone when he turned up for Leafs' camp in 1939 at the age of 20.

"He can't be kept out of line-up this year," Leafs managing director Conn Smythe proclaimed to the *Winnipeg Tribune*.

Stanowski wondered what all the fuss was about.

"I just grew up skating like that," Stanowski said. "That's the only way I know how to skate."

Boston Bruins' coach Cooney Weiland viewed Stanowski's stylish forays with the puck from his defensive position as what was to come in hockey. "He's full of colour, a wonderful rusher," Weiland said. "The model that young defenceman of the future will copy."

Handed the handle "the Whirling Dervish," Stanowski was known for his puck-carrying abilities and for the stylish threads he wore off the ice.

"All I want to do is play hockey and wear nice clothes," Stanowski explained.

He may also be the only player in NHL history to be benched for having sex with his wife. Stanowski's wife Joyce joined him at the hotel on the last day of Leafs' training camp in 1946, a no-no in the eyes of Leafs managing director Conn Smythe, so Stanowski rode the pine as the 1946–47 season got underway.

His stylish skating was the product of a youth spent participating in figure skating as well as hockey, as a stunned Boston Garden crowd found out the night of October 23, 1946.

Midway through the second period, Leafs' forward Bud Poile swung wildly at a loose puck near the Boston net. He missed the puck but the blade of his stick struck Bruins' goalie Frank Brimsek near the left eye.

Four stitches were required to mend Brimsek's wounds and with no back-up goalie on hand, the game was held up while Frankie was sewn up.

Leafs' coach Hap Day told Stanowski, who hadn't seen any ice time at all up to that point, to get out there and loosen up.

While doing so, Stanowski also decided to loosen up the crowd.

"I was embarrassed," Stanowski recounted to the Toronto Star. "So I just skated in front of the bench a little."

Day hollered at his defenceman to get out there and really get a good skate in during the delay.

Stanowski pushed off and glided to the centre ice faceoff circle, launching into a fabulous display of figure skating. The Garden organist launched into musical accompaniment and the crowd began rhythmically clapping along as Stanowski displayed his Salchow and Axel expertise during his free skate program.

"I could see Smythe sitting there (in the stands), mad as hell," Stanowski said. "But the crowd loved it. I skated back to the bench, backwards on one skate, with the other foot up behind me. My leg touched the boards so I knew I was there.

"When I turned around to look for Hap, I couldn't see him. He had his head below the boards. He was laughing like hell but he didn't want Smythe to see him."

THIS LEAF DECIDED THERE WAS MORE FOR LES

Reverend Les Costello was laughing uproariously as he relayed a story to writer Andy O'Brien about a letter he'd received from a fan in 1973.

"I watched you help score four playoff goals when the Toronto Maple Leafs won the Stanley Cup in 1948," the letter writer explained. "The way you were working left wing tonight showed you might still have been doing well in pro hockey.

"What made you go wrong?"

"Wrong?" Costello wrote to his interrogator. "You, sir, must either be a non-Catholic, or a non-enthusiastic Catholic, in which case you'll be surprised to learn that a stalwart Protestant inspired me to swap the Leafs for liturgy. His name was Conn Smythe.

"Mr. Smythe constantly impressed upon us the scriptural teaching that it's more blessed to give than to receive. He inspired me to extend his belief to the sinful world beyond the National Hockey League."

In May 1950, he told his brother, fellow NHLer Murray Costello, that he was leaving the game to enter the priesthood.

"He skated away from fame to seek another type of fame in his own way, in his own style," Murray Costello said.

Ordained as a priest in 1957, five years later Les Costello founded the Flying Fathers, a hockey-playing version of the Harlem Globetrotters. And he was their Meadowlark Lemon.

"He loved the Flying Fathers," Murray Costello said. "He knew they were special people with sterling characters."

The Flying Fathers traversed the world, raising more than $4 million for charity. In 1970, when the Department of National Defence flew the Fathers to Germany to play a series of games against Canadian Armed Forces' teams, they made a side trip to the Vatican to meet with Pope Paul VI. Presenting him with an autographed stick signed by all of the hockey-playing priests during their Papal visit, the Pope promptly held it upside down.

"When His Holiness seemed puzzled about how to hold the stick, I showed him how, adding that it could also be used to stir a big pot of spaghetti," Costello laughed.

As a player, Costello won two Memorial Cup titles with Toronto St. Michael's to go with his 1948 Stanley Cup, before he answered his higher calling.

"I never regretted my decision," Costello told writer Tom Hawthorn. "I've been playing hockey all my life anyways, and not only that but I've had the opportunity of dealing with people in the schools, in the jails, burying the ones that are deceased, baptizing, marrying..."

Costello served as organizer of the Flying Fathers as well, entitling him to fringe benefits.

"I stand in front of the net and if the young guys don't pass to me, I bench them," Costello joked.

Costello was still leading the Flying Fathers when during a 2002 game in Kincardine, Ontario he fell and struck his head on the ice.

Admitted to hospital, Costello slipped into a coma and died December 10, 2002, at the age of 74.

BASHING BILL

He is remembered romantically for the most famous Stanley Cup-winning goal in Leafs' history, and recalled tragically because his death in a plane crash that summer would ensure it was also his last goal.

A falling, gleeful Bill Barilko, caught forever in that position by the photographer's lens a split second after his one-timer found the Montreal Canadiens' net behind goalie Gerry McNeil in overtime of Game 5 of the 1951 Cup final to give the Leafs the title, is the image maintained of the man by the masses.

What isn't recalled is how close Barilko came to not being there at all for his magical moment.

Bashing Bill, as he was known, often found himself in the doghouse of Leafs' coach Joe Primeau, GM Hap Day, and managing director Conn Smythe.

His style of play was often described as crude and Barilko was roundly criticized early in the 1950–51 season for a punishing hit into the boards that fractured the collarbone of New York Rangers' forward Jackie McLeod. Barilko hit McLeod from behind with just ten seconds remaining in the game.

Two years earlier, another Barilko hit severed the Achilles tendon of Boston's Ed Sandford. The same season, one of his checks separated the shoulder of Montreal's Ken Reardon.

The husky Leaf rearguard thrived on dishing out punishment. "I get a bang out of it," Barilko told *Canadian Press*. "You can feel it when it's a good one.

"There aren't too many trying to go through centre on me now. That cuts down on their chances. Makes me look good."

For that reason alone, Barilko saw no reason to change his game. "Why?" he asked. "What else can I do to stay up in the big league? I'm not much of a skater, not much of a stickhandler, not much of a scorer.

"I have to be good for something or else I'm back in the leaky roof."

Barilko led the NHL in penalty minutes with 147 in 1947–48. "I don't mind getting a penalty when I have it coming," Barilko said. "Now I think the referees are watching me too closely and are giving me chippy penalties.

"That's the only trouble about being the league's badman. That won't stop me, though."

The Leafs tried to stop Barilko. On several occasions they benched him due to his penchant for committing costly infractions.

In fact, just a couple of weeks before his historic tally, there was strong speculation that the Leafs had grown weary of Barilko and *Montreal Herald* sports editor Elmer Ferguson reported that he would be traded to the Habs after the season.

"I don't admire his methods, but I'd rather have him on our side than against," Canadiens' GM Frank Selke told Ferguson.

Then the playoffs began and Barilko seemed to find another level of play. He was outstanding in Toronto's semi-final win over the Bruins.

"Barilko was just about their best man in the series and he didn't do a thing against us all season," Boston coach Lynn Patrick told the *Montreal Gazette*. "We'd hardly noticed him."

In the final series, Barilko scored the biggest goal of the season and the last goal of his life and ensured that he would be remembered forever.

PORTRAIT OF A LEAF

The official NHL statistics show that Dick Gamble played three games as a Leaf.

He scored a power-play goal in his Toronto debut on March 7, 1966, in a 5–3 win over the Bruins at Boston. It was Gamble's first NHL goal since November 4, 1954, when he was a member of the Chicago Blackhawks and scored on Gump Worsley of the New York Rangers.

Gamble played one more game for the Leafs that season and another during the 1966–67 campaign and that was it for his NHL career, but he continued to play for the Leafs for years in households across Canada.

Every Canadian youngster from the 1950s through the 1970s knows that nobody scored more goals or played more games in a Leaf uniform than Gamble.

There were few households across the country in those days that didn't own a table hockey game, and the most popular brand was produced by the Montreal-based Eagle Toy Company, featuring the Leafs playing the Canadiens, with smiling metal players outfitted in Montreal red and Toronto blue uniforms.

That smiling face belonged to Dick Gamble.

In 1954, Ben Stein, owner of the Eagle Toy Company, approached Canadiens vice-president Ken Reardon to learn how to acquire an NHL license for his table hockey game. The Canadiens were the first NHL team to sign on in 1954 and the following season, the Leafs came on board.

Stein's next mission was to design his players. He poured through photos of all the Montreal players and settled on Gamble, at the time a Habs forward. When the Leafs signed on, Stein simply took Gamble's likeness and lightened the hair colour for the Toronto players.

So you could say that Gamble actually played for the Leafs 11 years before he actually played for the Leafs.

TEEDER'S ILL-FATED COMEBACK

Riddled with injuries, mired in fifth place, the Leafs turned to one of their living legends to help resurrect their 1956–57 season.

They lured former captain and Hart Trophy winner Teeder Kennedy out of retirement.

"If I can help get Leafs going I'll be only too happy to do so," Kennedy told *Canadian Press*. "I don't expect any favours. If I'm convinced I'm able, I'll play wherever they think they can use me."

Kennedy scored a club-record 225 goals over 12 seasons, seven of them as Leafs' captain. He won five Stanley Cups and originally planned to retire following the 1953–54 season, but was lured back with a $17,000 contract, at the time the highest single-season pact in Leafs' history, and Kennedy won the Hart Trophy as NHL MVP that season.

Several times after his retirement Leafs' GM Hap Day sought to lure Kennedy back into the fold. Kennedy finally took him up on his offer, showing up unannounced for a November 27, 1956 practice.

"Kennedy is bound to help our team," Day said.

"I think Kennedy's biggest contribution will be with the kids," Leaf coach Howie Meeker said.

Kennedy worked hard to drop his weight from 206 to 185 pounds. "This club might still start to go without any help. If it does, I might forget all about a comeback," Kennedy said. "But if I get back into action and the team starts to click, I'm certainly going to stay with it."

Kennedy made his return to game action January 6, 1957, in a 2–1 loss at Detroit. He produced 22 points in 30 games, but it wasn't enough.

The Leafs came up nine points short in pursuit of a playoff spot and Kennedy retired for good at the end of the season.

OFF THE MARC

Marc Reaume didn't ask to be the answer to a trivia question. He didn't seek out a trade.

Reaume was the other player in one of hockey's most famous trades. On February 10, 1960, the Leafs dealt Reaume, then a 26-year-old defenceman, to the Detroit Red Wings for future Hall-of-Famer Red Kelly. Leafs' coach Punch Imlach switched Norris Trophy winner Kelly to centre and Toronto won four Stanley Cups with him in their line-up.

Fortune did not smile in the same manner on Reaume.

While Kelly played a starring role as the Leafs eliminated the Wings during the 1960 Stanley Cup semi-final, Reaume sat out the series due to a shoulder injury.

"I was ready to play but injuries started to happen as soon as I got to Detroit," Reaume said. "Little small injuries that prevented me from playing properly."

Reaume played just 47 games as a Red Wing.

"The writing is pro Red Kelly and I can certainly see it," Reaume said of historical accounts of the deal. "The man played fantastic hockey."

Maybe he wasn't a superstar, but Reaume was talented enough to play 317 games in the six-team NHL and lists significant hockey firsts on his resume.

An original Vancouver Canuck in 1970–71, thanks to a three-game stint with the Montreal Canadiens in 1963–64, Reaume became the first to skate with what then were all three of Canada's NHL clubs.

The Leafs originally found Reaume, or should we say divine intervention led him to Toronto.

Playing for Windsor's Assumption College, Reaume caught the eye of Rev. Ronald Cullen, who contacted his counterparts at Toronto St. Michael's, where the Leafs operated a junior club.

"The Basilian priests were running both schools," Reaume explained. "He said, 'I've got a boy down here who shows some promise, would you give him some schooling?' That's how it turned out that I went to Toronto."

In those days, it would appear that the Leafs had God on their side.

Reaume made his NHL debut with the Leafs during the 1954–55 season.

To Reaume, the funniest part of the Kelly trade is that both men share a bond. "He's an old St. Michael's boy and of course we always stick together," Reaume laughed.

Some might think of him merely as the answer to a famous trivia question, but Reaume is amazed at how often people recall him as an NHLer.

"So many people still send me (hockey) cards in the mail," he said. "I still get a couple every week, 30 years after playing professional hockey.

"It's nice to be remembered."

VIENNA CALLING

At first, the Leafs didn't want Larry Regan. When they did finally get him, he helped them make back-to-back runs to the Stanley Cup final.

So when Regan wanted to go, the Leafs weren't about to let him.

After playing with the Toronto Marlboros, the Leafs' OHA junior affiliate, Regan wasn't signed by the team.

"The boss doesn't like him," Toronto scout Squib Walker explained, referring to Leafs' managing director Conn Smythe.

Unwanted, Regan bounced around the minor leagues for six years, playing for five teams in four different leagues.

Acquired by the Boston Bruins in 1956, Regan put up 14–19–33 totals in 1956–57 and won the Calder Trophy. But he soon fell out of favour in Beantown and was claimed on waivers by the Leafs midway through the 1958–59 season. New Leafs' coach-GM Punch Imlach coached Regan in Quebec and, unlike Smythe, was a fan of his work.

After helping the Leafs to reach consecutive Stanley Cup finals, Regan ended up as player-coach with the AHL Pittsburgh Hornets in 1961–62.

From there, he shocked everyone, signing to be player-coach of Innsbrucker EV of the Austrian League, among the first NHLers to go play in Europe.

It was a move that didn't sit well with the Leafs, who insisted they still owned his rights. The NHL would not release Regan and he was ordered to return to Canada by International Ice Hockey Federation president Bunny Ahearne, who labelled Regan a pro and ineligible to play in Europe.

Regan filed a $50,000 lawsuit against the NHL and the Pittsburgh club and was granted permission to return to Austria, where he worked for three years.

"It was really appealing to me," Regan told the *Ottawa Journal* of his Austrian experience. "I found the fans very enthusiastic and very appreciative of any sharp stickhandling."

In 1965, Regan planned a hockey clinic to run 16–18 days in Innsbruck and featuring NHLers Gordie Howe, Terry Sawchuk, Marcel Pronovost, Alex Delvecchio, Tim Horton, and Ron Stewart.

While the plan received NHL endorsement, it didn't sit well with Ahearne, who feared the presence of all these pros in Europe could lead to some sort of barnstorming tour across Europe featuring some of the world's best players and threatened an IIHF ban on any rink that hosted Regan's school.

"I guess it's understandable," NHL president Clarence Campbell said. "Ahearne isn't anxious for Europeans to see what real hockey is all about."

Regan admitted that the Austrian people found it hard to believe that someone with his skill level wasn't still performing for the Leafs.

"Naturally the number of good hockey players by Canadian standards is restricted in that European territory," Regan said. "I used to point out that there were 150 hockey players in Canada better than me and truthfully they found this hard to believe."

Regan thrived in Austria, insisting the hockey was more conducive to his type of game, which was skating and stickhandling with less emphasis on physical punishment.

"The rules were hand-made for me because it offered a lot more freedom to stickhandle," he said. "And they really liked that part of my play."

THE KEON THE LEAFS

At 5'9" and 163 pounds soaking wet, Dave Keon hardly struck an imposing figure. Yet perhaps no player in the history of the Leafs imposed his will on the game as effectively or as consistently as Keon.

Joining the Leafs straight out of the junior ranks in 1960, Keon scored 20 goals in each of his first six seasons, something no Toronto player had ever done before.

"Give me a whole team of Keons and the rest of the league wouldn't have a chance," Leafs' coach Punch Imlach told writer Andy O'Brien in 1967.

It wasn't Keon's offence that made him a star as much as it was his 200-foot game. Had there been a Selke Trophy for the best defensive forward in Keon's day, he'd have been a frequent winner.

"Dave never quits on a play," Imlach explained. "If somebody takes the puck from him he goes right after the guy and gets it back."

On the big stage, Keon loomed large, even if his stature was diminutive. He accounted for all of Toronto's goals as the Leafs beat Montreal 3–1 in Game 7 of their 1964 Stanley Cup semi-final series at the Forum. His tenacious penalty killing and checking work against the Habs during the 1967 final earned Keon the Conn Smythe Trophy as playoff MVP.

Keon felt his lack of size made him a better all-around player because it forced him to always use his brain as opposed to relying on his brawn.

"Sure, there are times I'd give a lot for more weight," Keon once explained. "Sure, I'd love more weight for those scrambles around the goal-mouths. Sure, I'd often like to plow through the defence instead of trying to circle unscathed, but having to think my way conceivably gives me an edge over big players who rely over much on their size."

As far as Toronto fans were concerned, Keon might have been the littlest Leaf, but when it mattered most, no Leaf stood taller.

HE SHOOTS ... HE SPELLS

He was called colourful, a loafer, both fearless and careless.

Eddie Shack was all that and more. He wasn't the best Leaf who played for all four of the club's Stanley Cup winners during the 1960s, just the most popular one.

No one got longer and more passionate ovations from the Maple Leaf Gardens faithful than Shack.

"I just toss him out there and confuse them a little," Leafs' coach Punch Imlach said of Shack, who could best be described as a free-lancer on the ice. He was listed as a left-winger but Shack swooped all over the rink. He was just as likely to flatten a teammate as check an opponent.

Joining the Leafs in 1960 via a trade with the New York Rangers, Shack made instant waves. He laid out Detroit's Gordie Howe, the NHL's best player, cutting Mr. Hockey for 12 stitches and leaving him concussed.

And Shack didn't stop there, classifying Howe as a dirty player.

"He'll give you the stick," Shack said. "He'll cut you open with it."

Not that Shack was afraid of Howe's legendary policy of exacting revenge on anyone who got the better of him on the ice.

"I can take care of myself," Shack said. "Don't worry about that.

"I think Howe will be wary of me now, because when I go, I go all out."

All this talk didn't sit well with Detroit GM Jack Adams, who took a jab at Shack's limited education. Shack was illiterate.

"You should learn to read and write," Adams bellowed at Shack during the first period of a November 11, 1961 game at Maple Leaf Gardens.

The score was tied 1–1 at the time and Shack tallied to give the Leafs the lead, the eventual game winner in a 5–1 Toronto victory.

Skating by the Detroit bench, Shack stopped abruptly and locked his gaze on Adams.

"S-C-O-R-E," Shack spelled out.

Such antics caused hockey people to bristle at the mere mention of Shack's name. "He's just a clown who doesn't belong in the league," Montreal Canadiens' coach Toe Blake said.

That wasn't the case at all.

They called him The Entertainer and the clown prince of hockey—there was even a song, "Clear The Track, Here Comes Shack," written about him—but to suggest Shack couldn't play is pure fallacy.

"There wasn't a stronger forward in the league than Eddie," former Leafs teammate Bert Olmstead once said.

Shack connected for double digits in goals in five of his nine seasons as a Leaf, including a 26-goal campaign in 1965–66. And he was always willing to stick up for his teammates, ever ready to tangle with the other team's tough guy.

"He's a good hockey player when he's not trying to be a clown," suggested no less a source than Canadiens' legend Maurice (Rocket) Richard. "He's big and strong and when he doesn't get silly, he can help that Toronto team."

THE MIGHTY HERCULES HORTON

There's a line in *Pride Of The Yankees*, the 1942 film about New York Yankees' legend Lou Gehrig, who played 2,130 consecutive games before succumbing to ALS, where actor Gary Cooper, portraying Gehrig, is asked, "What do we have to do? Kill you to get you out of the line-up?"

Tragically, that's what it took to end the NHL career of legendary Leafs' defenceman Tim Horton.

Horton was killed when he crashed his Italian sports car on the Queen Elizabeth Way en route to Buffalo February 21, 1974, just hours after he played his 1,446th NHL game for the Sabres against Toronto.

Horton was 44 and in his 22nd NHL campaign when he died. A Leaf from 1949–70, he won four Stanley Cups with the team during a Hall-of-Fame career, and for his feats of strength, was compared to the mythical figure of Hercules, the Greek strongman.

Horton's last defensive pairing in Buffalo was with Jim Schoenfeld.

"Tim was going to give you all he had as a partner, a teammate and a friend," Schoenfeld said. "He played hard. He worked hard. He partied hard. He was a guy that lived life to the fullest and left nothing on the table."

Horton assembled an impressive resume as an entrepreneur, turning doughnuts into dollars.

Horton's name has become synonymous with baked goods and hot beverages, making him famous to a generation that never saw him play.

To many the name Tim Horton means nothing more than a honey-glazed and a large double-double.

Fellow Hall-of-Famer and former Leafs' defenceman Larry Murphy, who broke Horton's NHL record for games played by a defenceman, was fond of both the Leafs and Horton.

"I was a diehard Leaf fan as a kid," Murphy recalled. "I remember when the Leafs won the Stanley Cup in 1967. I knew everybody on the team. I remember Tim Horton well off that team."

Horton's teammates remember his steadfastness and reliability most of all.

"Steady. I never knew a player so steady," Frank Mahovlich said of Horton. "No flash. No polish. All hard work."

Horton never had his name inscribed on the Norris Trophy as the NHL's best defenceman, although he was a losing finalist in 1964 and again in 1969.

"He was the strongest-skating defenceman in hockey, and one of the cleanest players I ever saw," former Montreal Canadiens' GM Sam Pollock told *Canadian Press*. "The kind of guy everybody wanted on his team."

For 32 years, Horton held the Toronto playoff record for points by a defenceman in one playoff campaign, garnering 3–13–16 numbers during Toronto's run to the 1961–62 Stanley Cup—at the time it was also an NHL mark—but the ever-modest Horton, who had a uncanny knack for knowing when to join the rush without getting caught up ice, downplayed the accomplishment.

"Points are funny," Horton said. "Either they're going in for you or they're not.

"When they're going for you, you get a lot."

Horton's durability allowed him to play a Leafs record 468 consecutive games from February 11, 1961, to February 4, 1968, the NHL mark for defencemen until 2007 when it was surpassed by Karlis Skrastins of the Colorado Avalanche.

"Horton was a tremendous competitor, a great person," former Leafs' coach King Clancy recalled to *Canadian Press*. "Nothing was too much, no task too great. There were no ifs, ands or buts. He did the job, injured or not."

It was Horton's brute strength which separated him most of his NHL brethren. "He was the strongest man I've ever met and it was all natural," said Don Rope, a two-time Canadian Olympian who roomed with Horton in junior with Toronto St. Michael's.

"Every night before bed, he'd go to the sill over the door and do 500 chin-ups. Then he'd do 500 finger-tip push- ups."

Rope recalled one night in the dorms at St. Mike's when the players opted to empty the furniture out of the common room for an impromptu game of ball hockey.

"Tim was carrying desks out all by himself," Rope said.

Even into his 40s, Horton was still operating like a bull in a china shop.

"He was built like Hercules and did everything to the fullest degree," Schoenfeld said. "There was an expression he taught me—the hard way is the easy way.

"I didn't understand it at the time. But over the years, the more I thought about it, the more I realized what he meant, the more it made sense."

THE SWEDE VS. THE MEATBALLS

In Toronto they called him in the king. In all the other NHL rinks they sought to crown him.

When Borje Salming arrived from Sweden to play defence for the Leafs in 1973, every other NHL team followed the same game plan—rough up the European, they thought, and he'll head for the first flight home.

Worst offenders of all were the Philadelphia Flyers. Salming arrived at the dawn of the Broad Street Bullies era and his second game was at the Philadelphia Spectrum, where the Flyers committed every sort of hockey atrocity on the books against him, and he ended up in a slashing-fighting duel with the toughest Flyer of the all, Dave (The Hammer) Schultz.

"If they did some of those things today, they would be suspended for life," Salming said. "They really tried to kill you."

In the 1976 Stanley Cup quarter-final series between the two teams, Flyers' forward Mel Bridgman was charged with assault causing bodily harm for pummelling Salming in a fight.

"Swedes don't know how to fight," Salming explained. "In Canada kids are brought up fighting. In Sweden, never."

Enduring through the abuse, Salming rose to become what former Leafs' captain George Armstrong described as "the most talented player ever to wear the Toronto Maple Leaf uniform."

When the first Canada Cup was held in 1976 and Canada played Sweden at Maple Leaf Gardens, Salming was afforded the longest ovation of any player on either team during the pre-game introductions, and that didn't sit well with some Canadian players.

"They stand up and cheer some bleeping Swede for three minutes and they give the Canadian players hardly nothing," complained

Montreal Canadiens' centre Peter Mahovlich to *Canadian Press*. "What kind of bleeping fans do we have in Canada anyway?"

In Toronto, they were fans who appreciated a great player no matter where he came from.

"Borje is a living legend in Canada and Toronto, but he's even bigger in Sweden," former Leafs' captain and fellow Swede Mats Sundin said.

Salming played 16 seasons with the Leafs. He holds the NHL record for most points by a defenceman (787) who wasn't selected in the NHL entry draft and is the Leafs' all-time leader in assists (620) and plus-minus (181). His 148 goals and 768 points are records for a Toronto defender.

IT WASN'T HAMMAR TIME

As much as Borje Salming opened the doors to Europeans in the NHL, Inge Hammarstrom only served to reinforce the stereotypes some North American hockey people held of the "Chicken Swede."

Even though he was a three-time 20-goal scorer as a Leaf, the six-foot, 180-pound left-winger never grew comfortable playing the NHL brand of game.

"The biggest problem for me was the ice surface was so much smaller," Hammarstrom explained to United Press International. "Everything happened so much faster.

"But the biggest difference was the checking. They hit you most of the time."

Bombastic Leafs' owner Harold Ballard lashed out at Hammarstrom's unwillingness to mix it up. "You could send Hammarstrom into the corner with six eggs in his pocket and he wouldn't break any of them," Ballard said of his Swedish winger.

The blast led to Hammarstrom being hung with the nickname "Inge Omelette" and the tag stuck with him no matter how much he worked to adapt to the North American game.

Hammarstrom made no apologies for the way he played hockey.

"My game is the one of skills we were taught in Sweden," Hammarstrom said. "We also were taught self-discipline.

"I hate to be roughed up and am tempted to drop my gloves and fight at times, but I do not believe that is the way the game should be played."

Hockey seemed to embrace Hammarstrom's way of thinking as time passed and for nearly two decades he served as European scout for the Philadelphia Flyers, the same team that tormented him and Salming as players.

Among his many finds over the years was Peter Forsberg.

ELLIS SHARES HIS STRUGGLE

On the shelf in Ron Ellis's office, his two prized possessions sit side-by-side.

There's the miniature replica Stanley Cup he earned as a member of the 1966–67 Toronto Maple Leafs, the most recent Leafs' club to capture Lord Stanley's mug.

It represents his greatest accomplishment as a hockey player.

Right next to it rests the Courage To Come Back Award that Ellis received in 2000 from the Centre for Addiction and Mental Health.

It represents his greatest accomplishment of all—the battle Ellis waged and won to regain control of his life.

"I look at that award as a symbol of the work that I did to get back on my feet," said Ellis, diagnosed in 1986 with clinical depression.

He chronicled his battle in *Over the Boards*, the 2002 best-selling book he co-authored with writer Kevin Shea.

"It's certainly not something that happened overnight," Ellis said of his decision to not only go public with his own battle with depression and use his celebrity status to help get the message to the general public, but to say it's okay to admit having a problem, and it's essential to seek help.

"The information is out there today," Ellis said. "It certainly wasn't as accessible when I was first diagnosed. That's one of the reasons why I decided to speak out, to see if I could make others aware of the help that's out there and to connect them to the people who could supply the help they require."

More than three million Canadians are affected by depression. Knowing that Ellis, a man who lived the Canadian dream—playing for the Leafs and for Team Canada in the 1972 Summit Series—is afflicted by the illness, the message is that we are all susceptible.

"I've done appearances with Margaret Trudeau, who was the youngest first lady in Canadian history (when she was married to Prime Minister Pierre Trudeau)," Ellis said. "When people see someone like that admitting they suffer from depression, the message gets through that it could be anyone."

For Ellis, the diagnosis explained a lot. Leafs fans will recall that he walked away from the game for two years in the prime of his career in 1975.

"I was coming off my best season in the NHL," Ellis said. "I came to training camp in great shape and played in every pre-season game."

The desire to go on was gone, though.

"I remember turning to Brian Glennie, who was my roommate, and telling him: 'I'm going to retire tomorrow,'" Ellis said.

Ellis came back to the Leafs in 1977 and played until 1980. After leaving the game, his conditioned worsened.

"It got to the point where I couldn't even function at work," recalled Ellis, who today serves as director of public affairs for the Hockey Hall of Fame.

"With the support of my family, my friends and my employer, I was given the opportunity to get well and get back on my feet again."

Now, he seeks to do the same for others, a reward that keeps on giving.

SITTLER'S TEN-SPOT

It is the defining moment for a generation of Toronto Maple Leafs fans, as Darryl Sittler continues to discover whenever he's recognized in public.

Without a recent Stanley Cup memory to grasp, Leafs supporters hold the night of February 7, 1976, dear to their hearts.

The night that Sittler was a perfect ten.

"The number of people who tell me exactly where they were, what they were doing that night, it's staggering," said Sittler, the former Leafs' captain, of the game in which he registered an NHL-record ten points in an 11–4 win over the Boston Bruins.

"It was Saturday on *Hockey Night In Canada*—the Leafs were broadcast from coast to coast in those days—so there really was a nation watching."

The hockey landscape was much different in that era. The Ottawa Senators were a team that left the NHL in 1934. Calgary, Quebec, and Edmonton played in the WHA and, while pockets of left coasters worshipped at the altar of the Vancouver Canucks, the majority of Canadian NHL fans held vested interests in the Leafs or Montreal Canadiens.

It was a difficult time to be a Toronto fan. After winning four Stanley Cups between 1962–67, the Leafs had endured a nine-year drought without Lord Stanley's mug.

Meanwhile, the Habs won six Cups in that span and were about to launch a four-year run as champions.

Toronto supporters sought a reason to pump their fists skyward.

Sittler's sensational performance provided that moment.

It was a remarkable night with rather unremarkable beginnings. Sittler registered a pair of assists in the opening frame, then lit it up in the second period, scoring three times and setting up two other counters.

The captain knew he was on fire and the bean counters soon arrived to advise him that he was on the verge of breaking a long-standing record.

"Stan Obodiac, who handled publicity for the team, he came into the dressing room after the second period and told me the NHL record was eight points," Sittler recalled.

"That was the first I'd heard about it."

He equalled that mark early in the third period with a goal, and then broke it with a 40-foot wrist shot past unfortunate Boston goalie Dave Reece, who, as it turned out, was making his farewell NHL appearance.

"The last one was one of those things where you just know it's your night," Sittler said. "I threw the puck out from behind the net, it struck Boston defenceman Brad Park's leg and bounced in the net."

Sittler erased the 32-year-old mark established by Maurice Richard of the Canadiens in 1944 and equalled by the Habs' Bert Olmstead in 1954.

That his grip on the standard is 40 years and counting astonishes Sittler.

"The way they were scoring goals in the 1980s, I thought for sure that Wayne Gretzky or Mario Lemieux would better it," he said. Neither superstar produced more than eight points in a night, as have six others since Sittler put up his ten-spot.

These days, Sittler figures his figure is somewhat safe from assault.

"How often today do you see both teams combine for ten goals in a game?" he asks.

Those who bleed blue and white aren't the only ones who can recall each moment of Sittler's spectacular show.

"It's a game which has remained vivid in my mind," Sittler said.

As it has with all Leafs fans, Darryl.

TURNBULL TURNS IT ON

When Leafs' defenceman Ian Turnbull took to the ice February 2, 1977, for a game at Maple Leaf Gardens against the Detroit Red Wings, he'd gone 30 games without a goal since he scored the final tally of a 4–2 win over Boston on Bruins' goalie Gerry Cheevers.

An injury replacement for Darryl Sittler in the NHL All-Star Game one week earlier, Turnbull endured the embarrassment of playing a couple of early shifts and then being benched for the remainder of the game by Wales Conference coach Scotty Bowman.

"I don't care what he thinks of me for not playing him," Bowman said. "And I don't think the fans do, either."

Soon, Turnbull would have everyone in the NHL talking about him.

He scored five goals, a record for NHL defenceman that continues to stand today, as the Leafs drubbed the Wings 9–1.

Leafs' fans booed the team off the ice after a sluggish first period, but then Turnbull ignited. Just 1:55 into the second period, Turnbull took a pass from Lanny McDonald and rifled a 20-foot shot past Detroit goalie Ed Giacomin. He put one behind Giacomin on a breakaway midway through the frame.

In the third, he scored three more times on Jim Rutherford, who replaced Giacomin to start the period. Turnbull tallied on all five shots he took during the game.

"It had been a long drought," Turnbull admitted to *Canadian Press*. "Although I had just as many chances in the last 30 games and nothing happened.

"When they go in, you smile. When they don't, you try again."

The previous NHL record for goals in a game by a defenceman was four and was shared by four players, including former Toronto rearguards Hap Day, and Harry Cameron, who turned the feat twice.

TORONTO'S ALL-STAR BENCH JOCKEY

When former Leafs' defenceman Jim McKenny was invited to serve as honourary coach during the 2000 Ontario Hockey League All-Star Game, a thought immediately came to his mind.

"The first question I asked when they called was: 'Who cancelled?'" laughed McKenny, recalling the invitation from OHL president David Branch.

As a junior with the Toronto Marlboros, McKenny's offensive skills were compared with Bobby Orr.

It says so right there on the back of his 1971–72 O-Pee-Chee hockey card.

As a 14-season NHLer—13 of them with the Leafs—McKenny's play was often compared to iron ore by irate Leaf fans.

"People come up and tell me how great I played for the Leafs," McKenny said. "They forget the standing ovation boos I used to get."

It wasn't all bad.

McKenny skated in the 1974 NHL All-Star Game and had two 14-goal seasons, but it's his sense of humour which is deserving of Hall-of-Fame recognition.

"The only way you could have had more fun would have been if they had 26-hour days," McKenny said of his NHL time. "It was like having 20 of your best buddies together on a tour of North America, with an unlimited supply of cash."

Roger Neilson arrived as Leafs' coach in 1977 and didn't laugh at McKenny's minus-26 rating from 1976–77, shipping him to Dallas of the Central League.

"At first, I was mad but then I called to thank Roger," McKenny said. "I loved Dallas. I golfed every day. The only problem was I had to play. I hadn't done that in three years."

McKenny suggested he employed the pine more often than the hickory, once penning an article for *The Hockey News* extolling the virtues of being a bench jockey.

"Official NHL stats credit me with 184 games played completely on the bench," McKenny noted. "I used to tell the reporters: 'Catch me during the game when I've got some free time. I have to work in practice.'"

That ability to laugh at life's foibles helped McKenny make the transition to sports journalist, working for Toronto's CITY-TV for decades after he retired from the NHL in 1979.

His unique perspective from having been on both sides of the interview sometimes leaves McKenny wondering what's up with the modern athlete.

"Hockey players are still pretty much the same and the Toronto Argonauts are good guys," McKenny said. "Basketball is like pulling teeth—and baseball? I'd rather watch a guy fish than talk to them."

He blames sports talk radio and social media for the indifference of athletes towards the media.

"They're ruining it for everyone else," McKenny said. "They want these lengthy interviews so they can run them over and over again. They could do shorter interviews and write copy to fill the space between quotes like the rest of us do, but that would require work."

This former Marlie thinks Toronto fans are missing the boat by not watching more OHL games and fears today's juniors are missing out on the enjoyment the game gave him.

McKenny's sage advice to up-and-coming hockey stars?

"Forget about winning or losing, about your agents, about the scouts, and about the draft. Just have fun."

Spoken like a man who's learned how not to let life ruin his life.

WALT WAITED AWHILE

As a rookie with the Minnesota North Stars in 1967–68, centre Walt McKechnie appeared in nine Stanley Cup games, scoring three goals.

By the time he was acquired by the Leafs on Oct. 5, 1978, those were the only NHL playoff games on McKechnie's resume.

Naturally, McKechnie was an excited participant on April 10, 1979, as the Leafs prepared to open the Stanley Cup playoffs at Atlanta against the Flames.

The game is remembered for a second-period brawl that established six Stanley Cup records—most penalty minutes in a game (219) and against one team (115, Atlanta), and most penalties assessed in a game (35) and one team (19, Atlanta). The 181 second-period PIM and the 99 assessed to the Flames in that frame were also new marks.

Beyond the scrapping, McKechnie's big night was relatively overshadowed, even though he scored both goals in Toronto's 2–1 victory.

"That first goal (a shorthanded tally) was probably the best shot I ever made in hockey, my best shot in 12 years," McKechnie said.

It was also the first shot he'd put past a goaltender in a Stanley Cup game since May 3, 1968, a span of 3,993 days, but amazingly, McKechnie had tallied in the last two NHL playoff games he'd played. And he'd scored the last three goals his teams had tallied in Stanley Cup play, since his previous goal came for the North Stars in a 2–1 loss to the St. Louis Blues.

McKechnie's Leafs debut in 1978 came 15 years after the team had made him their first-round choice, sixth overall in the NHL's first-ever amateur draft on June 5, 1963. McKechnie never made it to the big club during his first stint as Toronto property and on Oct. 15, 1967, the Leafs traded him to the Phoenix Roadrunners of the Western Hockey League.

By 1980, McKechnie was no longer a Leaf but that was just par for the course for the NHL's travelling man. Between 1967–83, McKechnie made nine NHL stops—twice in Detroit with the Red Wings and also with the California Golden Seals, Boston Bruins, Washington Capitals, Colorado Rockies, and Cleveland Barons, as well as suiting up for the Leafs and North Stars. But after a six-game run with the 1978–79 Leafs, McKechnie would never again see action in a Stanley Cup game.

BASHING BILL, THE SEQUEL

Bill McCreary's only claim to fame might have been that he shared the same name with a Hall-of-Fame referee and original St. Louis Blues forward, if it weren't for his fateful meeting with Wayne Gretzky the night of January 3, 1981, at Edmonton's Northlands Coliseum.

In the third period of a game the Leafs would lose 4–1, Toronto forward McCreary caught the Great One himself, Oilers superstar Wayne Gretzky, with a thunderous body check at the Toronto blue line that left Gretzky on his back and briefly motionless.

"I meant to get out of the way," Gretzky told the *Edmonton Journal*.

The rest of the Oilers meant to get at McCreary. "It wasn't just me," remembered Oilers tough guy Dave Semenko. "Our whole team went after the guy."

McCreary wasn't surprised by the unfriendly reception. "When you hit a guy like him, I guess you're going to expect some questions from the other team," McCreary reasoned.

If the goal was to derail Gretzky, it didn't work. The Great One finished with a goal and two assists on the night.

"I've only been hit that hard once before," Gretzky said. "Jim Dorey hit me in almost the exact same spot, on almost an identical play, in my first year of pro.

"If I can keep it down to once every three years, I don't mind."

Over the years, a myth has been purported that McCreary never played another NHL game, that he was blackballed from the league for running Gretzky.

It isn't true. That game was McCreary's third in the NHL. He'd play another nine before the Leafs returned him to New Brunswick of the AHL.

Never to play in the NHL again, McCreary spent his final five seasons of pro with the IHL's Milwaukee Admirals. He put his down time to good use, attending the Milwaukee campus of the University of Wisconsin at night during the season and full-time in the summer and earned a business degree from the school.

THE BELLEVILLE TRIO

The Leafs were well positioned to restock their prospects cupboard when they arrived in Minnesota for the 1989 NHL entry draft.

For the first time since 1973, the Leafs owned three first-round picks.

They began their bonanza by taking Scott Thornton, a left-winger from the Ontario Hockey League's Belleville Bulls, with the third overall pick.

Nine picks later, the Leafs selected Rob Pearson, a right-winger with the Bulls, and eyebrows were raised. The strange looks changed to utter disbelief, when with the 21st pick, Toronto completed its Belleville trilogy, tabbing Bulls defenceman Steve Bancroft.

"We had high expectations for all three players but to have them go to the same team is a strange, amazing coincidence," Belleville coach-GM Dan Flynn said.

The players could only chuckle as they each donned the Leafs sweater at the podium.

"I guess the Leafs had a limited scouting budget, or there was a pretty good watering hole in Belleville," Thornton figured.

The Leafs actually figured they'd done quite well at the draft table.

"We asked ourselves if there was something wrong with doing this and said no," Toronto general manager Gord Stellick said. "We got a good feeling on all three and they're all thrilled to play in Toronto."

No one was surprised to see Thornton go so high, but the other picks certainly raised question marks. Pearson's season was limited to 26 games due to wrist surgery, while Bancroft had a pin in his shoulder following a 1988 surgery.

It wasn't long until the jokes began to fly.

Question: Why did the Toronto Maple Leafs pick as their top draft choices three players from the Belleville Bulls?

A: They got a deal at a Belleville hotel.

B: The scouting staff could only afford bus tickets as far as Belleville.

C: It was buy-two, get-one free.

The last time the Leafs made three first-round choices, all ended up playing for quite a while with the Leafs, two of them very successfully—right-winger Lanny McDonald (fourth overall) and defenceman Ian Turnbull (15th). Bob Neely (10th) wasn't as successful as the other two, but did enjoy a 283-game NHL career.

"I have the same feeling today as I had back in 1973," Stellick said. "I feel the three guys we picked today will play prominent roles in the future of this team the same way as the three guys picked in '73 did."

Think again.

Thornton enjoyed a 16-season NHL career, but played just 33 games as a Leaf, scoring once. Pearson played three seasons as a Leaf, netting 23 goals in 1992–93. Bancroft never played for the Leafs at all and saw action in just six NHL games.

Among those the Leafs passed on to assemble their Belleville trio were Bill Guerin (fifth), Bobby Holik (10th), Olaf Kolzig (19th) and Adam Foote (22nd).

A KILLER MOVE

The Leafs rang in the New Year in 1992 by making the biggest trade in NHL history and one of the best deals in the history of the franchise.

Cliff Fletcher, who'd taken over as GM of the club at the start of the 1991–92 season, made a 10-player trade with his old club the Calgary Flames, sending forwards Craig Berube and Gary Leeman, defencemen Michel Petit and Alexander Godynyuk and goalie Jeff Reese to the Flames for goalie Rick Wamsley, defencemen Jamie

Macoun and Ric Nattress and forwards Kent Manderville and Doug Gilmour.

Gilmour, nicknamed Killer for the aggressive style he played despite his slight build, was the key to the trade. He was always a solid performer and a significant contributor to Calgary's 1988–89 Stanley Cup win.

Placed in a lead role in Toronto, he'd blossom into an NHL superstar.

"Dougie was the ultimate competitor," former Calgary teammate Joe Nieuwendyk said. "He wasn't a big guy, but he played big."

Gilmour (Cornwall, 1981, Calgary 1989) and another ex-Leaf, Andy Bathgate, are the only players in hockey history to score Memorial and Stanley Cup winning goals. Bathgate, added like Gilmour in a blockbuster trade with the New York Rangers in 1964, tallied Toronto's Cup winner that spring. He also scored the winner for the Guelph Biltmore Mad Hatters in the 1952 Memorial Cup final.

But while Bathgate enjoyed his finest individual seasons as a Ranger, Gilmour would rewrite the Toronto record book in his first full season with the Leafs.

In 1992–93 Gilmour established new franchise marks for assists (95) and points (127) as the Leafs enjoyed their first winning season since 1978–79. In a 6–1 win over the Minnesota North Stars on February 13, 1993, Gilmour collected helpers on every Toronto goal to match the 1944 team record Babe Pratt established for assists in one game.

In the playoffs, Gilmour set another Toronto record with 35 points as the Leafs went all the way to Game 7 of the Western Conference final before falling to the Los Angeles Kings, the closest the Leafs have come to reaching the Stanley Cup final since their last win in 1967.

Gilmour finished second in Hart Trophy voting to Mario Lemieux of the Pittsburgh Penguins, the best showing by a Leaf since Johnny Bower also finished second in the balloting to Bernie Geoffrion of the Montreal Canadiens in 1960–61.

"It's amazing," Gilmour said of playing for the Leafs. "The opportunity to play in Toronto is something I'll never forget and I'll never regret. When you play in Toronto, you're put up on this pedestal.

"Yes the media's there, but you accept that. It's a challenge. You just go out and play. Your teammates are with you and you kind of accept that.

"If you ever have the chance to play in Toronto, I'm the first one to say, 'Go for it.'"

BASHING BILL, PART THREE

When ESPN came looking for a member of the Leafs to appear in one of the television network's National Hockey League promotional spots, it wasn't Doug Gilmour or Wendel Clark they sought.

It was checking winger Bill Berg.

"I had a good time doing that," Berg recalled of the ad he filmed for the all-sports network, while admitting at the same time the offer came as a complete surprise.

A gritty checking forward for the Leafs from 1992–96, Berg caught people by surprise from the moment the New York Islanders selected him in the 1986 NHL entry draft and converted him from defenceman to winger.

Wayne Gretzky, Marty McSorley, and actor Dennis Leary were among those featured in other ESPN spots.

"I remember thinking, 'what am I doing here with these guys?'" Berg said of his acting debut.

In Berg's bit, he skated towards the camera while a voice asked if it was true that he was such a dogged competitor, he'd even check his mother into the boards.

"Sure," answered Berg. "But I wouldn't go in with the elbows up."

Berg indicated that while he had fun, it was McSorley who provided the most vivid memory of his TV experience.

"They wanted him to go into the camera like he was throwing a bodycheck," Berg said. "But the producer yelled at Marty because he wasn't going into the camera hard enough, that it didn't look realistic, so the next time, Marty winds it up, goes full tilt at it—and puts his elbow right through a $25,000 lens."

Full tilt was the only way Berg knew how to play the game. Berg's work ethic, penalty killing ability and determination made him a valuable Leaf.

"I knew what my job was," Berg said. "It was to forecheck, to skate hard and to make sure the other team doesn't score when I'm on the ice."

His task was in stark contrast to that of younger brother Bob. A left-winger just like his older brother, Bob was a minor-league sniper who four times produced 100 points.

"If you could have put the two of us together," said Bill the checker said of Bob the scorer, "you'd have had one heckuva hockey player."

IN THE NIK OF TIME

"I'm ticked off," Leafs' general manager Cliff Fletcher said moments after Toronto's 4–3 Game 7 victory over the Detroit Red Wings in the opening round of the 1993 Stanley Cup playoffs, although his ear-to-ear grin said otherwise.

"Before the series started, I was in a room with about 20 people and I told them that we would win the series in seven games and (Nikolai) Borschevsky would score the winning goal," Fletcher explained.

"If only I had gone public," Fletcher moaned playfully. "I'd have looked like a genius."

Borschevsky's goal at 2:35 of the extra session is remembered by a generation of Leafs fans with a fondness greater than any other Toronto goal in the past three decades.

Much like those Leafs' fans, to Borschevsky, the goal meant much more than just a win for one team over another.

It was also an example of a son's love for his father.

Playing with a fractured orbital bone, which had kept him sidelined since Game 1 of the series, Borschevsky was more concerned with the health of his father, whom he has flown across the Atlantic Ocean from their Siberian homeland in Russia for heart surgery.

The surgery would cost $45,000 and Borschevsky used the $12,000 each Leaf player got for winning the first-round series, as well as the other playoff bonus money he earned that spring as Toronto advanced to the Stanley Cup final four for the first time since 1978, to put toward his father's life-saving bypass operation.

"Happy, very happy," Borschevsky said. His grasp of the English language was limited at the time, but no translation was necessary for the gleam in his eyes or his sparkling smile.

"I score big goal for team."

Along with Lanny McDonald's goal to capture Toronto's 1978 quarter-final series over the New York Islanders, they are the only two Game 7 OT winners scored in Leafs' history.

THE SEASON THAT EVERYTHING WENT IN FOR ANDREYCHUK

Game over, his goal-scoring exploits responsible for another Leafs' victory, Dave Andreychuk grabbed his trousers from a hook in his dressing room and could only look on helplessly as the gold wedding band fell from the pocket, one-hopped the bench and landed in the garbage can.

"Oh, geez," Andreychuk said as he watched his wedding ring sink into the mass of mangled hockey tape and gauze. "The wife's not going to like that."

That's life in the big city. Some days they bounce for you, some days they don't.

During the 1993–94 season, everything was going in for Andreychuk. He set franchise marks for a left-winger with 53 goals and 99 points while skating alongside centre Doug Gilmour.

"We had some good times together in Toronto," Andreychuk said. "Dougie liked to carry the puck, go behind the net and then find that man in the open. Getting open was something I've always been good at doing. We had good chemistry together."

A guy who scored the vast majority of his goals by going to the net and finding rebounds didn't figure to have much trouble unearthing his wedding ring, a piece of gold amongst the sea of white in the waste basket. When you made a living mucking about and picking up garbage goals, it wasn't too difficult a task.

PRIME TIE

Putting his best foot forward, Deion Sanders was advised to move aside. Prime Tie had topped his act.

When Leafs' winger Tie Domi kicked a field goal and a conversion for the Toronto Argonauts in 1996 and 1997 Canadian Football league exhibition games, he officially became a three-sport professional athlete.

In 1995, Domi played in the professional Canadian National Soccer League.

Sanders, a cornerback who won the Super Bowl with the Dallas Cowboys and San Francisco 49ers, also played for the Atlanta Braves in the 1992 World Series against the Toronto Blue Jays.

George Hadre figures he was the only person who knew Domi would be successful kicking field goals for the Argonauts.

"In 1984, he kicked us to the ECSSAA junior football championship," Hadre recalled. "He kicked a 42-yard field goal in the final."

"It was a 47-yarder," Domi said, correcting his former coach and teacher at Belle River District High School.

Hadre remembered Domi as a dominant athlete at Belle River, a star of both the soccer and football teams in his two years at the school before he left town to play junior hockey with the Peterborough Petes.

There was just one dilemma during Domi's football days.

"We couldn't keep him in football pants," Hadre said. "His thighs were so powerful, he just kept ripping open the legs."

The school also needed to borrow a football helmet from the University of Windsor's football team, because none of Belle River's helmets were large enough to fit Domi's massive head.

Domi recalled a championship game against rival General Amherst when he scored all 24 of Belle River's points. "I still have the headline from *The Windsor Star*," Domi said. "It read 'Domi the whole story for Nobles.'"

QUINN'S QUEST

From the beginning of his hockey career, Pat Quinn was a study in contrast.

A hard-nosed defenceman who hit the books with equal authority. A defensive blue-liner who embraced attacking hockey.

"My two main aims in life were to play in the NHL and get a college degree," said Quinn, a Leafs' player from 1968–70 and coach of the Leafs from 1998–2006.

The man diligently combined both desires, even after losing a hockey scholarship to Michigan Tech when NCAA officials ruled Quinn was a pro because he had played for the OHA's Hamilton Tiger-Cubs, a club sponsored by the Detroit Red Wings.

Undaunted, he continued to pursue higher education after turning pro—attending college at Tennessee, Tulsa, and Memphis State during tenures with minor-league clubs.

"I remember Ted Lindsay telling me 'why are you wasting your time getting an education?'" Quinn said.

After making the Leafs in 1968, Quinn studied at the University of Toronto and York, completing his degree in economics by attending summer classes while skating for the Vancouver Canucks and Atlanta Flames during the 1970s.

"There were times in both hockey and school when I wondered if I'd ever make it," Quinn admitted. "At one time, I was pretty sore at hockey for holding up my education."

Making the grade in hockey also proved a chore for Quinn, who failed chances with Detroit and St. Louis.

Quinn recalled a training camp stint with the first-year Blues in 1967. "(Coach) Scotty Bowman called me into his office and said, 'Son, do you want to play in the NHL?'" Quinn remembered. "'Yes sir,' I said. 'Well,'" Bowman told me, 'You'll have to get a lot better than that then,' and he sent me to the minors.

He finally hit the big time with Toronto during the 1968–69 season.

"The Leafs had a lot of skill on defence, but they needed a lunkhead," Quinn recalled. "I said, 'Over here.'"

Three decades later, this low-skill lunkhead taught the Leafs how to play the game with talent.

"What we tried to do was copy the style which Detroit used to win two Cups," Quinn said in 1999.

"The Red Wings play an up-tempo, puck-possession game, but they're relentless on defence and that's the way I want our team to play."

As a coach, Quinn would assess his personnel and design a system to fit them. Quinn's Leafs were laden with European skill players, so Detroit's style was a natural.

In Philadelphia, rugged hockey was his recipe for success. When *Sports Illustrated* took Quinn's Flyers to task for their brutality, he groused that it "was just another commie magazine."

A decade later, the fall of the Soviet empire freed Russians to play in the NHL and Quinn spoke out against outdated stereotypes.

"Canadians don't have a lock on courage," he said.

Quinn has never been afraid to take a stand. One night in Boston, he ran Bobby Orr, touching off a bench-clearing brawl.

"When the cop in the penalty box turned against me, I knew I was in trouble," Quinn remembered.

He always displayed a knack for trying new things.

One afternoon in Atlanta, Quinn decided to take a spin on his daughter's skateboard. A few feet and one broken leg later, he was done as a player.

Quinn turned to coaching and when the Flyers handed him a pink slip, headed back to school.

The guy who worked behind the Leafs' bench was equally qualified to work in front of one.

Plenty of NHL coaches have been known to lay down the law. Quinn was the only one who earned the right to practise it.

Quinn thought his law degree made him a better coach.

"You were trained to look beneath a situation that appeared to be cut and dried," Quinn said.

To see both sides of the coin and realize there is value in each.

The sort of theory a fellow like Quinn could embrace.

WENDEL'S WORLD

The presence of his image on the Air Canada Centre scoreboard unleashes uncontrollable emotional response from the Leafs' faithful.

Wendel Clark still has Toronto supporters in the palm of his hand, even though he left the game more than a decade ago.

Surprisingly, the end came easily for Clark.

"I really didn't have to dwell on it for long," Clark said of his 2000 decision to hang up his skates after 15 NHL seasons.

Clark entered the pro ranks a Leaf, the top player selected in the 1985 NHL entry draft. As a rookie, he led the team in both goals (34) and penalty minutes (227) and finished second to Calgary Flames' defenceman Gary Suter in the Calder Trophy voting, the closest a Leaf has come to being named the NHL's top rookie since Brit Selby won the award in 1965–66.

"They love him," former Leafs' coach Pat Quinn once said of Clark.

Growing up in Endiang, Alberta, former Leaf Darcy Tucker was glued to the set every Saturday night, listening intently as his dad told him to watch the way No. 17 for Toronto handled himself on the ice.

Learn to be more like Wendel Clark and you'll learn what it takes to be an NHLer, Dale Tucker advised his son.

"When I watched *Hockey Night In Canada*, No. 17 was always the main man," Tucker said. "He played the game with heart and character."

"Some people have unrealistic expectations of certain players," former Leafs' coach Pat Burns said of Clark. "They size them up as franchise players just because they were taken first overall."

The love affair with Wendel was never about numbers for Leafs' fans. It was about how he played the game; that he was willing to trade blows with the toughest of the tough and yet could still produce like an all-star.

Five of his six 30-goal seasons came in a Leaf uniform, as did his career-high 46-goal campaign in 1992–93. Eight times he also topped the 100 penalty minute plateau in Toronto, including a career-best 271 PIM in his sophomore season of 1986–87.

Clark earned a reputation as a punishing hitter and someone who never backed away from a challenge.

"I'd rather be hated than be a guy that no one ever knew was around," Clark said. "I just treated all of it as competition. Usually, the guys you hate the most as opponents are the guys you're going to love the most as teammates.

"That's what fans should be doing. Good fans love the home team and hate the guys on the other team."

A heart-and-soul guy, Clark maintained the same quiet humility throughout his career.

"He's a farm boy," close friend Joe Kocur said. "He's the product of parents who brought him up the right way."

Clark wore the uniform of the Quebec Nordiques, New York Islanders, Tampa Bay Lightning, Detroit Red Wings, and Chicago Blackhawks during his career, but that blue-and-white Maple Leafs sweater was the only one that ever truly fit.

Clark played with Toronto from 1985–94, 1996–98 and again in the second half of the 1999–2000 season.

"You don't often get a second chance to come back to your first team," Clark said.

Or your first love, for that matter.

"I was lucky enough to get a third chance," said Clark, who didn't want to press his luck.

He'd closed out his last season with the Leafs—20 regular-season games and six more in the playoffs. The love affair had been rekindled.

To keep playing would have most certainly meant playing elsewhere. Clark didn't feel like packing, he felt like packing it in.

He came to the realization that the final chapter had been written. It just felt right to him to retire as a Leaf.

"After the playoffs were over, I took some time, then I sat down, looked at everything and gave the decision some serious thought," Clark said.

"It really came quickly. There wasn't a lot of indecisiveness."

Timing is everything, even when it comes time to exit.

"There aren't very many times in your life when everything just feels right," Clark said.

DANNY BOY

When you think about Russian hockey players, you likely think in terms of skill, speed, and sublime creativity.

Danny Markov was living proof that Russians could also play it rough.

A Leaf defenceman from 1997–2001, Markov delivered a physical payload, agitated the other team, stood up to much larger opposition and stuck up for his teammates.

At 6'1" and 186 pounds, Markov was hardly a physically imposing specimen, but he carried himself on the ice like someone who owned a significant size advantage.

"Sleeper tough," was how former NHL forward Kyle Calder described Markov. "He was a wiry guy, but those are always the toughest. Different body physique. Same mentality.

"It was not very forgiving to go to the net when he was there."

Markov's game was to get the other team off theirs.

"I tried to be a little bit (Vladimir) Konstantinov, a little bit (Darius) Kasparaitis," Markov said, invoking the names of two other legendary rugged Russian defencemen and smiling at the notion. "I just play like I play. I like to hit people.

"I always play like this, a physical, fiery game."

Others offered up the superlatives that confirmed the comparison.

"The way he played the game was much the same to the way Vladdie would play," said Dmitri Yushkevich, who was Markov's defence partner in Toronto and a former teammate of Konstantinov's with the Russian national squad.

Attitude was always served as a side dish with Markov's main course of "take no prisoners" physical hockey.

When Toronto eliminated Pittsburgh from the 1999 Stanley Cup playoffs, Markov sought out Penguins' star Jaromir Jagr and saluted him, the trademark move Jagr made after every goal he scored.

"He knew no fear," former Leaf tough guy Tie Domi said.

Even the Phantom knew not to mess with Markov. Well, at least he learned that lesson.

Back when Markov was still being schooled on the NHL game with St. John's of the AHL, the mascot for the Philadelphia Phantoms hung over the glass during a stoppage, taunting the opposition.

Markov drilled the boards in front of the costumed character, sending the mascot spilling backwards into the seats.

"You really hit a mascot?" someone asked Markov.

"A little bit, yes," Markov said, the devilish smile widening.

Markov smiled a lot. Only a little less often than the Mona Lisa.

The Leafs discovered early that Markov danced to the beat of his own drummer. After a sampling of his swagger and fashion sense, his teammates quickly dubbed Markov 'Elvis.'

"He dressed like Elvis, he walked like Elvis, he even talked a little like Elvis," Yushkevich explained.

And sang like Elvis?

"No," Yushkevich said with the tone of someone who had listened to Markov try to mimic The King one too many times.

TO THE MATS

He is the only Leaf to finish in the NHL's top five scorers over the past 16 seasons. He is the club's all-time leader in goals (420) and points (987). Yet when Leafs' fans wax poetic about the team's all-time greats, seldom is the name of Mats Sundin invoked.

And that's just wrong.

Sundin led the Leafs in scoring in all but one of his 11 seasons in blue and white. Sundin finished fourth in NHL scoring with 80 points in 2001–02 as he led the Leafs to the Eastern Conference final, the closest they've come to the Stanley Cup in the past 16 years. That matched Doug Gilmour's fourth-place finish in NHL scoring in 1993–94 and those remain the best results recorded by a Leaf in the scoring race since Darryl Sittler came home third overall in 1977–78.

"I look at Toronto as my home," Sundin said. "Being there, this was the most fun I had as a hockey player."

He served 11 seasons as Leafs captain, the longest run of any non-North American born captain in NHL history. Sundin played more games for Canadian-based teams (1,346) than any player in NHL history. He's the NHL's all-time scoring leader among Swedish-born players (1,349 points) and averaged more than a point per game during his NHL career.

Internationally, Sundin won three world championship gold medals (1991, 1992, 1998) and one Olympic gold medal (2006) with Sweden, serving as team captain at that Olympiad.

"He was just a very consistent player throughout his whole career," Daniel Alfredsson, second in Swedish NHL scoring, said of Sundin. "We had a lot of battles with him in Ottawa against Toronto, and he was always the guy we keyed against. We knew if we gave him space and time he was going to hurt you.

"I don't think anybody is going to beat his record in a long time. He had longevity, he had skill, and he had consistency and one very impressive career."

In 2007, Sundin broke an 83-year-old franchise record when he recorded a point in 15 straight games. Babe Dye had established the previous mark of 14 games in 1924–25, when Toronto's NHL team was still known as the St. Patricks.

Sundin never brought the Leafs a title and like all Toronto captains, dealt with the expectations of Leaf Nation.

"The pressure was there for me to perform, but I don't think it was any more pressure than what I put on myself," Sundin said.

In 2012, Sundin was inducted into the Hockey Hall of Fame in his first year of eligibility, following Borje Salming, another Leaf star, as the second Swede to be enshrined in the Hall.

Three years later, the Leafs appropriately added statues of Sundin and Salming to the club's Legends Row at the Air Canada Centre and Sundin raved about his time in Toronto.

"I don't think that there's a better place to play hockey," Sundin said.

KESSEL A MODERN-DAY DRILLON?

Gordie Drillon? The name elicited a blank stare from Phil Kessel.

He didn't know the name of the last Toronto Maple Leafs player to lead the National Hockey League in scoring.

"I didn't even know about that," Kessel acknowledged.

He also didn't realize that it occurred during the 1937–38 season, nearly a decade before the league began awarding the Art Ross Trophy.

In the last decade, no Leaf has come closer to emulating Drillon than Kessel, who played for the team from 2009–15.

Kessel finished sixth in NHL scoring in both 2011–12 and 2013–14 and eighth overall in 2012–13, the best performance by a Leaf since Mats Sundin came fourth overall in 2002–03. His 82 points in 2011–12 are the most recorded by a Leaf in a single season since Sundin put up 83 points in 1998–99.

Kessel also finished his Leafs career riding a 456 consecutive game streak, the second-longest stretch in franchise history and the longest by a Toronto forward.

The parallels between Drillon and Kessel are obvious. Like Kessel, Drillon shot right and played right wing. He scored at least 20 goals in four of his five full seasons as a Leafs. Kessel tallied at least 20 goals in each of his six seasons with Toronto.

Drillon, like Kessel, was a pure goal scorer whose overall game was often questioned.

The first time Leafs' managing director Conn Smythe saw Drillon in action with the junior Toronto Young Rangers, he left unimpressed, feeling Drillon was too slow and too small to make it as an NHLer.

"He might go all right in that amateur stuff but heavy checkers like (Earl) Seibert and (Red) Horner would power him to pieces," Smythe told Ed Wildey, manager of the Young Rangers.

The following season Drillon came under the tutelage of former Leafs' right-winger Ace Bailey and improved so much that Smythe added him to Toronto's negotiating list.

He made a Western Canadian tour with the Leafs' in the spring of 1936 and upon returning, Drillon was offered a contract by the team.

Called up a few weeks into the 1936–37 NHL campaign, Drillon was seated nervously on the end of the Leafs bench during a game against the Montreal Canadiens when Toronto coach Dick Irvin nudged him.

"Say Gordie, old (Montreal winger Aurel) Joliat isn't going very fast tonight," Irvin said. "Let's see what you can do out there."

On his first NHL shift, Drillon set up Bill Thoms for a goal.

"Kids come up from the minors and muff that first chance and it seems to do something to them," Smythe said. "Few of them make good later.

"When I saw Drillon score a point on that play I knew we had a hockey player."

Soon, they would know that they had a hockey player who tended to work only at one end of the ice. Backchecking was a foreign concept to Drillon.

Similar questions have been posed about Kessel's game, concerns which were even shared by some of his teammates.

"You hear things," admitted former Leafs' defenceman John-Michael Liles. "I think that as goal scorers go, sometimes they get knocks on them.

"Everything you hear about him, his strength is his goal scoring, being an offensive player.

"People said his defence wasn't that strong, or maybe he doesn't compete coming back."

When Kessel was the October 2011 NHL player of the month, he was the first Leaf to be so honoured since Felix Potvin in 1993. Kessel's seven goals in his first five games that season were the most over that span to start a season by a Leaf since Dave (Sweeney) Schriner scored eight during Toronto's first five games of the 1944–45 campaign. Kessel joined Schriner and Rick Vaive (1983–84) as the only Leafs to hit double-digits in goals through the first ten games of the season and he was the first Leaf to reach the 20-point plateau in 12 games since Doug Gilmour in 1992–93.

Not that it seemed to matter to him.

"I don't think about it," Kessel said.

When the Leafs continued to flounder, Kessel was dealt to the Pittsburgh Penguins in the summer of 2015, where he was finally able to combine team success with his individual accomplishments, winning a Stanley Cup title.

When Drillon finally got his name on the Stanley Cup in 1941–42, it was as a spectator. After losing the first three games of the Stanley Cup final to Detroit, Leafs' coach Hap Day benched

Drillon for the remainder of the series. He sat and watched Toronto win the next four and take the Cup.

He'd never play for the Leafs again, and was traded to Montreal in October of 1942.

"Bring your scoring stick and your backchecking skates," advised Irvin, now coach of the Habs, via a telegram he sent to Drillon. "We can use them."

Drillon played one season for Montreal, scoring 28 goals, and then was done the NHL at the 30, just five years after leading the league in scoring.

Ace Foley of the *Halifax Chronicle* described Drillon as "a sports specialist."

"He could get goals," Foley wrote. "He didn't bother to backcheck and he wasn't very interested in skating up with the others—unless he figured he'd get a chance to score.

"But when he got the puck in close even the best goalies in the business knew the effort the big boy made to get in there wouldn't be wasted."

Sure sounds an awful lot like Kessel.

THE PHANEUF FROWNY FACE

Remember when your mother would tell you not to make that face because it might freeze like that?

Well, that's exactly what his Leafs teammates thought might have happened to former Toronto captain Dion Phaneuf.

Amongst the Leafs, it was known as the Phaneuf frown—the combination scowl/death stare that seemed to permanently occupy Phaneuf's face.

"We'd joke about it," teammate Joffrey Lupul said. "We were saying it's one of those things where people say if you frown too much, your face gets stuck that way.

"Maybe he's stuck in that frown."

Some players are viewed as the face of the team. In Phaneuf's case, he was the frown of the franchise.

Some suggested that as captain of Canada's most popular National Hockey League franchise, Phaneuf filled the most glamorous job in the country.

In times of distress, though, wearing the C for the Maple Leafs and carrying the expectations of Leaf Nation can prove to be a C of trouble. "It was an honour to be the captain of such a storied franchise, but I definitely learned a lot," said Phaneuf, traded in 2016 to the Ottawa Senators.

If he'd finished his new pact with the Leafs through its completion and continued as captain, Phaneuf would have tied George Armstrong (1957–69) as the longest-serving Maple Leafs captain.

Armstrong lifted the Stanley Cup four times as captain of the team, a club record, and that may have been the key to his long sojourn in the role, according to someone else who understands the burden of captaining Canada's most talked-about NHL club.

"Everything about how tough a job it is really comes down to how well the team is playing," said Wendel Clark, leader of the Leafs from 1991–94, carrying the club to a pair of conference final appearances during his tenure.

"When you're winning, you get more and more support for the captain and that group stays together and plays together for a longer time."

When the team isn't winning, however, the captain is the one expected to have the solution.

That's when the stress and pressure often proves to be overwhelming.

"It can be," Clark admitted, regarding the pressure he felt while captaining the Leafs. "It's the whole win-lose thing. Nobody likes to lose and when you lose, the captain is kind of the focal point of the team."

When the dealt to acquire Phaneuf from the Calgary Flames during the 2009–10 season, it was with the belief that like Armstrong and Clark, he'd be the type of fiery leader who take the Leafs to great heights. Instead, they made the playoffs just once under his leadership and never won a post-season series.

In 2016, the Leafs frowned on Phaneuf and traded him to, of all teams, their cross-province rivals the Ottawa Senators.

THOSE GOOFY GOALIES

Some of the most interesting characters to wear the Maple Leaf on their chest also wore goalie pads on their legs.

A HALL-OF-FAME QUARTET

It's a great trivia question, one you can utilize to stump your friends.

Name the four Hall-of-Famers to play goal in the NHL for Toronto and Detroit.

The first three are fairly easy.

There's Terry Sawchuk, who backstopped the Leafs to their most recent Stanley Cup in 1967 after winning three Cups as a Red Wing.

The man Sawchuk replaced in the Detroit net—Harry Lumley—found his way to Toronto and in 1953–54 set the Leafs' single-season mark for shutouts with 13 and won the Vezina Trophy. Lumley won a Cup with the Wings in 1949–50.

You've got to go back a ways to get the third one, Harry (Hap) Holmes. He was the goalie when the Toronto Arenas won the NHL's first Stanley Cup in 1917–18 and was Detroit's No. 1 goalie when the team joined the NHL as the Cougars in 1926–27.

Holmes, who was balding, was famed for the ballcap he wore in net, with good reason. Unruly fans were fond of spitting tobacco at his chrome dome.

The fourth? Now that's the toughie. It was Charlie Conacher, a right-winger by trade but an emergency goalie on four occasions during his NHL career—three times as a Leaf and once as a Red Wing.

Conacher's netminding debut came November 20, 1932, as the Leafs lost 7–0 to the New York Rangers. During the second period, Toronto goalie Lorne Chabot wandered from his net and Murray Murdoch of the Rangers bodychecked him. Chabot countered by whacking Murdoch over the head with his stick and both were penalized.

Goalies served their own penalties then, so Conacher, who'd tended goal in youth hockey, took over in goal for the duration of Chabot's two-minute infraction and kept a clean sheet, making six saves.

Later that season in a March 16, 1933 game at Detroit, Chabot again ran afoul of the rules. He engaged in a fistic bout with Ebbie Goodfellow of the Wings, a battle that continued as both men sat in the penalty box, and was assessed a roughing minor.

Conacher once more filled the breech, this time easily, as Detroit wasn't able to muster a single shot on goal.

Exactly two years later on March 16, 1935, George Hainsworth was in the Toronto net when he was clipped over the eye with a shot. Instead of waiting for Hainsworth to be patched up, Conacher took his goal stick and parked himself between the posts, putting on a show for three minutes of scoreless hockey until Hainsworth returned to finish the game with a plaster holding his cut closed.

Conacher was the star of the night, netting a hat trick as the Leafs beat the Habs 5–3.

After a move to Detroit in 1938, Conacher's netminding career would end where it started, against the New York Rangers. During a 7–3 loss to the Rangers on February 21, 1939, Detroit goalie Tiny Thompson was struck over the left eye by a shot from the stick of New York's Mac Colville with four minutes to play.

Blood streaming down his face, Thompson handed his goal stick off to Conacher, who played the rest of the way, though the Rangers went easy on him. With a significant advantage on the scoreboard, they opted to sit back and defend and Conacher wasn't asked to block a single shot.

So there you have it, the four Hall-of-Famers to play goal for Toronto and Detroit. Interesting to note, isn't it, that the guy with the best career goals-against average was the only one who wasn't a netminder.

ULCERS WASN'T MCCOOL WITH HIS JOB

Coming off military service and with only senior and U.S. college hockey on his resume, Frank McCool hardly seemed like the solution to the Leafs' wartime goaltending woes when he arrived at training camp in the fall of 1944.

Out the entire previous season due to stomach ulcers, McCool surprised everyone by winning the starting job. He then posted 24 wins and a league-leading four shutouts to earn the Calder Trophy as the NHL's rookie of the year.

Backstopping the Leafs to the Stanley Cup final, McCool set a record that continues to stand when he posted shutouts in each of the first three games of the series against the Detroit Red Wings.

"It looks as if the puck is never going to go in again for us," Detroit manager Jack Adams lamented.

Detroit rallied to win the next three games, but McCool rebounded in Game 7, carrying the Leafs to a 2–1 win and the Stanley Cup.

Although he was on top of the hockey world, McCool never seemed to take a shine to his chosen profession. Nor did Leafs fans take a shine to him.

Constantly battling his chronic ulcers, McCool was required to take daily medication. McCool's teammates thanked him for his gallantry by playfully hiding his ulcer medication.

One morning, McCool showed up early for practice and asked a young equipment assistant if he could borrow a hammer.

The youngster went about the business of setting out rolls of tape and sticks for that day's workout, but couldn't help notice the methodical pounding coming from inside the dressing room.

He entered to find McCool hammering each player's skates to the bench by carefully driving a nail through the eyeholes where the laces would go.

The players stopped hiding his medicine.

McCool was known for his ulcers, but there were times when he could give an ulcer or two to his Leafs teammates.

"I had a habit of moving out of my net," McCool explained to the *Saskatoon Star-Phoenix*. "Babe Pratt was one of our defencemen.

He'd back up and snarl over his shoulder, 'Get back in your cage McCool. We'll do the checking. Or else take off that mattress and join us.'

"So I stayed in my little hut, but sometimes I thought I was guarding a soccer goal and my pals had deserted me, like the night the Canadiens beat me ten times."

So where was Pratt to take care of the checking on that night?

"I'm not sure," McCool said. "But the next time I see him, I'll ask."

The year after his Stanley Cup heroics, McCool missed the start of the season in a contract holdout. Then Turk Broda returned from military duty looking to resume his job as Toronto's netminder.

McCool was speaking to children at a Toronto boys' club one day, when one kid went right for the jugular.

"Mr. McCool—do you think Turk Broda will beat you out of your job?"

"Anything can happen in hockey, son," McCool answered. "Anything."

Not long after, Broda took over between the posts and the ailing McCool almost seemed relieved. "I feel right for the first time in a long while," he told *Canadian Press*.

"I shouldn't be playing anyway. I find it too tough. I get jitters before, during and after a game in goal and just burn myself up."

At the end of the season, McCool retired from hockey. He was 28.

"I never thought of myself as a professional goalie even after I quit hockey," McCool told *Canadian Press* in 1963. "I would have never reached the NHL if I hadn't been given a medical discharge from the army before the end of the war and if it was not for a shortage of professional goalies."

ANGULAR AL

They called him the Elongated Netminder and Angular Al. They said he was awkward and unspectacular and counted him out, insisting he'd never amount to anything.

Yet during the 1950–51 season, Leafs' goalie Al Rollins was called a Stanley Cup champion and the Vezina Trophy winner, though the latter honour arrived with some questioning and cat-calling his performance.

Rollins (40 games) and Turk Broda (31 games) combined to allow 138 goals, one fewer than Detroit's Terry Sawchuk, who had appeared in all 70 of the Red Wings' games.

In those days, the Vezina was awarded to the goaltender playing the most games for the team that allowed the fewest goals. Under those terms, the Vezina winner was Al Rollins.

This, some felt, was a controversial decision.

"Al Rollins has finished up with the Vezina Trophy and the ($1,000) bonus that goes with it," wrote Bill Westwick in the *Ottawa Journal*. "A fine thing for Rollins but rather tough on Detroit's Sawchuk, whose record over the entire season would seem to stand out as the greater achievement."

Detroit proposed to the NHL that the Vezina regulations be altered to read that a goaltender must play in at least 55 of the 70 scheduled games. At the time, empty-net goals were still charged against netminders and Sawchuk had one of these counted against him, the difference in the outcome.

Toronto also argued about the Vezina stipulations, reasoning that both Leaf goalies should get their names on the trophy. At one point during the season, Leafs' managing director Conn Smythe suggested that he would see to it that both Rollins and Broda would each appear in exactly 35 games, forcing the league to put both names on the award.

Prior to the season, Rollins' entire NHL experience consisted of two games played near the end of the 1949–50 season in relief of Broda.

"It would give the Turk a rest," Smythe said at the time. "He has a tough grind ahead of him. We want to take a look at Rollins anyway."

The 1950–51 season began as if it would remain Broda's net. He played six of the first seven games and 14 of the first 17. But then Rollins got on a roll. The rookie went 7–0–2 in his first nine games.

"It's a tough one," Smythe admitted of his goalie situation. "I've got to decide whether to keep the thin man in there and let him get thinner or whether to go back to the thinned-down fat man."

At 6'2" and 180 pounds, Rollins was built more like a modern NHL goalie than the short, stocky types who gravitated toward the net. Broda, for example, was 5'9" and 165 pounds, and had been known to balloon up to as much as 190 pounds.

In mid-January, the Leafs decided to ride Rollins. Broda played just four of Toronto's last 32 games. At 36 and the NHL's oldest active player, Broda admitted he was contemplating retirement.

"I probably will hang up my skates after this season," Broda said. "I don't know for sure.

"I'll have to talk it over with the boss."

Rollins, meanwhile, was doing his best to silence his critics. He went 21–6–5 once the Leafs handed him the No. 1 job and posted five shutouts while only allowing more than three goals just once all season.

Regardless, Sawchuk still held a five-goal lead in the Vezina chase with five games to play. But Rollins bricked up his net down the stretch, going 5–0, allowing just three goals for a 0.60 goals-against average.

Rollins credited Leafs' assistant GM Hap Day and coach Joe Primeau for turning him into an NHL goalie. "They've been getting me to stand up a little more and are helping to smooth out the rough edges," Rollins explained to the *Ottawa Journal*. "Turk helps too. We talk over the games all the time."

The Leafs had acquired Rollins from the American Hockey League's Cleveland Barons the season before as Broda's understudy, choosing him over Cleveland's other goalie, a fellow named Johnny Bower.

It had been a long road to the top for Rollins. Attending the training camp of the New York Rangers in 1943 at the age of 16, Rollins contracted rheumatic fever and was sent home and advised to give up the game.

The Rangers gave Rollins a less-than-glowing scouting report. "He's first rate when he's in front and coasting, but he's likely to go to pieces when things are going against him," New York coach Bun Cook said. "He's also a member of the old ulcer fraternity."

Rollins ignored their advice, won an Allan Cup with the Edmonton Flyers in 1947–48, and less than eight years after he'd been cast adrift by New York, Rollins was the talk of hockey.

"He's come up with flashes of mighty good goaltending," Primeau said. "He has been particularly good on close-in plays."

Rollins would continue to shine in the NHL but would do so elsewhere. After the Leafs were swept in the 1951–52 playoffs, Toronto dealt Rollins to Chicago. In 1953–54, rollins won the Hart Trophy as the NHL's MVP while playing for the Blackhawks.

FALSE ALARM

Johnny Bower was someone who bought into Leaf coach Punch Imlach's theory of long, hard practices and usually, Bower was one of the last players off the ice.

One such day, when Bower came clomping into the Leaf dressing room in his bulky goalie gear, unbeknownst to him, all eyes were on the Toronto netminder.

The first thing Bower would do upon reaching his dressing room stall would be to grab his false teeth and pop them back into place. The upper plate slipped into his mouth without issue but for some reason, the lower plate was resisting all attempts.

As he fumbled with his dentures, Bower became aware of the quiet that surrounded him, and he knew something was up. Upon closer examination, Bower realized the choppers in his hand were in fact, not his false teeth.

Suddenly, the room was filled with uproarious laughter with the exception of Bower, who was steaming mad. He immediately pinned the blame on Eddie Shack, the most notorious prankster on the team, but Leafs' captain George Armstrong, Bower's close friend and road roommate, fessed up to the crime.

"Where'd you get the teeth?" Bower asked Armstrong.

"Well, it's like this," Armstrong explained. "I have a friend who works in a funeral home and he gave them to me."

DANDY DON

Things looked grim for the Leafs midway through the 1962 Stanley Cup final. Dead-even in the set with the defending champion Chicago Blackhawks at two wins apiece, the Leafs not only lost

Game 4 by a 4–1 count, they lost goalie Johnny Bower when he did the splits to make a save and pulled a hamstring.

Trailing 1–0 at the time, Reg Fleming whistled Chicago's first shot past Simmons 61 seconds after he'd entered the game to make it 2–0.

Simmons was no stranger to Stanley Cup play. His pinch-hit appearance in Game 4 was the 22nd of his NHL career and he'd backstopped the Boston Bruins in losing efforts against the Montreal Canadiens in the 1957 and 1958 Stanley Cup finals.

"Simmons isn't to be taken lightly," Chicago coach Rudy Pilous told the *Montreal Gazette*. "He stoned us in Boston."

Pilous also feared the Leafs would rally in front of their back-up goalie.

"The Leafs may be more inspired," he reasoned. "They will play better defensively as a team to help Don Simmons.

"It could work against us more than if Bower were in the nets."

Goaltending didn't exactly decide the outcome of Game 5. Trailing 3–2 in the second period, the Leafs scored four straight goals en route to an 8–4 victory. Simmons made 26 saves, 12 of them in the first period.

In Game 6, after two scoreless periods, Bobby Hull beat Simmons to give Chicago the lead, but Bob Nevin and Dick Duff countered and the Leafs had a 2–1 win and Lord Stanley's mug.

Finally a Stanley Cup champion in his third try, Simmons seemed more relieved the rejoiced. "What happened before doesn't matter," Simmons told writer Bill Westwick as he took a drag from a cigarette. "All that matters is we win the Cup.

"I wasn't nervous, though this was a tougher game for me than in the high-scoring last one at Toronto. Anytime you have one of those scoreless games going, the pressure's tougher on a goalie. But if I wasn't nervous, I still wasn't moving in the net for shots the way I wanted to, or would with more regular net time."

The Cup was won, but Simmons was done. Though he'd remain an NHLer until 1969, he'd never play another game in the Stanley Cup playoffs.

A SNOWSTORM SAVED DON SIMMONS' NHL CAREER

As far as likely occurrences go, it would rank right up there with Kenya winning an Olympic hockey medal.

When the Boston Bruins came to Maple Leaf Gardens for a Saturday *Hockey Night In Canada* game on January 18, 1964, the Bruins were a last-place team—albeit one riding a two-game winning streak—and the Leafs were two-time defending Stanley Cup champions.

That it was going to be an ominous event was evident less than a minute in, when Boston rookie Garry Dornhoefer opened both the scoring, and as it turned out, the floodgates.

When the night was done the Bruins were the authors of an 11–0 shutout rout, the worst loss in Maple Leafs' history.

Dean Prentice and Andy Hebenton recorded hat-tricks and Murray Oliver scored twice. John Bucyk and Jean-Guy Gendron also scored, and Ed Johnston made 26 saves for the shutout.

The Bruins shattered both the Leafs and the supposedly unbreakable Herculite glass that surrounded the rink when Boston forward Bob Leiter slammed Eddie Shack hard into it with a bodycheck. Shack took offence and fisticuffs immediately ensued.

It was about the only time all night that the Leafs put up a fight.

Seeking to stem the tide, coach Punch Imlach kept juggling his lines and gave plenty of ice time to defenceman Arnie Brown, just called up from Rochester of the American League, and forward Pete Stemkowski, a junior on an amateur tryout from the Toronto Marlboros.

Nothing worked and when the night concluded, perhaps not surprisingly, Imlach decided that it was Millar time.

The ultimate scapegoat for Toronto's night of embarrassment was goalie Don Simmons. In net due to a hand injury to Leafs' regular goaltender Johnny Bower, Simmons had allowed 22 goals in three games as Bower's replacement, and Imlach decided that even though Simmons was an NHL veteran who had appeared in three Stanley Cup finals and backstopped Toronto to the 1961–62 Stanley Cup in place of the injured Bower, it was time to audition another understudy.

He put in a call to Denver of the Western League for veteran pro puck-stopper Al Millar. Millar had played for Imlach when he was coaching senior hockey in Quebec and the Toronto coach planned to give Millar the start the following night in Chicago. But Millar never got closer than Des Moines, Iowa.

His flight to Chicago was grounded there by a snowstorm, leaving Imlach with no choice but to go with Simmons once more. Handed a reprieve, Simmons was stellar, blocking 27 shots for a 2–0 shutout at Chicago, earning himself a pardon.

Imlach advised Millar to return to Denver, that he was going to stay with Simmons. Simmons finished out the season as Bower's understudy but lost his spot in the summer of 1964 when Terry Sawchuk was claimed on waivers from Detroit in the NHL Intra-League Draft.

Simmons played one more season in Toronto's minor-league system with the Central League's Tulsa Oilers and, in 1965, he was acquired by the New York Rangers.

ALL FOR ONE AND BOTH FOR VEZINA

Toronto coach-GM Punch Imlach thought it was a stroke of genius when he claimed veteran netminder Terry Sawchuk from the Detroit Red Wings in the 1964 NHL Intra-League Draft.

Not only did it give the Leafs the two goalies who'd just gone head-to-head in a thrilling seven-game Stanley Cup final, in Sawchuk, 34, and Johnny Bower, 39, he had two veterans who would be comfortable in their own skins and equally comfortable with sharing the workload between the posts.

"With Sawchuk and Bower I've got the two goaltenders from the Stanley Cup final," Imlach boasted. "What could be better than that?"

Detroit coach-GM Sid Abel anticipated that Imlach would make a move for Sawchuk. "We knew that everybody else would probably pass on Sawchuk and that Toronto would probably take him," Abel told *United Press International*. "Actually, it may have solved a problem for us because we may have had to ask Terry to play at (AHL) Pittsburgh next year."

Others wondered what Imlach was up to. "What's Imlach going to do with Sawchuk?" Wings superstar Gordie Howe asked. "He has a great goalie in Johnny Bower."

Imlach knew exactly what he was doing. He intended to alternate his two cagey veterans in the Leaf cage, giving both of them breathers during the 70-game workload.

Even Leafs' president Stafford Smythe, often Imlach's harshest critic, had to agree the plan was brilliant.

"We now have Sawchuk to divide the goaltending with Bower," Smythe said.

The Leafs had seen this plan work to perfection once before. During the 1950–51 season, the Leafs utilized Al Rollins, who Smythe's father Conn acquired the year before from the AHL Cleveland Barons, to spell veteran Turk Broda in the Toronto goal. Rollins played in 40 of the 70 regular-season games and when the Leafs finished with the lowest goals-against average in the NHL, Rollins was awarded the Vezina Trophy.

That spring, the Leafs also won the Stanley Cup.

History repeated itself on one count during the 1964–65 season. Sawchuk (36 games) and Bower (34) would split the workload and in doing so, allowed an NHL-low 173 goals.

In a tight race with Detroit's Roger Crozier, the man who'd replaced Sawchuk in the Red Wings goal, Crozier carried a two-goal edge over Bower and Sawchuk into the regular-season finale between Toronto and Detroit at Olympia Stadium.

With Bower in goal blocking all 37 shots aimed his way, the Leafs won 4–0 and the Vezina was theirs. But whose Vezina was it?

According to the regulations governing the award, it would go only to Sawchuk.

The NHL originally insisted it would stick by its policy of awarding the Vezina and its $1,000 prize to the goalie who played the most games for the team that allowed the fewest goals.

Bower and Sawchuk had already made a personal pact that they would share the prize money. But at the end of the season Sawchuk insisted he wouldn't accept the award unless the names of both netminders were inscribed on it.

On June 9, the NHL board of governors altered the Vezina regulations so that the prize could be awarded to both netminders, assuming each netminder played at least 25 games, and made the ruling retroactive to permit Bower and Sawchuk to both get their names on the award.

BIGGER THAN THE BEATLES

Johnny Bower, pop star?

As the holiday season of 1965 approached, that was indeed the case.

Bower was approached by CBC personality Chip Young and songwriter Orville Hoover to record a pair of songs they'd written for a 45 record they planned to release in time for Christmas.

On the B-side would be Banjo Mule, but the tune they projected to be a hit single was "Honky The Christmas Goose."

Bower's son John Jr., 11, was among a group of children who accompanied him on the song, their band being billed as Johnny Bower with Little John and the Rinky Dinks.

None of them could have imagined how much of a smash their recording would prove to be.

The first week provided sales of 20,000, even outselling the Beatles as "Honky The Christmas Goose" took off and left the Fab Four in his dust.

Suddenly, Bower was being mentioned on the entertainment pages with the likes of Bob Dylan, Mick Jagger, and Sonny & Cher.

Honky made it to No. 29 on the CHUM charts in Toronto and as high as No. 45 on the *Toronto Telegram*'s After Four's Hot 100, ahead of Frank Sinatra's "A Very Good Year" in 51st place and "Yesterday" by the Beatles, which sat at 72nd overall.

The first 7,000 singles sold before the record even hit the stores. The 45 ended up selling about 40,000 copies, which at the time made Honky the top selling Canadian-produced record. All of the proceeds from the sales went to charity.

"I remember Honky well," Bower said. "It's got a nice tune to it, but they claim the singer's lousy."

Bower performed a duet of the tune with Canadian country music star George Fox on the latter's 2002 Christmas TV show and the song was re-released in 2012 as part of the *A Moose In A Maple Tree: A Canadian Christmas Compilation album.*

HELLO, BRUCE

Perhaps no goaltender in Leafs' history made a more auspicious debut than Bruce Gamble.

Things looked grim for the Leafs as they entered the stretch run of the 1965–66 season. When Johnny Bower suffered injured ribs after being crashed into by Jean Ratelle during a February 28 game against the New York Rangers, Terry Sawchuk, just back from a charley horse, sought to rush back into action but in doing so reinjured his leg during practice.

"I think the groin is really gone this time," said Sawchuk, who was helped from the ice by teammate Eddie Shack and trainer Bobby Haggert.

On top of Sawchuk's woes, in the past month Bower had endured a groin injury and a 24-stitch cut over his eyes when cranked by a shot during a practice session. Gary Smith, recalled from the minors, hurt his leg in his third game for the Leafs.

Ever the superstitious sort, Leafs' coach Punch Imlach liked to avoid green taxis, black cats, ladders, and throwing his hat on a bed.

He went out for coffee while contemplating his goaltending dilemma and paid for his brew with a $5 bill.

"Don't give me back any two dollar bills," he cautioned the waitress."

Oh yeah. Punch didn't much like deuces, either, although on this day he was desperately seeking a second goalie.

With 19-year-old junior Al Smith his only healthy goalie, Imlach didn't want the kid's confidence to be destroyed by the defending Stanley Cup champion Montreal Canadiens, Toronto's upcoming opponent.

"Al Smith is a fine prospect but I don't want to play Al unless it's absolutely necessary," Imlach explained to Pat Curran of the *Montreal Gaze*tte. "His progress would be set back a long time if he got bombed by Canadiens."

At the same time, he advised Smith to stay prepared just the same.

"He's got strict orders to go home and stay there. If he watches television he mustn't get too close to the set in case the picture tube explodes."

Imlach was a perplexed man. His only two available pros were a pair of minor-league journeymen with limited NHL experience, Al Millar and Bruce Gamble.

Imlach opted to recall Gamble from their Tulsa farm club in the Central League.

The portly Gamble hardly looked like a solution to their problem. His last NHL game also involved the Leafs, when he backstopped the Boston Bruins to a 5–4 victory over Bower and Toronto on March 25, 1962, at Boston Garden.

Since leaving the Bruins, Gamble, 27, saw duty with three teams in three leagues—the Portland Buckaroos of the Western League, the Kingston Frontenacs of the Eastern Pro League and the Springfield Indians of the American League. He so despised his time in Springfield that Gamble opted to sit out the 1964–65 season under suspension rather than return for another season under the tyrant that was Springfield owner Eddie Shore.

"Shore didn't give me much of a chance and wanted to change my style," Gamble explained.

Gamble was solid in his Toronto debut, making 33 saves and earning the third star in a 3–3 draw with the Habs. But the best was yet to come.

Travelling to the Forum the next night, Gamble turned aside 31 shots in a 4–0 shutout of the Canadiens. Two days later, Dave Keon fired a hat trick and 33 Gamble saves blanked the Chicago Blackhawks 5–0.

Gamble opened as a Leaf with a shutout streak of 171 minutes and 55 seconds before John McKenzie of the Bruins finally got a puck past him in Toronto's 5–3 road win. Gamble had more goose eggs on order, though.

His 35 saves made Frank Mahovlich's first-period goal stand up for a 1–0 victory over the Detroit Red Wings on March 9. Facing the Bruins again March 12 at Maple Leaf Gardens, Gamble blocked 27 shots and Shack scored twice in a 6–0 win.

"I must be living right," Gamble said.

Amazingly, Gamble posted just one shutout in his first 80 NHL games tending goal for the Rangers and Bruins. He surpassed that total in his first four days as a Leaf.

"I don't think I ever saw a goaltender play as good a six-game stretch as that," Imlach told the *Ottawa Journal.*

SUITCASE UNPACKED A NEW RULE

A few days before Christmas, on December 21, 1967, at the Montreal Forum, Gary Smith gave the 13,829 in attendance a unique gift that they'd never forget.

The victim of a 6–2 thrashing at the hands of the Habs, Toronto coach Punch Imlach opted to switch goalies midway through the contest, replacing Bruce Gamble with rookie Gary Smith.

Known as Suitcase because he'd been shipped around the minor leagues so frequently he never had time to unpack, and in an era when most goalies were the smallest players on the ice, Smith towered over other players at 6'4". So he stood out in the crowd whether he liked it or not.

Fortunately for Smith, he liked to be the centre of attention, and fearing that he might not ever get another chance, he decided that this was his opportunity to make history.

"I didn't know if I'd ever play another game," Smith explained. "What can I do to make people remember that I played in the NHL?

"So I thought I would go down the ice and try to score."

Smith gloved a shot fired by Montreal forward Dick Duff, dropped the puck at his skates and began stickhandling his way toward the Canadiens end.

As astonished as the fans were in the seats, the Montreal and Toronto players on ice looked on dumbfounded as Smith worked his way to within three feet of the centre red line.

"Montreal defenceman J. C. Tremblay didn't know what to do," Smith remembered. "He never hit a guy in his life, but then he decided to take a run at me. He nailed me. I was at the red line and I was spinning around. I saw Punch Imlach pull his hat down over his head on the first spin, and on the second spin I saw Marcel Pronovost make a great save on Tremblay's long shot."

Smith's memory of the play might be somewhat embellished for dramatic effect. According to reports of the game, he tried to pass the puck as he reached the red line and Tremblay intercepted Smith's pass and immediately wired a long shot toward the vacated Toronto net.

Pronovost, who had opted to guard the goal while Smith set off on his offensive foray, made a nifty skate save.

"I was so surprised when I saw Smith that all I could think of was to shoot," Tremblay told Pat Curran of the *Montreal Gazette*. "Maybe I should have skated in closer."

Canadiens' coach Toe Blake, who'd been given many headaches over the years by Jacques Plante, his own innovative netminder, who also loved to roam from his net to play the puck, could only chuckle at Smith's foray.

"He makes Jacques Plante look like a chicken," Blake quipped.

As a direct result of Smith's attempt, and to avoid future chaos caused by adventurous netminders, the NHL imposed a rule forbidding goaltenders from crossing the red line.

As for Smith, he'd stick around the NHL until 1980, sharing the 1971–72 Vezina Trophy in Chicago with Tony Esposito and finishing fifth in Hart Trophy voting in 1974–75 while stopping pucks for the Vancouver Canucks.

Fred Glover, Smith's coach with the Oakland Seals, described his goalie as "a dedicated non-conformist. He was opposed to anything which smelled of The Establishment."

He also never gave up his wandering ways. Playing against the Leafs as a Seal at Maple Leaf Gardens during a February 7, 1970 game, Smith, facing a 54-shot barrage in a 5–1 loss, gathered up the puck on his blade and lumbered to just shy of the red line, upon which he fired a shot toward the Toronto net. He didn't score this time, either.

YOU CAN CALL HIM AL

If you happen to be wandering the hallways of the Air Canada Centre and are walking past the entrance to the Leafs dressing room, pause for a moment to study the photo directly across from the door.

It's a colour snapshot of the Leafs and Montreal Canadiens shaking hands moments after the Leafs had captured Game 6 of the 1967 Stanley Cup final at Maple Leaf Gardens and, with it, the most recent title in franchise history.

You'll notice a goaltender wearing No. 29 in the photo. It isn't Johnny Bower, who was the back-up that night. It isn't Terry Sawchuk, who blocked 37 shots in Toronto's 3–1 win.

So who is it then?

Why, none other than Al Smith.

Toronto's third goalie for the playoffs, Smith was pressed into duty when Bower pulled a hamstring in the warm-ups for Game 4 of the final series.

He dressed hurriedly and was on the Leafs' bench by the second period as Montreal won 6–2 to deadlock the best-of-seven set at 2–2.

"It was bound to give us a lift when Bower was out," Canadiens centre Ralph Backstrom said. "After all he's stoned us before."

Sawchuk was shaky in the game and there was concern that the Leafs were done without Bower, a feeling that the Leafs obviously didn't share.

"You'd think this was a wake," Leafs' assistant GM King Clancy told the *Ottawa Journal*. "Don't count us out, we'll bounce back. It's not the end of the world.

"Why if Bower isn't ready we'll simply go with Sawchuk. And don't think he can't come up with the biscuits! Terry helped put us where we are, and he'll do it again.

"As for Bower, he's going across the net in the warm-up and stretched and pulled a muscle. The doctor gave us a high sounding name for it, but I don't know what he meant. They say it's a groin but for me it's the back of his thigh and Punch will make up his mind tomorrow."

To Montreal captain Jean Beliveau, it didn't matter who donned the pads for Toronto.

"They're all tough," Beliveau said. "There's no weaknesses I can see. When I see part of the net, I let go."

It wasn't the first time that Smith was asked to pinch-hit in the Toronto net. He saw his first NHL duty during the 1965–66 season.

Both Bower and Sawchuk were felled by injury. The Leafs recalled Gary Smith (no relation) from their Rochester AHL farm club and also brought in Al Smith, 19, from the junior Toronto Marlboros to serve as back-up for a February 23 game against the Chicago Blackhawks.

If Al Smith thought he'd enjoy a view of the game from the end of the Leafs' bench, he was sadly mistaken. His namesake suffered a leg injury just 2:15 into the contest, pressing the teenager into service, and he was sensational, stopping 27 shots in Toronto's 3–2 victory.

"Smitty played a whale of a game," remembered Leafs' coach Punch Imlach. "I can still see everybody crowded around him after the game. He was probably the happiest person in Chicago.

"I remember he couldn't get out of the rink fast enough to phone home."

Smith also played one game during the 1966–67 season, one of five goalies to see action for the Leafs that Cup-winning campaign along with Bower, Sawchuk, Gary Smith, and Bruce Gamble. That's the most goaltenders ever used in a season by a team that won the Cup, a mark the Leafs share with the 1984–85 and 1989–90 Edmonton Oilers.

Smith dressed as Sawchuk's back-up for Game 5 of the Cup final series, a 4–1 Toronto win at the Montreal Forum, but when the series shifted back to Maple Leaf Gardens for the decisive sixth game, there was Bower back on the bench, even though he hadn't practiced since his injury.

"I would certainly want Bower on the bench as back-up instead of some minor leaguer," Leafs' coach Punch Imlach snarled.

All three goalies took the warm-up, but Smith disappeared once the game got underway. So where did Smith, in full uniform, come from at game's end? Well, it was a little bit of the old Imlach skulduggery at work.

"Before the game, Punch said, 'you're dressing,'" Bower recounted in his book *The China Wall*. "I could hardly put my pads on. Bobby Haggert, our trainer, had to tie the straps.

"It was useless for me to be on the bench. Punch said, 'If anything happens, you'll have to go in.'"

In such an emergency, the contingency plan was for Bower to fall down at his first chance, grab at his leg and tell the officials he was injured.

"Al Smith was there, waiting in the dressing room," Bower explained.

Smith saw no regular-season game action with the Leafs in 1967–68, but did play in the NHL All-Star Game for the Leafs, the final season in which the defending Cup champs faced the league's all-stars. He was in the Toronto net seven times during the 1968–69 campaign, but was not protected in the NHL Intra-League Draft that spring and was claimed by the Pittsburgh Penguins.

"I would have liked to have stayed in Toronto but I was not really surprised because I knew that neither general manager Jim Gregory, nor (co-owner) Mr. Stafford Smythe, had any confidence in my ability," Smith said.

"Naturally, I was a little bitter, but there is only one way to handle that kind of situation—prove they made a mistake."

In 1969–70, Smith helped the Penguins qualify for the playoffs for the first time and go all the way to the Stanley Cup semi-finals. Jumping to the WHA in 1972, he backstopped the New England Whalers to the first Avco Cup title.

Suppose Sawchuk had been hurt in that 1967 final series and Smith was called into action. Would he have proven to be another among the many like Lester Patrick, Alfie Moore, and Earl Robertson, emergency goaltenders who performed legendary Stanley Cup feats?

Or would Leafs' fans be left today to lament the club's last Stanley Cup title in 1964?

BOWER'S NEW DEAL

A 40-save performance produced a 5–0 shutout win for the Leafs and Johnny Bower over the Montreal Canadiens in a rematch of the 1967 Stanley Cup final on November 1, 1967, at Maple Leaf Gardens.

It also earned Bower, 43, a big payday.

After the game in the Toronto dressing room, Leafs' coach Punch Imlach symbolically tore up a piece of paper in front of Bower and indicated that they would hammer out a new contract the next time they met.

Imlach was pleased to see his veteran goalie, who had been struggling, rediscover his game.

"He's been having trouble," Imlach told *Canadian Press*. "I think it was mostly a matter of bad breaks.

"So we worked with him on long shots—the ones he seemed to be missing—earlier in the week and it seems to have helped.

"I told him he played so well, I'll tear up his contract and he'll get a new one. He'll get a good raise.

"Only players over 40 get that opportunity."

Bower groused about the latest reference to his senior status in the NHL. "For God's sake boys, give me a break and say, 'The young Johnny Bower,'" he joked.

The next day, Imlach gave Bower a $100 a week raise, worth $2,400 over the course of the season.

GAMBLE STUMPED THE STARS

A new era began for the NHL in 1967 and an old one came to an end in 1968.

With the addition of six expansion teams, the NHL doubled in size from six to twelve teams for the 1967–68 season, so following the standard protocol of including at least one member of each team in the All-Stars' line-up for the NHL All-Star Game January 16, 1968 at Maple Leaf Gardens proved far more challenging than during the six-team era.

From its beginnings in 1947 through that 1968 game, the traditional format of the NHL All-Star Game pitted the defending Stanley Cup champions against the stars from the remaining teams in the league.

That was again the plan as the Leafs readied to tangle with the NHL All-Stars at Maple Leaf Gardens, the eighth time that the Leafs would provide the opposition.

The Leafs owned a rich history of All-Star Game participation. They played host to the NHL All-Stars in the first unofficial NHL all-star contest, the Ace Bailey Benefit Game on February 14, 1934, which aided former Leaf forward Bailey, whose career was ended earlier that season when he suffered a head injury in a game at Boston.

When the game became an official part of the annual NHL landscape 13 years later, it was the Leafs who again provided the opposition, falling 4–3 in the debut game.

The 1968 game would be the final all-star game of its kind. The league would switch to a divisional format, East vs. West, in 1969, so the Leafs would be the last NHL team to face the All-Stars.

They wanted to go out winners. And they did.

Ron Ellis, who'd also scored in Toronto's Cup-clinching win over the Montreal Canadiens the previous spring, netted the deciding goal early in the third period as Toronto vanquished the NHL All-Stars 4–3.

Pete Stemkowski and Allan Stanley, also members of the 1967 Cup winner, tallied for Toronto, as did Murray Oliver, acquired in an off-season trade with Boston for Eddie Shack.

Detroit's Norm Ullman, who'd be traded to the Leafs later that season, scored for the All-Stars, along with Chicago's Stan Mikita and Ken Wharram. One of the three All-Star goalies was Terry Sawchuk of the Los Angeles Kings, the winning goalie for the Leafs in their 3–1 victory over the Habs to wrap up the 1967 title. Defenceman Bob Baun, representing the Oakland Seals, was another member of the 1966–67 Leafs who suited up for the All-Stars.

It was a wide-open affair, the two teams combining for an NHL All-Star Game record 88 shots. Goaltending was the difference for Toronto, but neither of the Leafs' goalies had played for the team during the 1967 playoffs.

Johnny Bower, who'd shared the post-season netminding workload with Sawchuk, was out with an elbow injury, so journeyman Bruce Gamble got the start for the Leafs and was sensational, stopping 28 of the 30 shots he faced in two periods, including 18 first-period stops.

"The turning point came in that first period when we had all those chances and couldn't beat Gamble," All-Star coach Toe Blake of Montreal told *Canadian Press*.

The save of the game was turned in by youngster Al Smith, called up from Tulsa of the Central League to fill in for Bower. He made a spectacular glove save on a slapshot by Chicago's Bobby Hull.

"I had planned to use Smith in the third period no matter what the score," Toronto coach Punch Imlach explained to the *Montreal Gazette*. "He played real well and made several big stops before that (save on Hull)."

Playing in his first NHL All-Star Game, Boston Bruins' defenceman Bobby Orr picked up an assist but his history of bad luck against the Leafs continued when he suffered a shoulder injury in a collision with Toronto's Frank Mahovlich.

"He cross-checked me," said Orr, who remained in the game. "It's tender now but I don't think it's too serious."

Orr turned heads with his performance. "He's some passer that Orr, some player," Detroit's Gordie Howe said.

Added Blake: "(Orr) was certainly one of the best players out there."

Howe took a pair of penalties, giving him an NHL All-Star record of 11 trips to the sin bin for 25 minutes. The second came later in the game when Howe tangled with Toronto's Mike Walton and both were assessed roughing minors by referee Bill Friday.

"It wasn't a fight," Howe scoffed. "I've been around long enough that if I was going to take anything but a token swing I wouldn't miss.

"Besides, I didn't do anything else in the game so I had to get my name in the paper somehow."

While pleased with his team's performance, Imlach also felt chagrined.

"The only thing is that we can't get two points in the standings," Imlach said. "I think we should get two points from every other team in the league."

The victory secured, Leafs' owner Stafford Smythe couldn't help but get in a playful dig at the coach of their Montreal rivals.

"If Blake couldn't coach this team to a win, how's he going to do it with the Canadiens?" Smythe wondered aloud.

THE NIGHT THEY BOOED JOHNNY BOWER OFF THE ICE

He is a Maple Leafs icon, beloved by all, as much as fixture on the Toronto scene as the CN Tower and the city's trendy theatre district.

Hall-of-Famer Johnny Bower isn't merely a four-time Stanley Cup champion and a two-time Vezina Trophy winner, the affable legend is the honourary grandfather of every Leafs' fan.

Hard to believe then that on the night of January 8, 1969, many of those same Leafs' fans booed Bower off the ice.

Forty-four years old at the time and in his last full NHL season, Bower got the nod in goal against the second-year Philadelphia Flyers, but it wasn't his night. The Flyers got just 17 shots on Bower, but four of them found their way past him before Bower was hooked from the net in favour of Bruce Gamble early in the third period. The Leafs were left to settle for a 4–4 tie even though they pelted Flyers' goalie Doug Favell with 44 shots.

"I was lousy," Bower said after the game. "That's all there was to it. I blew four easy shots.

"What else do you want me to say?"

Punch Imlach felt that there was plenty left to say. He was appalled at the way the Toronto fans had heckled such a Leafs icon.

"Sure Bower was shaky," Imlach admitted. "He was as nervous as hell and I had to get him out of there or we might not have even got one point.

"But you know why he's so nervous? It's because they are giving him such a hard time. This will kill him faster than anything. On the road he isn't nervous. He's a lot sharper."

Bower appeared in just seven more games the rest of the regular season, making only one more home appearance on February 8, 1969, against the Oakland Seals. He played in all four of Toronto's playoff games as they were swept in the quarter-finals by the Boston Bruins, but his only start was in the Leafs' 3–2 loss in Game 4 at Maple Leaf Gardens.

Bower saw action in just one game during the 1969–70 season, making his farewell NHL appearance in a 6–3 loss to the Montreal Canadiens on December 10, 1969.

MARVELOUS MARV

As a 15-year-old rookie with the Junior A St. Catharines Teepees in 1950–51, netminder Marv Edwards was invited one day to practice with the Toronto Maple Leafs, the team that would win the Stanley Cup that spring.

Leafs' coach Joe Primeau offered Edwards a piece of advice, teaching him how to hug his post to prevent costly short-side goals.

Eighteen years later, Edwards would get to wear the Leafs' uniform again, and this time, it would be for real.

With just one NHL game on his resume, the Leafs claimed Edwards in the NHL Intra-League draft and utilized him in a three-goalie rotation during the 1969–70 season with veterans Bruce Gamble and Johnny Bower.

"Edwards never had a real good shot with any other club," Toronto general manager Jim Gregory told *Canadian Press* of their 34-year-old rookie goaltender. "He'll get it here."

Edwards' only previous NHL game came February 20, 1969 when he made 30 saves and earned the third star with the Pittsburgh Penguins in a 3–0 loss to the Detroit Red Wings.

Although his NHL experience was limited, Edwards' body of work was still impressive.

He won back-to-back Memorial Cups with the Barrie Flyers in 1952–53 and the 1953–54 Teepees. Edwards was a world champion in 1959 when he played for the Belleville McFarlands, who represented Canada at the world tourney that year, and one of his teammates was John McLellan, the new Leafs coach in 1969–70.

"He's a guy who may surprise a lot of people," Gregory predicted of Edwards, and the early returns backed up the optimism of the Leaf GM.

In his first three games as a Leaf, Edwards turned in a 36-save performance for a 4–1 win over Chicago, blocked 27 shots in a 4–2 decision against St. Louis and then earned the game's first star with a 40-save effort to beat the Boston Bruins 4–2.

Edwards started 4–0–1 before finally suffering a 6–3 defeat at Montreal.

He was also just the fourth Leafs' netminder to don a mask, following Don Simmons, Terry Sawchuk, and Bower, and Edwards admitted at the time that the decision led hockey people to question his performance.

"If we happened to let in an easy-looking goal, the mask would always be blamed," Edwards said. "But the mask has come to stay. I will be surprised to see a goalie who is not wearing one by the end of this season."

By the beginning of the next season, Edwards was no longer wearing a Leaf sweater. A knee injury slowed his season and Edwards finished 10–9–4 with a 3.25 GAA and one shutout. When Toronto missed the playoffs, the Leafs moved to acquire future Hall-of-Famer Jacques Plante during the summer of 1970.

Though his tenure was brief, the memory of his time in Toronto is something that Edwards still savours.

"I always wanted to wear that Maple Leaf sweater," he told the *St. Catharines Standard*. "That was the highlight of my whole career."

THE POPCORN KID

And pop goes another myth.

They called Leaf goalie Mike Palmateer The Popcorn Kid because, supposedly, he munched on popcorn prior to every game.

A reporter caught Palmateer with some popcorn prior to a junior game when he played for the Toronto Marlboros and just like that, a legend was born.

"While I was in Toronto, I noticed that if I happened to have some (popcorn) in my locker I'd generally have a good game," Palmateer told *Sports Illustrated*. "But it was more habit than superstition. Then somebody wrote about it.

"I'd like to kill the guy that wrote the popcorn thing, because that's the first thing anyone associates with me."

Palmateer, who backstopped the Marlies to the 1972–73 Memorial Cup and was drafted by the Leafs in 1974, would rather be remembered as the first Toronto goalie to carry the team to a victory in a best-of-seven playoff series since their 1967 Stanley Cup triumph when he was the goaltender of record as the Leafs took out the New York Islanders in seven games in the 1978 quarter-finals.

Unfortunately, the good times were short-lived and in 1979, when Punch Imlach took over as GM of the Leafs, Palmateer's relationship with the team turned sour.

"This is one of the lowest years of my career," Palmateer told *Canadian P*ress at the end of the 1979–80 season. "As a matter of fact, it's right at the bottom of the totem pole. The way things have gone, I don't expect I'll be back next year."

Palmateer had little respect for either of the coaches hired by Imlach, former Leafs Floyd Smith and Joe Crozier.

"With Smitty, the guys never learned anything at all," Palmateer said. "Joe Crozier is a man you can't talk to."

Palmateer was dealt to Washington that off-season, but made a return to Toronto in 1982, though it was hardly triumphant. Slowed by wonky knees, Palmateer won just 30 of 87 games over two seasons, and in 1983–84, his farewell NHL campaign, Palmateer's goals-against average soared to 4.88.

CHANGING ON THE FLY

During an October 4, 1979 pre-season game at Maple Leaf Gardens against the Chicago Blackhawks, Toronto goalie Mike Palmateer raced to the bench during a delayed penalty call. Upon arriving at the Leaf bench, Palmateer was surprised to see Jiri Crha with his mask on.

"I asked him if he was going in and he said, 'Yes,'" Palmateer said. "I thought it was a bit unusual after I was supposed to play the complete game, but I took a seat."

Crha played goal for 5:28, making one save, before startled Leafs' coach Floyd Smith discovered the goalie change and immediately sent Palmateer back into action at the next stoppage in play.

The duo ended up sharing a shutout in a 5–0 Toronto victory.

The first Eastern European goalie to play in the NHL after he defected from Soviet-controlled Czechoslovakia, Crha made his Leaf regular-season debut several months later on February 16, 1980, relieving starter Curt Ridley in a 5–3 victory over the Hartford Whalers. That earned Crha his first NHL start the next night at New York, where he recorded a 6–4 win over the Rangers at Madison Square Garden.

HERE'S JOHNNY

The 1979–80 campaign was a season of chaos and conflict for the Leafs, but it nearly went from sublime to ridiculous as Toronto readied for a January 9, 1980 date with the Montreal Canadiens.

The Leafs found themselves short on goaltenders. No. 1 goalie Mike Palmateer was out with an ankle injury and back-up Paul Harrison was bedridden with flu.

Vincent Tremblay was recalled from the AHL New Brunswick Hawks and slated to make his NHL debut. And if Harrison were too ill to suit up, his spot on the bench would be filled by Leafs' 55-year-old legend Johnny Bower.

Bower practised with the Leafs on January 8—a scout with the team, he still put the pads on in a pinch—and the ever-loyal Bower was ready to answer the call if need be.

"I volunteered for this job, but I just hope and pray I'm not needed," Bower told *Canadian Press*. "I feel pretty good and I guess if I can help the team out of a bind, I will do it."

Leafs' GM Punch Imlach, who'd won four Stanley Cups in the 1960s with Bower as his goalie, was certain of this—if Bower dressed, he would see action.

"If Tremblay ever got hurt, I wouldn't hesitate for a minute to send Bower in there," Imlach said. "He has to be the greatest competitor I've ever seen. I coached him last year in an old timers' game and he still showed me a few things.

"I don't know whether Johnny can see that well, but I used to say that when I coached him and he never let us down."

Bower's last NHL action came December 10, 1969, in a 6–3 loss to the Habs at the Montreal Forum. And it would remain his last action.

Harrison was well enough to dress, but Tremblay, even though he gave up four goals before the game was 10 minutes old, settled down and went the distance in a 5–3 loss to the Canadiens.

Bower was on hand, suited up and sitting in the Leafs' dressing room, just in case disaster struck and he was called upon for duty.

THE PIPER WHO COULD BUTTERFLY

The No. 1 goalie for the Highland Creek Pipe and Drum band proved to be a more than adequate backup for the Toronto Maple Leafs.

"When I was brought in here, I knew there was more expected of me than just stopping the puck," said Glenn Healy, a free-agent signee who backed up both Felix Potvin and Curtis Joseph during a Leafs career that spanned from 1997–2001.

Today a *Hockey Night In Canada* analyst, Healy was known as one of the wittiest players in the National Hockey League and one of the best players at keeping a dressing room calm and upbeat.

"He's a comical, bright guy who can read the environment well," former Leafs' coach Mike Murphy said of Healy.

A Western Michigan grad, Healy saw just about everything during a 15-season NHL career.

He broke in with Los Angeles in 1985, during the Kings purple uniform stage. "We still wear those for Halloween," Healy said of his old L.A. jersey.

In 1993, Healy backstopped the New York Islanders to a playoff upset of the Stanley Cup champion Pittsburgh Penguins.

Left unprotected in the expansion draft that summer, Healy ended up with the New York Rangers after a series of deals and was Mike Richter's understudy on the Ranger team that won the Stanley Cup in 1994.

"Each job has its ups and downs," Healy said of the variables of being the main guy or the No. 2 man between the pipes. "A lot of guys can't do both.

"Some guys can't play every day and there are a lot of guys who aren't able to go a month without playing and then come in and be on top of their game."

Like most goalies, there was more to Healy than pads and blocker saves. Behind the mask was a man of many talents.

While with the Islanders, Healy combined with teammate Pat Flatley to co-host an offbeat cable-access program, "The Heals and Flats Show"—a sort of *Wayne's World* on skates.

He's worked as a counsellor at a drug rehabilitation centre in Long Island, N.Y. and has done extensive work with handicapped children through the National Center for Disability Services in the United States.

When he wasn't situated between the pipes, Healy could often be found playing them.

The bagpipes, that is.

While he gained a reputation around the NHL as someone who can keep a dressing room loose, Healy never considered piping a tune for his teammates as a realistic option.

"Not everybody likes the bagpipes," he said, "though I can't imagine why."

THE GOALIE WHO SCORED A CAR

Goaltender Corey Schwab's career as a Leaf was brief—30 games during the 2001–02 season—but he's better known for scoring than puck stopping anyway.

During the mid-1980s, Schwab tended goal for the North Battleford, Saskatchewan AAA midgets, but bled the blue and gold of the Western Hockey League's Saskatoon Blades.

"I was a huge Blades fan," Schwab said. "I never missed a Blades game on the radio."

Or a chance to see them in person.

On a cold, Saskatchewan night in the winter of 1987, the Schwab family made the one-hour trek southward towards Saskatoon to visit relatives.

En route, the car radio informed them of that night's Blades game.

"Can we go?" Schwab asked from the back seat, a query that was met with silence.

"I could see in his eyes that my dad wanted to go," Schwab said. "He was just afraid to say so in front of my mom."

Schwab kept working his parents, wearing them down. In the end, Arlene Schwab stayed to visit family. Ken Schwab and his son headed to Saskatoon Arena.

"When we got in the rink, I asked my dad to buy me a program and he said, 'No,'" Schwab remembered. "I asked him to go halves—50 cents each—and he still wouldn't do it.

"I only had five bucks and when you're 16 and don't have a job, a buck seems like a lot of money."

Nonetheless, Schwab made the plunge. During the second period, he heard his program number called for the intermission shootout.

"I went down to check and they said, 'You're shooting for the car,'" Schwab said.

One chance, from the far blue line, to slide a puck though a hole in a board barely big enough to accommodate a rubber biscuit and take home a brand new Dodge Omni.

"I wasn't nervous," Schwab said. "My dad told me to aim for the middle of the faceoff dot at centre and that's what I did. I can still see that puck sliding down the ice, going through that hole."

Winning him a new car.

Schwab still has the stick that he used to score his only goal, a Wayne Gretzky model Titan. The car, he kept for nine years.

When he turned pro, Schwab handed the keys to his sister Carla.

ACKNOWLEDGEMENTS

Much like many of the tales of former Leafs players that populate these pages, there are plenty of people who toil behind the scenes and don't necessarily shine in the spotlight but are nonetheless so deserving of recognition for their efforts.

Dan Wells and the staff at Biblioasis would be at the top of that list. Through their tireless work they've taken my words and turned them into something that is both colourful and a keepsake for all fans of the Toronto Maple Leafs.

I've been fortunate enough through my 30-plus years work as a sportswriter to get to know and interview many of the people whose tales are featured in these pages, and some of the stories you read within were witnessed first hand by my own eyes. Many others were shared with me over the years by Leafs legends like Johnny Bower, Red Horner, King Clancy and Ron Ellis. I thank them for their time and consideration.

If I had a dollar for every time I've been asked whether I am a Wings fan or a Leafs fan, I'd be richer than Bill Gates and Warren Buffett combined. The fact of the matter is that I am a fan of hockey. I've loved this game for as long as I can remember and I have a passion for telling its stories.

Bob Duff
November 2016

ABOUT THE AUTHOR

Bob Duff has covered the NHL since 1988 and is a contributor to *The Hockey News*, *HockeyBuzz.com*, *NHL.com* and *TAP Digital Marketing*. Duff's book credits include *Marcel Pronovost: A Life in Hockey*, *The China Wall: The Timeless Legend of Johnny Bower*, *Hockey Dynasties*, *Without Fear*, *Nine: Salute to Mr. Hockey*, *On the Wing: A History of the Windsor Spitfires*, and *The Hockey Hall of Fame MVP Trophies and Winners*.